4/2015

A **NAOMI SCHNEIDER** BOOK

Highlighting the lives and experiences of marginalized
communities, the select titles of this imprint draw
from sociology, anthropology, law, and history, as well
as from the traditions of journalism and advocacy, to reassess mainstream
history and promote unconventional thinking about contemporary
social and political issues. Their authors share the passion, commitment,
and creativity of Executive Editor Naomi Schneider.

Blind Spot

CALIFORNIA SERIES IN PUBLIC ANTHROPOLOGY

The California Series in Public Anthropology emphasizes the anthropologist's role as an engaged intellectual. It continues anthropology's commitment to being an ethnographic witness, to describing, in human terms, how life is lived beyond the borders of many readers' experiences. But it also adds a commitment, through ethnography, to reframing the terms of public debate—transforming received, accepted understandings of social issues with new insights, new framings.

Series Editor: Robert Borofsky (Hawaii Pacific University)

Contributing Editors: Philippe Bourgois (University of Pennsylvania), Paul Farmer (Partners In Health), Alex Hinton (Rutgers University), Carolyn Nordstrom (University of Notre Dame), and Nancy Scheper-Hughes (UC Berkeley)

University of California Press Editor: Naomi Schneider

Blind Spot

HOW NEOLIBERALISM INFILTRATED
GLOBAL HEALTH

Salmaan Keshavjee

Foreword by Paul Farmer

UNIVERSITY OF CALIFORNIA PRESS

University of California Press, one of the most distinguished university presses in the United States, enriches lives around the world by advancing scholarship in the humanities, social sciences, and natural sciences. Its activities are supported by the UC Press Foundation and by philanthropic contributions from individuals and institutions. For more information, visit www.ucpress.edu.

University of California Press
Oakland, California

Library of Congress Cataloging-in-Publication Data

Keshavjee, Salmaan, 1970– author.
 Blind spot : how neoliberalism infiltrated global health / Salmaan Keshavjee ; foreword by Paul E. Farmer.
     p.   cm. – (California series in public anthropology ; 30)
 Includes bibliographical references and index.
 ISBN 978-0-520-28283-4 (cloth : alk. paper)
 ISBN 978-0-520-28284-1 (pbk. : alk. paper)
 ISBN 978-0-520-95873-9 (ebook)
 I. Title.   II. Series: California series in public anthropology ; 30.
 [DNLM: 1. Health Services—economics—Tajikistan.   2. Health Policy—Tajikistan.   3. Health Services Administration—economics—Tajikistan.   4. Organizations—Tajikistan.   5. Socioeconomic Factors—Tajikistan.   6. World Health—Tajikistan.   W 84 JT23]
 RA395.A783
 362.109586—dc23   2014008620

Manufactured in the United States of America

23 22 21 20 19 18 17 16 15 14
10 9 8 7 6 5 4 3 2 1

For my parents, Sherbanu and Ameer Keshavjee.

Born in apartheid South Africa, they brought us to a place that many in this world can only dream of and taught us to be courageous, persistent, and vigilant in the struggle for equity and justice.

The inner meaning of history . . . involves speculation and an attempt to get at the truth, subtle explanation of the causes and origins of existing things, and deep knowledge of the how and why of events. History, therefore, is firmly rooted in philosophy.

Ibn Khaldun, fourteenth-century historian, *The Muqaddimah*

Fyodor Pavlovitch was drunk when he heard of his wife's death, and the story is that he ran out into the street and began shouting with joy, raising his hands to Heaven: "Lord, now lettest Thou Thy servant depart in peace," but others say he wept without restraint like a little child, so much so that people were sorry for him, in spite of the repulsion he inspired. It is quite possible that both versions were true, that he rejoiced at his release, and at the same time wept for her who released him. As a general rule, people, even the wicked, are much more naïve and simple-hearted than we suppose. And we ourselves are, too.

Fyodor Dostoyevsky, *The Brothers Karamazov*

Contents

Illustrations

Foreword

Paul Farmer

It is rare that a scholarly work can be called soul-searching as well as wrenching, but *Blind Spot*, by physician-anthropologist Salmaan Keshavjee, is just such a book. Based on ethnographic research conducted after the collapse of the Soviet Union, in a remote and mountainous part of Central Asia at the margin of armed conflict, this is a haunting account of a goodwill effort to replace an inadequate public health system with a "sustainable" (and privatized) one. This new system is to be based, Keshavjee learns, on a post-Communist ideological framework even more impervious to course correction than the one preceding it. Lost in the battle between partisans of competing frameworks, one ascendant and one in the throes of collapse, are the poor and vulnerable and hungry who live in the Pamir Mountains, through which the storied Silk Road improbably winds.

For the reader who hasn't heard of the Pamir Mountains or the region called Badakhshan, Salmaan Keshavjee offers rich detail. Its inhabitants, citizens of Tajikistan, might not find the word *rich* in any way apposite. When the young graduate student arrived at the tail end of a civil war, the lives of his hosts were precarious in every sense: the Soviet political system had collapsed, and the economy along with it. But beyond these dramatic events towers the immutable and cold rock face of the mountains. Much of the region looks like moonscape—were moonscape to be blanketed in snow.

In terms of health care and other basic social services, or even food and clothes, the poor of Badakhshan might as well have been lost on the moon. But this is also the story of those who are lost in other ways: the architects and implementers of programs and projects, blinded by ideologies cooked up in Geneva and Washington and other centers of soft (and not-so-soft) power. They assert that health care, to be sustainable, must be sold as a commodity even when and where the majority of its potential beneficiaries are unable to buy it. They have become the gatekeepers, sometimes reluctant, of a veritable "House of No." The gates are barred to those unable to pay.

But who is convinced and who is really pressed (or press-ganged) into service? Take the example of a young Tajik dentist, Misha, who meets Keshavjee while seeking funding from an international nongovernmental organization in the hope of sparing some of his patients—the destitute, children, aging veterans, and others once protected, however feebly, by the Soviet health system—the closed-door fate that awaits them. The organization is one of several that have come to Tajikistan to address a humanitarian crisis provoked by the collapse of the Soviet Union, which triggered war and strife and privation.

Misha is portrayed as a sympathetic character, but he eventually gives in to the inevitability of the "reform" (a term used by aid officials and their advisors, apparently without irony) that rips even more holes in Tajikistan's ragged safety net. Soon there are few patients in his waiting room or in any others. There is no viable alternative to privatization, Misha is forced to conclude.

Keshavjee's account of the privatization of the dental clinic is piercing because the dentist comes to the same conclusion as the architects and apostles of neoliberal ideology. There aren't many doors open to him, and even fewer for his patients. But how did the options before Misha, and others, come to be so powerfully constricted? Why are so many doors closed? How was the House of No erected, from what materials, and on what foundations?

Keshavjee's book is an experience-near case study of the impact of "dogma over data" in a little-studied part of Central Asia. Here, the nineteenth-century Great Game of empire was followed by a century of Russian influence and then, suddenly, the collapse of the Soviet system, with attendant conflict and demographic decline. The extent of the contracture of the public services was of epic proportion. In a review of *Capital in the Twenty-First Century,* Thomas Piketty puts it like this: "At the global level, the most extensive privatization in recent decades, and indeed in the entire history of capital, obviously took place in the countries of the former Soviet bloc."[1]

But it's not that the dissymmetries are new in Badakhshan, as Keshavjee's history of the place, which is populated mostly by Ismaili Muslims, shows; the region's inhabitants have known centuries of neglect or worse. In Badakhshan, the rapid erosion of public institutions, such as they were, fueled emerging social inequalities, themselves exacerbated by the rending of social safety nets. The Soviet health care system that preceded the collapse reached, if unevenly, into the highlands of Badakhshan. So did, surprisingly, the pensions and public works we associate with welfare states. But the quality of care was never very good, nor was a centralized system able to avoid shortages of medicines, perverse incentives, or demoralization among care providers. Claims of the effectiveness of this system prior to its erosion are suspect.

In the years of Keshavjee's fieldwork, which began in 1995, this collapse was followed by the chaotic proliferation of what were termed, in developmentspeak, "civil society institutions" with very different and competing agendas. In the mid-1990s, disparities and asymmetries of all sorts—public-private, center-periphery, urban-rural, mountains-lowlands, practitioner-patient, foreign-local—abounded and were growing. Above all, and quite new, was the gulf between the tottering public health system and the well-resourced aid agencies and nongovernmental organizations (NGOs) new to the region.

As a graduate student, Keshavjee served as a consultant for one of the NGOs caught up in the irresistible logic of neoliberalism, or that part of it that claimed all health care should be marketed and sold as a commodity like any other in the market. But what if need isn't matched by an ability to pay? This is the daily drama of the destitute sick, especially in rural areas; it's why, across the world, they bang on the door of the House of No. They seek to be patients but are asked to be customers. It was during Keshavjee's assessment of a revolving drug fund—some fraction of receipts from the direct sale of pharmaceuticals would go to replenish the fund and the rest to finance primary health care—that one of his Tajik informants told him, ruefully, "You can't sell medicines to starving people." This was the working title of this book and stands as a concise assessment of both the promise of such projects and a demolition of the premise on which they rested.

Anthropology graduate students rely heavily on comments like these, a marker of their presence and proximity. *Blind Spot* is thus about *translocal* power, but not all of it is ethnographically visible: the dentist, a lucky professional in Badakhshan, is hardly powerful if he is obliged to beg Keshavjee, a student, for a pittance to keep his clinic open to those who need it most. Such personal narratives are woven together so artfully with the historical backdrop that dominates this account that it is difficult to put this book down. But even after reading the book twice and hearing iterations of it over the course of years, it's hard for me to recollect many details about the Tajik characters in this account.

It's not that these folks are there to serve up local color. It's rather that Keshavjee's strongest portrait is of his patrons and peers, those who funded the projects so openly designed less to improve health outcomes than to "change the mentality" of those seeking access to health services. Many of the new aid givers seem to speak in tongues, spouting a glossolalia replete with doublespeak about "privatization," "user fees," and new and "more efficient" ways of "managing" health care delivery. "Free trade" and "competition" are liberally invoked. Erstwhile patients become "clients," "consumers," or even "customers."

Blind Spot is magisterial and scholarly, but the book is also humane and doleful and reflective: after all, Keshavjee was himself pulled into an effort, thus far fruitless, to sell essential medicines to the poor. He tells with sympathy the stories of hapless aid workers and care providers caught in the middle of a bitter struggle that has left them unable to serve the sick or to prevent unnecessary illness and suffering. It's this wistful tone that packs the greatest punch. The study has a psychological depth (and reflexiveness) associated with his Harvard mentor, Arthur Kleinman, even as it brings to mind the work of fellow anthropologist James Ferguson and of sociologists like C. Wright Mills and Pierre Bourdieu.

It's easy, especially looking back almost two decades later, to deride some development efforts as ineffectual or wasteful or cruel or ineffective or costly. Such derision is easy enough. It's less easy, but not for lack of information, to parse carefully the reasons for failure (or success). And it's downright difficult to identify reasons for failure in such a fraught enterprise and then to differentially weight them.

What's stunning about this book is its suggestion that such an analytic effort, even if honest and painstaking, probably wouldn't have made a difference, not in the short run. At least, such are the conclusions to be drawn from Keshavjee's critical review of the Bamako Initiative upon which the Badakhshan project was based. The reader unfamiliar with health programs for the world's poor may be unfamiliar with the terms of this debate, and might well ask, "Wait: isn't Bamako in the West African country of Mali? Wouldn't a program devised there be based on different kinds of data and dynamics than those encountered in the high reaches of the Pamir Mountains as the Soviet Union collapsed?"

Yes, Bamako is in Mali, but in truth, as Keshavjee shows, the influential Bamako Initiative, launched in 1987, was never based on much in the way of data. It was, rather, based on ideology and dogma of the neoliberal flavor.

Why didn't it matter that these efforts, expected to fail, did fail, and early? Wasn't there any "feedback loop" to correct or halt them, in either Badakhshan or Bamako? Keshavjee's central thesis is that the proposed privatization of health care, termed "reform" across the former Soviet Union as in Africa and Latin America, not only engenders the curious doublespeak mentioned above but also creates, when handsomely funded, realms of *neoliberal programmatic blindness*. Keshavjee shows us how and why such logic becomes irresistible, in part because it is almost invisible, not to those on the receiving end nor to mediators like Misha, but rather to many of the rest of us, who fail to interrogate the models of "cost recovery" that have come to dominate discussions of public health and health care for the poor.

It's not always clear how invisible such frameworks are to those convinced, as Margaret Thatcher put it, that "there is no alternative" (TINA) to an imperious logic that shapes programs and plans, limiting the choices not only of the world's destitute sick but of those who might serve them. Are they confident ideologues, like Thatcher, or are they cowed into accepting mediocrity when faced with dramatic circumstances? Or do they go through cycles of confidence and uncertainty, as the architects and implementers of the neoliberal reforms outlined in *Blind Spot* seem to do?

To answer these questions, Keshavjee turns to the specifics of the Bamako Initiative. Bamako encouraged health officials of African nations, already heavily indebted to international financial institutions and private banks, to finance a slender package of health care for the poor by having the "consumer" pay for care when sick, in order to "recover costs" and thus finance health care through "community participation." The dignity conferred by paying for one's own (or one's children's) care would magically render such programs "sustainable." Such responsible approaches would also cut down, suggested Bamoko's most ardent cheerleaders, on the sort of "frivolous spending" and "moral hazard" one encountered so often (or so you'd believe) in places like rural Mali. Such cost shifting to private payers—meaning patients and their families—would also decrease public expenditures in health care and "decentralize" care.

Why so many quotation marks? Could a Rosetta Stone of sorts help us decipher a language (developmentspeak or, in Orwellian terms, doublespeak) like this one? If there were key code breakers, they would surely include the Mont Pèlerin Society and the structural adjustment programs adopted in the 1980s by the World Bank and other institutions described in detail in *Blind Spot*. Let me first summarize Keshavjee's description of the latter:

> Bamako's solution to the bank's policy of structural adjustment—a policy that restricted public sector health spending—was to turn to financing and organizational mechanisms that promoted user fees to raise revenue and decentralization so that funds would be raised "close to the point of service" and not go into central government coffers. Viewed this way, it was the perfect "common sense" outcome. What was perhaps not obvious to most of those endorsing the proposal was that its principles were born from the mission of the Mont Pèlerin Society, the result of a decade of intense ideological construction. It was as if there was no alternative. (98)

And the health officials all signed on, as did the various United Nations agencies involved, from UNICEF to the World Health Organization. But there must have been many misgivings in Bamako. After all, the initiative contradicted, in so many ways, the 1978 Alma Ata declaration, whose slogan, "Health for all by the year 2000," had been enthusiastically endorsed by the world's health ministers: same signatories, more or less. But just as it's difficult to find empirical studies to shore up claims that programs like the revolving drug fund would be able to recover a substantial fraction of costs, so too is it hard to find many dissenting voices where it matters most. This is true even though it's clear, as the editor of the *Lancet* suggested in 1988, that several claims made for Bamako were extravagant, even when data from the World Bank were considered: "Any cost recovery system would disqualify a considerable proportion of poor inhabitants of rural areas. A World Bank study in Kenya showed that any fee would exclude 40% of the population, and these are the people who most need access to the services. Charging the sick to pay for preventive services is also open to criticism."[2]

And this wasn't just felt in Africa: Bamako metastasized. In 2000, in a book called *Dying for Growth*, physician-anthropologist Jim Yong Kim and colleagues offer a lucid and detailed report from urban Peru, written at about the time Keshavjee found himself entangled in the ostensibly anodyne revolving drug fund in Badakhshan:

> According to several analysts, the success of these smaller, rural [clinics] at recovering costs owes more to the fact that they are residents' only health-care alternative rather than to their true "affordability." And even in these venues, Bamako Initiative funds were far from self-sustaining, in part because they suffered under a flood of inappropriate and expensive drug exports to Africa from pharmaceutical companies in industrialized countries. In the end then, decentralization of this kind has not proved sustainable; it has, however, accelerated the push toward private economies among people who can often ill afford them. This is apparently true even for public services that are supposed to be free, as underpaid government employees supplement their income through informal charges.[3]

The reason for such widespread support for an unproven notion was not a temporary *folie à N*, with Africa's health leaders suddenly espying epidemics of frivolous use of health services in the slums and villages of their home countries. Nor did they unanimously replace the previous slogan ("Health care for all by the year 2000") with a new one ("Health care for some if they can pay for part of it when they're sick, as we shrink our public budgets"). The officials signed on because adopting the Bamako plan was linked, if not always clearly so, to what the international financial institutions called "structural adjustment," the linchpin of neoliberal policy. It was a sort of hidden conditionality, a "natural" part of the market globalism that sought to commoditize health care and shrink social sector spending. Kim and his colleagues explain how it works:

> The World Bank does not and cannot directly force poor-country govern-ments to reduce spending in the public health sector. But, as a lending insti-tution charged with ensuring repayment of debt, the Bank is in a position to offer guidance on how poor countries can best "streamline" their economies to meet their debt service obligations. As a result, in recent years, the World Bank has had an enormous impact on the health of impoverished popula-tions. The design of privatization policies, and their manner of implementa-tion, suggests that bettering poor people's health outcomes is often inciden-tal to their budget-cutting function.[4]

For Kim and colleagues, the intentions of the architects of Bamako and other neoliberal strategies were less important than the health outcomes: "Whatever their ultimate intention, is it possible that privatization poli-cies are ultimately beneficial to the health of the poor? If we base our answer on currently available data from both rich and poor countries, the answer seems to be no."[5]

But don't expect either an apology or a retraction or a published erra-tum, since the TINA refrain works even better in retrospect: with condi-tionality of this sort, *there was no alternative.* Much of this story is a par-able about the golden rule of neoliberalism (he who has the gold, rules). To link programs to the grant proposals that fund them is to unearth the doublespeak of dozens of bureaucracies in control of funds and thus of access to health care, such as it was and is. *Blind Spot* casts a light, some-times harsh, on some of the most vexing problems of what is these days termed "global health," and also on the relationship between citizen and state, between the poor and the powerful, and between shifting centers of power and periphery.

So, did the program in Badakhshan succeed or did it fail? Yes, replies Keshavjee. In Orwell's usage, "double-speak" meant the ability to assert two contradictory claims as fact. High up in the Pamir Mountains, as in the fetid lowlands of Bamako, it was impossible not to feel a certain Orwellian chill. In Badakhshan, there was no need for any success beyond imposing the reform, just as had been the case in Bamako.

This uncoupling of interventions ("reform") and assessment of their effectiveness in improving health, or at least in preventing catastrophe, is often pathognomonic of dogma over data. We've met some of those who served up dogma to the hungry and the sick, but who cooked up the dogma? Keshavjee introduces us to some of the people he believes were injured by neoliberalism but also tries to identify the mechanisms of the injury, and why some are spared. He also, and sometimes brashly, makes claims about the etiology of such injury. If one Rosetta Stone is the World Bank's structural adjustment programs, what of the other code or key—the role of the Mont Pèlerin Society?

If there's one smoke-filled room, it's to be found, argues Keshavjee, in an obscure Swiss resort town called Mont Pèlerin. There, in 1947, a veritable who's who of neoliberalism convened to lay out a plan for, well, global domination.

Such statements can sound sweeping, even ex cathedra, if not buttressed by ethnographic research, and here Keshavjee has helped fill the void between assertion and documentation. Many discussions of neoliberal policies and "the Washington Consensus" have an almost paranoid ring to them, and Keshavjee echoes it simply by quoting those among his informants who struggle directly for survival amid the anomie and confusion and disorder of economic and social collapse. But his close reading is not only of the documents laying out the revolving drug fund and health reform project, but also of the historical record. This allows us to follow him from the smoke-filled hovels of craggy Pamir to those smoke-filled rooms in which policies are hammered out and messages hammered home until they seem to be "just common sense."

Mont Pèlerin is home to some of those smoke-filled rooms. The effort to achieve hegemony ("There is no alternative") required, Keshavjee claims, a decades-long campaign designed less to promote a specific school of economics or any other type of analysis, and more to promote a specific political and social program. This book offers an analysis of how that scaffolding was erected and what it propped up in specific places and times. Keshavjee names names, bringing into view the "organic intellectuals" (and their approach was at times Gramscian) of neoliberalism and how they worked to promote this program and ensure its inevitability.

In a recent review, Manfred Steger observes that "market globalism is without question the dominant ideology of our time." He contrasts it to two competing forms, "justice globalism" and, from the Right, "religious globalism."[6] Pope Francis and many other social justice advocates from liberation theology might dispute this typology. In his first major exhortation, issued in November 2013, Pope Francis attacked neoliberalism specifically and related "ideologies which defend the absolute autonomy of marketplace . . . reject[ing] the rights of states . . . to exercise any form of control."[7] But Steger's observation about how neoliberalism gets in our minds is worth noting: "Market globalism has become what some social theorists call a 'strong discourse'—one that is notoriously difficult to resist and repel because it has on its side powerful social forces that have already pre-selected what counts as 'real' and, therefore, shape the world accordingly. The constant repetition and public recitation of market globalism's core claims and slogans have the capacity to produce what they name. As more neoliberal policies are engaged, the claims of market globalism become even more firmly planted in the public mind."[8]

The aspirations of the Mont Pèlerin Society were not, in any sense, unambitious (then again, nor was "Health for all by the year 2000"). These aspirations touted "free markets" as a panacea for the world's economic *and* political ills; the health problems of the poor were not a ranking concern. Reporting from the Pamir Mountains, Keshavjee recounts how health care expenditures can often lead to the ruin of people already living on the edge, at the close of war and upheaval. This is nothing new, as studies from around the world, in poor countries and in rich ones, show that catastrophic health care expenditures are the number one cause knocking people from poverty into destitution.[9] To link such unhappy tales to the deliberations of those who argued that markets alone should determine what sort of welfare programs should exist is a perilous enough task. It is more so when those deliberations take place far away (and long ago, in terms of medical history). But it is not a long road, Keshavjee shows us, from the mountains of Badakhshan to a resort town on the shores of Switzerland's Lake Leman.

If health outcomes and social protection are, in the words of Jim Yong Kim and colleagues, "often incidental" to the design and financing of health systems, it must be, as in Tajikistan, that that such reforms have other goals. And so they did, from privatization to the reduction of public budgets and staff. What were the "transfer mechanisms" by which neoliberal programmatic blind spots were overlooked when convenient?

Keshavjee suggests that this role was played largely by international NGOs, new players who showed up in places like Tajikistan as the Soviet Union was becoming the former Soviet Union, and also seasoned USAID contractors. In developmentspeak, these, along with humanitarian groups, are the citizenry of "civil society." But there are NGOs and NGOs, and it is the *funders*, argues Keshavjee, who distorted the agendas of institutions such as those willing to implement the revolving drug fund described in *Blind Spot*. Funding for the transfer mechanism, at least in Central Asia, came less from the World Bank and more from the champion of a "reform" that looked a lot like the strictures of the Bamako Initiative, complete with a revolving drug fund. And yes, they were glossed as "RDFs." The U.S. Agency for International Development was among the largest.

This book is also a cultural history of the rise of the twentieth-century transnational institutions, public and private, that shaped and were shaped by neoliberal ideologies. It casts a bright light on the institutions mediating these relationships and webs of power. These include the too rarely examined roles played by NGOs in replicating, wittingly or no, a social order that promises enduring disparities as patients are transformed into consumers—or, as often as not, nonconsumers—of health care and other social services. And thus documents as anodyne as grant proposals become part of what Thomas Piketty has termed "the apparatus of justification" of social and economic inequality.[10] But Keshavjee, as noted, does not denigrate those who staff these bureaucracies; still less does he denigrate their motives. If anything, the anthropologist-physician has extended to them a hermeneutic of generosity and expunged some of their inculpatory (and exculpatory) correspondence. The staff of many, perhaps most, international nongovernmental and humanitarian organizations, including the one that sponsored Keshavjee's work, would flinch to hear themselves described as key sleeper agents for neoliberal policies. But he explains, better than anyone yet has, how these changing institutions relate to shifting development agendas and to public health and medicine in settings as far flung as Mali and the mountains of Badakhshan. This metastasis continues in settings across the world.

Five points are worth underlining in closing this foreword to Keshavjee's thoughtful and troubling book. The first is that it's difficult (perhaps almost impossible) to achieve equity of access to decent health care when neoliberal paradigms underpin care delivery. There are many ways to state this assertion, and it's important to try them all on for size. Amartya Sen and Jean Drèze, in their recent book about India—a country that has known fast economic growth but little improvement in the welfare of the poorest third or so of the population—note that building a strong *publicly* financed health system is critical to success, even if there are other, nonpublic insurers in the mix.[11] In the absence of fine-meshed public safety nets, quality services are by definition reserved for those who can pay for them. Holes in these nets— even the contraction of the notion of shared goods like social protection—is surely one of "the causes of the causes" of both ill health and the impoverishment it so often causes or complicates. As in post-Soviet Tajikistan, whenever and wherever social services are seen as commodities rather than rights, chances are that catastrophic health expenditures will serve as a brake on progress in the fight against poverty and for health.

A second point is that there's little sign we're nearing the end of a neoliberal period in global health. The problem lies not only in past policies, much excoriated by Keshavjee, of the Reagan and Thatcher era; nor does it lie in programs specific to the empire they sought to bring down. The neoliberal period is the moment we're in, right now, as study after study reveals growing inequalities between and within nations. From Tajikistan to Britain, safety nets are being stretched or rent or brought so low that they can no longer break the fall of those facing both poverty and serious illness. The problem is especially acute in the United States: as *Blind Spot* goes to press, a recession with roots in poorly regulated finance and a retreat from the state's responsibilities in social protection have led to similar reversals of fortune in a country responsible for many of the development policies Keshavjee unearthed on the other side of the world. Americans can also ask if and how and when NGOs and even churches (or other religious institutions) have served, wittingly or unwittingly, as "transfer mechanisms" for a heaping helping of economic and social pain that is visible in foreclosed houses, shuttered businesses, and the decay of cities built around manufacturing.

Third, there is ample room for resistance to the crass commodification of health and health care in the emerging arena of *global health equity*. There are a number of examples from the past few years, almost a decade after Keshavjee's fieldwork. Some would argue (at least I would) that global health equity is only now coming into being and that the role of neoliberal paradigms in this endeavor has yet to be determined. Take the example of user fees or the import of expensive pharmaceuticals, another problem mentioned by Jim Yong Kim and colleagues in their critique of Bamako.[12] This was published in 2000, well before the establishment of the President's Emergency Plan for AIDS Relief (PEPFAR) or the Global Fund to Fight AIDS, Tuberculosis, and Malaria. These are among the largest efforts or institutions in the new architecture of global health equity, and two of the reasons that ten million people living with both AIDS and poverty are now receiving treatment with antiretroviral therapy, or ART. If there were user fees associated with access to ART through PEPFAR or the Global Fund, many of the millions living with HIV would have died from it; most of the drugs were manufactured by the generic drug industry. There are many problems of the sort described in *Blind Spot*—for example, the ongoing weakening of public sector institutions or high overheads to contractors—but the success of PEPFAR and the Global Fund has sparked another recent turn toward ambition and equity.

Fourth, the "minimalists" and the "optimalists" continue to clash in professional debates about health care delivery. Selling medicines to starving people may not be wholly discredited in such circles, and the ideas that underpinned fantasies about revolving drug funds may be alive and well, but, twenty-five years after Bamako, universalism is emerging from its coma. Many health officials in the countries signatory to Bamako are now grappling with the challenge of providing health care services to all their citizens. The chief debate going forward seems to be between the optimalists who seek to build "universal health care" systems (whether with a strictly public care system or with a national health service that does not rule out private insurance) and those who advocate "targeting" the poor with a more minimalist package of services. In reviewing experience in India, the world's laggard in equitable access to care and protection from catastrophic illness, Jean Drèze and Amartya Sen summarize one part of a brisk global debate: "A health system based on targeted insurance subsidies is very unlikely to meet basic norms of equity in health care, as four different sources of inequality reinforce each other: exclusion errors associated with the targeting process; screening of potential clients by insurance companies; the obstacles (powerlessness, low education, social discrimination, among others) poor people face in using the health insurance system, where access to health care is linked to the ability to pay insurance premiums."[13]

Fifth and finally, things change. The ethnographic research informing this study was conducted in a time of rapid, indeed catastrophic, change. Such research is necessarily ethnographic and attuned to social change. Sometimes this is cataclysmic: war, natural disasters, and rapid social collapse reveal a lot about "the shock doctrine" in part because such extremity prompts spectators and those touched directly to ask why so many had to die. In Tajikistan, in the wake of civil war and food shortages, there was also a collapse of systems of meaning, of ways of making sense of the citizens' relationship not only to the state but also to each other. The commonweal, the sense of shared opportunities and misfortunes that bind us together—after all, what is "pooled risk" if not sharing?—is often one of the first casualties of hard-core neoliberalism. And things continue to change. More than a decade later, Keshavjee has learned that his old friend Misha is now in Badakhshan's government. Jim Yong Kim is president of the World Bank.

It's hard to point to empirical studies documenting the corrosive effects of neoliberalism in health care and education. But when the diagnosis is soaring inequality, what is the actionable agenda? Keshavjee hints at a response to this question at the end of this book. He may be ironic, but there's no cynicism here. Keshavjee shares the Enlightenment belief that it is possible to understand what's happening, to "measure outcomes" of great import to those who face punishing risk to health and well-being. Such outcomes, including the socially corrosive ones, will not be measured without bringing the mechanisms of social process into relief. They will not be gauged without understanding casuistry or seeking to understand how neoliberalism works itself into the lives and bodies of those who feel most keenly the impact of policies and programs like the ones examined in this book. *Blind Spot* acknowledges that claims of causality are difficult to make. But this is not because such effects don't ensue; it's rather that they are complex and far reaching and require, for any full measure of noxious effect, a commitment to the sort of research and reflection that Salmaan Keshavjee offers here. This is the work of an engaged and critical anthropology for which we all have cause to be grateful.

Preface

For many, Tajikistan is a faraway place, the Soviet Union an increasingly distant memory, and *neoliberalism* an ill-defined buzzword. It makes sense, therefore, for readers to ask how and why a book examining the intellectual and ideological roots of a small global health project, set almost two decades ago in the remote mountain valleys of that faraway place, is relevant to the contemporary understanding of global health and development. Even more, how is it relevant to readers' everyday lives?

As a practitioner and researcher trained in both internal medicine and anthropology, I have had the good fortune to spend significant time working with global health and development experts in a number of settings—Bangladesh, Tajikistan, Peru, Russia, Lesotho, and Switzerland—and have been involved in leading and implementing large and complex health projects. The idea for this book—an analysis that traces the intellectual and social history of one global health project but is really meant to inform our understanding of how we have approached international development over the last half century—stems from questions that have dogged me throughout my time working in some of the world's most vulnerable communities. Why are some development programs pursued in the face of clear and abundant evidence suggesting that they will not achieve their stated outcomes? How do social, political, and economic forces constitute a "metanarrative" capable of shaping events and choices? To be sure, the answers to these questions are complex. Yet, if we examine the latter half of the twentieth century, a defining ideological force does stand out, and its precepts appear to have played a significant role in shaping our social and economic landscape: *neoliberalism*. Because this political ideology has come to inform our "common sense," understanding its impact on global health and development—especially at the level of communities and individuals—requires thoughtful exploration of some strongly held beliefs. That is the aim of this book: to map the passage of neoliberal ideology from the powerful to the poor, and from policies to the lived experience of individuals.

The first belief—at the heart of what is often associated with neoliberalism as an ideology—is that "the market" is the best distributor of social goods and that the main role of government is to enable and facilitate markets. We hear arguments about this belief almost every day. Should we have vouchers for private schools rather than promoting a public education system? Should social security be privatized rather than ensured by the government? How best can health care be distributed to the most vulnerable? Why do bond or stock markets influence the behavior of governments more than the electorate does? From the effects of post-2008 austerity on the countries of the eurozone to debates about the best way to foster economic growth in poor countries, understanding the roots of neoliberalism and its ability to shape social relations—both among individuals and between individuals and the state—is at the heart of comprehending how we organize our own society and exhort others to organize theirs.[1] An abundance of data about the inability of markets to distribute health goods to those who need them most—such as the poor or those who become poor because of catastrophic or chronic health events—has been largely ignored.[2] The reason, I argue here, is because of the ascendancy of neoliberalism in Cold War and post–Cold War institutional and policy circles, ostensibly as a bulwark against totalitarianism. The result has been an emphasis on markets as the optimal distributor of social goods and, through this, a complete reshaping of our expectations of governments and our fellow humans. It has redefined how we help others, including the most vulnerable in society, and has reshaped our social world by penetrating our "common sense" about what is right and wrong. In the case of global health and development, it has led to blind spots—referred to in this book as *neoliberal realms of programmatic blindness*—that have contributed to poor outcomes for individuals and communities.

The second belief is that nongovernmental organizations (NGOs) are, de facto, the best institutions to provide social services to the poor. While many, including myself, view the efforts of international NGOs in some of the world's poorest communities as heroic, it is important to take the time for a deeper examination of how they have been used, for political purposes, to replace state functions. The idea of civil society is at the foundation of Western liberal thought: citizens and nongovernmental entities coming together around important issues or missions, representing the will of local communities or constituencies, and providing a check on state overreach.[3] Yet, from the 1980s on, donor-sponsored expansion of the activities of international NGOs—entities we previously associated with "grassroots" development and transnational civil society—has been promoted by neoliberal thinkers and policy makers as a means of halting the spread of communism and totalitarianism.[4] In some ways, this has turned the concept of civil society on its head and has increased the risk of NGOs becoming a conduit—or "transplantation mechanism"—for neoliberal ideology. The resulting conceptual realignment of the role of NGOs vis-à-vis society and the state—tied to de-emphasis of the state in ensuring the welfare of the poor—has contributed to what can best be called "mission capture" in global development. Moreover, it has exacerbated NGOs' lack of accountability to populations being served. This does not mean that NGOs are bad, or that they are unable to complement and enhance the services provided by governments. In fact, many do. It simply suggests that we need to understand and examine the relationship among NGOs, their funders, and their actions on the ground.[5] The exploration of how neoliberal ideology has permeated and shaped the practice of NGOs working in global health and development is at the core of this book.

The third belief worthy of careful examination is that if good people embark on a development project with good intentions, then good outcomes will follow. From my experience, especially in light of serious concerns about the first two beliefs, this is not a given. In fact, from the ethnographic case example I discuss in this book—about one of the world's preeminent NGOs working in what can only be described as an extremely difficult physical, economic, and political environment—it is clear that when left unchecked, dogma can prevail over data and shape the way we construct, execute, and evaluate development programs. Neoliberalism's success as an ideology, as a significant social force, is demonstrated by the way the components of this ideology have been absorbed by individuals, transplanted by NGOs, and—through its infiltration of practice—embodied in the local world in the form of poor health outcomes.[6] This can be prevented, but it requires actively orienting programs and practices around the outcomes that matter most to the communities being served. In the face of the large-scale funding required for many health and development interventions—along with the presence of often weak local institutions—this is certainly a challenge even for the best among us, as the case in this book highlights.

This book is intended to add to the conversation about how to more effectively bring the fruits of technology and innovation to those for whom it is a matter of life and death; how social, political, and economic forces have shaped practices in global health; and how ideological blind spots are traps along the path of achieving some of our most humane and important societal goals.

Acknowledgments

This book emerged from a dissertation that I wrote as a doctoral student in Anthropology and Middle Eastern Studies at Harvard University in the 1990s. Over the two decades during which I worked on the dissertation and several revisions of the manuscript, I have been blessed with the kindness and thoughtfulness of many wonderful people to whom I owe a debt of gratitude. I hope that those from whose goodwill I benefited but whom I have not mentioned below will forgive the omission.

First, I am grateful to those who made it possible for me to spend a year in Tajikistan collecting primary data. This research was made possible at various phases through fellowships and grants from the Harvard Center for Middle Eastern Studies, the Harvard Department of Anthropology, the Andrew W. Mellon Foundation, the Sir James Lougheed Award of Distinction (Alberta Heritage Scholarship Fund), the U.S. Department of Education (Foreign Language and Area Studies Fellowship), the Social Science and Humanities Research Council of Canada, the Aga Khan Foundation USA (through a grant from the U.S. Agency for International Development), the Harvard Forum for Central Asian Studies, and the Cora Du Bois Charitable Trust.

Collecting the ethnographic material presented in this book would have been impossible without the generous assistance and cooperation of the Aga Khan Foundation offices in Washington, D.C., Geneva, Dushanbe, and Khorog. I am especially grateful to Bob Shaw, Robert Middleton, Iqbal Noor Ali, Anne LaFond, Pierre Claquin, Najmi Kanji, and Hakim Feerasta for their encouragement and advice during my time in Tajikistan, and for allowing me to freely conduct my research. In Khorog, Mamadamin Mamadaminov and Yodgor Faisov helped arrange logistical support, and Peter, Nukhra, Dilawar, Mahmood, Natasha, Svetlana, Firuz, and many others at the Aga Khan Development Network offices were always most helpful. Banoz and Gulbargh used to bake little treats for me when I came back from the villages, and I shall not forget them for that. Special thanks are given to the following people for their assistance in conducting the surveys that guided this work: Khurshed Konunov, Kolya Konunov, Gulomsho Lutfaliev, the field staff for the Pharmaceutical Use Survey, Mansur Shakarmamadov and Farrukh Shakarmamadov for work on the Dental Survey, all the translators who worked on the long-answer surveys, the computer team at the Aga Khan Development Network for helping with data entry, and the many others, too numerous to mention here, who helped me. I am deeply grateful to the Badakhshani families who showed incredible kindness to me in Khorog and other villages. I cannot thank them by name because they are primary actors in this book. Not only did they look after me, but knowing that I was an anthropologist, they trusted me to convey their stories.

When I first arrived in Central Asia, I knew no one. Alisher Kassimov, Mubin Juraev, and Timur Hassanov helped me find my way. The families of Farrukh Asrarov, Lola Dodkhudoeva, Khayolbeg Dodhikhudoev, Abdulsalom Mamadnazarov, and Ebrahim Konunov opened their homes to me and made me feel welcome. For this, I am deeply indebted. I am especially grateful to Farrukh Asrarov, Farhad Asrarov, Firdaus Asrarov, Farrukh Dodkhudoev, Khurshed Konunov, and Kolya Konunov for their unwavering friendship and help. They, along with Jeanette Kuder, Isabel Hemming, Sadru Akbarali, Gulomsho Lutfaliev, Mahmood Khaled, Pierre Claquin, Mansur Shakarmamadov, Farrukh Shakarmamadov, Saifollah in Porshnief, Scott Simmons, and the gang at Médecins Sans Frontières (especially Cécile, Michel, and Vincent), made living in Tajikistan during trying times much more enjoyable.

At the Harvard Center for Middle Eastern Studies and the Department of Anthropology, I would like to give special thanks to Diana Abouali, Rasha Al Turki, Gulnora Aminova, Sahar Bazzaz, Michael Connell, Faisal Devji, Marilyn Goodrich, Rebecca Grow, the late Joan Gillespie, Bill Graham, Barbara Henson, Matthew McGuire, Munir Jiwa, Susan Miller, Eric Seivers, Chris Tennant, and Nargis Virani for all their help and support during my graduate studies and onward. I am especially indebted to John Schoeberlein, whose guidance and mentorship during my studies and research was constant and invaluable. I am also grateful to Ankur Asthana, Mercedes Becerra, Faisal Devji, Nadza Durakovic, Paul Farmer, Michael Fischer, Pamela Hunte, Ameer Keshavjee, Mohamed Keshavjee, Rafique Keshavjee, Tom Nicholson, Bob Shaw, Amin Tejpar, and Chris Tennant, all of whom either read parts of the original dissertation or one of the many versions of the manuscript and provided many useful comments and insights.

I am especially thankful to Paul Farmer, who has spent so much time teaching me to write more artfully, and who so generously offered to pen the foreword to this book. He read and commented on every page of multiple versions of the manuscript. His close friendship and mentorship over the last two decades—along with the intensity of his engagement on this project—has been a gift for which I am deeply grateful.

While finalizing the manuscript, I had the opportunity to present my findings at both the Harvard-Yale Anthropology Colloquium and Harvard's Friday Morning Seminar in Medical Anthropology, where colleagues provided important feedback and input. I am also grateful to the three reviewers for the University of California Press, whose guidance helped me markedly improve the final version.

To my three doctoral advisors at Harvard, Nur Yalman, Byron Good, and Arthur Kleinman, I cannot be thankful enough. Nur Yalman's support and encouragement began when I first considered entering the field of anthropology, and has been unwavering since. His wonderful ability to bring out the positive in every situation was a balm to me on many an occasion. Byron Good has been a demanding teacher, mentor, and friend for twenty years. He is one of the people in my life whom I know I can call any time and be met with warmth and thoughtful advice. I have many fond memories both in and outside the classroom of Byron and Mary-Jo Good.

I owe a great personal and intellectual debt to Arthur Kleinman, a mentor and a friend over the last twenty years. It was Arthur who encouraged and helped me to become an anthropologist, and who pushed me to pursue the global health scholarship that I have enjoyed so much. I cannot list all the ways in which he has taught me how to learn, how to work, how to teach, and how to engage as an anthropologist and a scholar. He and Joan Kleinman invited Mercedes and me to stay at their home when I returned from my fieldwork; he visited me as I went through my medical training; and he has supported me in every step of my career to date. He was the driving force in creating a nurturing space for critical reflection and practice of medical anthropology. I am one of many who had the good fortune to benefit from that rich and enabling environment—the Harvard school of medical anthropology—and can only hope that this book reflects the rich intellectual community of which I have been so privileged to be part.

I would be remiss if I did not also thank the wonderful team at Partners In Health for their warmth, kindness, and generosity during my graduate work and thereafter. Ophelia Dahl, Paul Farmer, and Jim Yong Kim, with whom Mercedes and I became friends in 1994, created a space at Partners In Health where ideas of social justice could re-enter the consciousness of people working in global health and development. Mercedes and I were privileged to work among an amazing group of people—some of whom, like us, lived for a time in the Partners In Health houses in Cambridge and Lima—who challenged the way that global health had become socially constructed, and worked tirelessly to improve the way care was being delivered in poor communities. In addition to Jim, Paul, and Ophelia, I am especially grateful to Jaime Bayona, Joaquín Blaya, Gene Bukhman, Mary Kay Smith-Fawzi, Hamish Fraser, Jennifer Furin, Irina Gelmanova, Alex Golubkov, Tim Holtz, Rocío Hurtado, Anne Hyson, Darius Jazayeri, Christopher Johnson, Keith Joseph, Kathryn Kempton, Serena Koenig, Younsook Lim, Carole Mitnick, Joia Mukherjee, Ed Nardell, Kristin Nelson, Oksana Ponomarenko, Michael Rich, the late Rocío Sapag, K.J. Seung, Aaron Shakow, Sonya Shin, Askar Yedilbayev, and Paul Zintl. Their support, warmth, kindness, and friendship are one of my life's treasures.

By the time I started writing the manuscript, I was a staff physician at Brigham and Women's Hospital in the Department of Medicine and, later, in the Division of Global Health Equity. I subsequently joined Harvard Medical School as a faculty member in the Department of Global Health and Social Medicine. I am grateful to the individuals at both these institutions who have mentored and encouraged me in my work on this book, including Anne Becker, Jaclyn Chai, Howard Hiatt, Steve Kadish, Joel Katz, Margaret Paternek, Jennifer Puccetti, and Susan Radlinski. Paul Farmer and Jim Yong Kim both served as chairs of the Department of Global Health and Social Medicine and the Brigham's Division of Global Health Equity during the writing of the manuscript, and helped me carve out the necessary time despite my other responsibilities. Funding for writing the final parts of the manuscript came from the Frank Hatch Fellowship at Brigham and Women's Hospital and the Zinberg Fellowship in Global Health Delivery at Harvard Medical School, for which I am very grateful.

Over the years, I received significant support for this project from my family—Fatima Keshavjee-Johnson; James, Roxana, and Odessa Johnson; and Corina, Genie, Guillermo, and Will Becerra—and from many close friends, including Aamir Khan, Adnan Mansour, Nora Osman, Islande Paul, Scott Plotkin, Candace Lun-Plotkin, Lubna Samad, Jacek Skarbinski, and Ali Velshi. Despite my misgivings, they had faith that I would actually finish this project. My dear friends Munira Padamsee and Tom White died before I finished the manuscript, but they were avid discussants about the topic of this book, and I would like to think that they would have enjoyed reading it.

While writing this book, I had the support of four dedicated coworkers, each hoping to be the one to send the final draft to the publisher. Sadly, my time working on other projects in Russia, Lesotho, and Geneva delayed its completion, but I will be forever in the debt of Catherine Oettinger, Vera Belitsky, Nadza Durakovic, and Ankur Asthana for their support and encouragement. Nadza and, ultimately, Ankur did the yeoman's task of helping me put the final pieces together.

Two additional friends deserve special gratitude: Suzanne Gordon and Steve Hubbell. They motivated me to take what was a dense and complex dissertation and make it into what they always referred to as a readable work. Steve is a brilliant writer and his cues made me think about how to make this story more accessible. Suzanne and I had long conversations at her kitchen table and in her living room, where she encouraged me to tell her stories of my time in Badakhshan. Together, Suzanne and Steve helped me think about the phenomenology of the post-Soviet transition at its most intimate levels. Their patience, friendship, advice, and input over a number of years have meant a lot to me as an individual and as a writer.

I am deeply grateful to Naomi Schneider, my editor at the University of California Press, who finally made this book a reality. She is a discerning editor and I am grateful for her friendship, guidance, and patience. It is thanks to her that the manuscript emerged in its final form.

Mercedes Becerra has been my closest friend, and her companionship for over two decades has been sustenance to me. We have been involved in an intense conversation about global health and development for more than twenty years. We were joined along the way by our son Zayn, who has been nothing but joy. He is still too little to learn about neoliberalism, but as soon as possible I am hoping he will read this book and understand why I worked to finish it, and why, as Mercedes says, health equity and neoliberalism cannot comfortably coexist. Lastly, I wish to thank my parents, Ameer and Sherbanu Keshavjee, for a lifetime of nurturing and kindness. It is to them that I dedicate this work.

Map of Tajikistan

1 Introduction

A WORLD TRANSFORMED

Spring in Badakhshan can be hauntingly beautiful. Ahmed and I had been traversing Tajikistan's Pamir Mountains for a week in an old Russian jeep when we paused at a juncture in the road to look at our map. I gazed out at the desolation of an almost treeless mountainside—endless rock formations standing in stark contrast to a powder blue sky—whose heights concealed roaring rivers, fertile pastures, and in the lower areas, small orchards. The local people say that when God created the world, he gave everybody something they could use. But by the time Badakhshan's turn came, almost everything had already been distributed, so God gave the Pamiri people rocks and stones.

We'd been moving along at a hectic pace, and in that instant, I had the weary sensation of having driven over every boulder, rock, and pebble in those barren hills. Studying the map, Ahmed asked if I wanted to continue along the same road or turn off toward the village of Kuhdeh.[1] It was the spring of 1996, and Ahmed and I had been visiting the medical clinics of Badakhshan's Roshtqala District to monitor the distribution of vitamins and polio vaccine. Known as the rooftop of the world, Badakhshan—which borders China to the east, Afghanistan to the southwest, and the Kyrgyz Republic to the northeast—has only 220,000 inhabitants scattered over

1

more than 64,000 square kilometers. Journeys between towns and villages—along some of the bumpiest thoroughfares I have ever encountered—can be formidable. Moreover, we had slept fitfully in our tent the night before, a night that in retrospect was too cold for us to have refused our host's insistence that we sleep indoors. To go to Kuhdeh now surely meant traveling up a valley for an hour only to find another closed health post.² I looked off the main road and saw what appeared to be a pile of dirt and gravel leading into the river. "There doesn't seem to be a road here," I said. The driver, who had been working in the district for more than twenty-five years, assured me that this was in fact the road to Kuhdeh, adding that it had been washed away. To get there, he said, we would have to cross the river in our jeep. I glanced over at Ahmed, who looked doubtful. If we did not feel like going to Kuhdeh because of the road, I reasoned, perhaps the health workers had not either.

So we set out through the river and along ten kilometers of rocky, bone-rattling road. The route at times towered over a deep gorge, and at other points descended to the level of the river. We were later to discover that the people of Kuhdeh had built the road themselves with the help of a neighboring village. As we crossed the river, this time over a worn wooden bridge, we happened upon some farmers and asked if anyone from the medical clinic had come by recently. They laughed and told us that it had been months since any health officials had visited. "Check with Rais [village leader]," they said, "just to make certain." We continued up the road, which ran between small fields bordered on one side by a steep cliff and on the other by a mountain, until we reached the home of the village head.

We were met by a lanky, taciturn man who eyed us with skepticism. We introduced ourselves, and he called us into his home to drink shir choi, *a local drink made with tea, milk, salt, and sometimes nuts, and to eat bread with sour cream. Light streamed from a central upper window into his single-room Pamiri-style house. I explained that we were there to monitor vaccination coverage and micronutrient distribution for the Aga Khan Foundation and asked about his contact with the health authorities. Like the farmers we had met, he laughed, telling us that our car was the first one that had come to Kuhdeh in almost a year; nobody else had made the effort, not even the nurse at the health post. "They've forgotten us," he said.*

I later discovered that Kuhdeh had had little assistance since the collapse of the Soviet Union, and that the clothes the villagers wore were, in most cases, the same ones they had owned on the day Tajikistan was forced into independence five years earlier. Rais himself had faced particularly hard times after the Soviet Union collapsed. His brother, after weeks of drinking, had fallen to his death in a ravine not far from his house; Rais had taken his brother's wife and children into his home. I never learned whether he fell or jumped, but Rais always intimated that it had been related to the collapse. Now fourteen people were living under Rais's roof. Despite the difficulties, Rais himself was cautiously optimistic: "Now that the Aga Khan Foundation is here and we're getting food," he would say, "things will be better." As I looked around the village, I desperately wanted to believe him.

Our chance turn onto the Kuhdeh road would prove fortuitous for my understanding of Badakhshan. Over the months that followed, I returned to the village dozens of times, and Ahmed and I lived with Rais's family for a few weeks. From countless conversations with people in Kuhdeh and other villages in Badakhshan, I was able to piece together a clearer picture of the myriad ways the collapse of the Soviet Union in 1991 had altered their lives. Although our mission focused on nutrition and vaccination—and later on pharmaceutical drugs—our trips to Kuhdeh and many other villages and towns in Badakhshan allowed us to witness firsthand the transformation of health care in the region from a universal, socialized system to a privatized apparatus guided by the priorities of donors from abroad. From the moment Moscow ceded control over the Soviet Union's vast Central Asian domains, Western governments, development banks, and international NGOs launched a remarkable experiment in privatization and economic liberalization. Some of these interventions have been productive, while others have exacerbated an already precarious situation, primarily for more marginal populations. Various aspects of this evolution—particularly in the banking, petroleum, and consumer goods sectors—have been well documented elsewhere. Relatively little attention has been paid, however, to the delivery of medical care at the village level.

This gap in the scholarship was very much on my mind when I was invited to Tajikistan's easternmost province of Badakhshan in the summer of 1995 by Dr. Pierre Claquin, the health officer at the Aga Khan Foundation (AKF), an international NGO based in Geneva, Switzerland. I had been conducting research for my doctoral dissertation in Tajikistan's capital, Dushanbe, which at the time was under curfew. The country was in the midst of a civil war that had started in 1992 and would continue until mid-1997. The origin of the war was itself a point of debate. According to some, it was driven by ethnic rivalries; according to others, it was a political conflict between supporters of reform and a conservative old guard holding onto power.[3] There were even those who attributed it to the rise of groups referred to as "Islamists" or "the mafia." It is likely that there were multiple contributing factors. Regardless, the violence resulted in an estimated 150,000 to 300,000 deaths across the political and ethnic spectrum.[4] Roughly 700,000 refugees who traced their origin to Badakhshan and its neighboring province, Gharm, fled from Tajikistan into Afghanistan; an additional 150,000 people are said to have fled to the Russian Federation.[5]

The war was a significant tipping point for Tajikistan. The country was one of the poorest republics in the Soviet Union, and although many gains in the population's health and education status had been registered during the Soviet period, Tajikistan emerged as an independent state in a precarious position. But even the most destitute citizens—many of whom were no strangers to deprivation even prior to the breakup—were not prepared for the sudden decline in living standards that began in 1991. The loss of subsidies from Moscow, exacerbated by the years of civil war, would ultimately plunge the newly independent nation into the ranks of the world's most impoverished states. Per capita GDP would fall from $2,870 in 1990 to $215 in 1998; by the end of the 1990s, almost 85 percent of the population was living below the poverty line.[6] By 1996, real wages were only 5 percent of their 1991 level.[7]

Although statistics offer only a hint of the suffering endured by the people of Tajikistan, they paint a dismal picture. Rapid inflation severely eroded purchasing power and food consumption, and health, nutrition, and educational services were on the brink of collapse.[8] In the midst of this crisis, the central and regional governments no longer paid the cost of providing health services. The Health Ministry could no longer purchase medical supplies, including essential pharmaceutical drugs that, though subsidized during the Soviet period, had consumed from 13 to 16 percent of the state budget.[9] As social sector spending dropped, the effects on the quality of life for most Tajiks were immediate and devastating. Life expectancy at birth for both men and women dropped during the early 1990s from 72.3 years for women and 67.1 years for men in 1991 to 68.5 for women and 63.2 for men in 1994. By 1998, the figures were 67.5 and 61.1, respectively.[10] By 1995, infant mortality exceeded 30.7 per 1,000 live births (compared to an EU average of 5.8 and a former Soviet Union average of 21.7),[11] mostly due to respiratory infections, diarrhea, and developmental disorders causing death in the first few weeks of life.[12] Maternal mortality increased from 41.8 per 100,000 live births in 1991 to 93.7 in 1995, almost ten times the European Union average. The breakdown in clean water supply, proper sewerage, and the public health system led to an upsurge of communicable diseases, including waterborne diseases, tuberculosis, malaria, typhoid fever, measles, and diphtheria.[13]

In Badakhshan, the situation was even more desperate due to its remoteness and sparse population.[14] Winters there are long and extremely severe, making travel almost impossible and leaving the region isolated most of the year. The region had become even more inaccessible with essential supply lines cut because of war: fighting had severed the only road to the rest of Tajikistan. One could still fly to Khorog, Badakhshan's capital—a hair-raising trip on a Soviet-made Yak-40 aircraft, described to me by a seasoned pilot as one of the most harrowing landing approaches in the world—or drive in via Osh in the Kyrgyz Republic through eastern Badakhshan's desolate and sparsely populated Murghab region, a route along the Pamir Highway at more than 3,650 meters (11,975 feet) above sea level. Although many Badakhshanis had been killed during Tajikistan's civil war, the region itself, for the most part, did not suffer much active conflict because of its isolation. This, however, did not stop the influx of more than 60,000 ethnic Pamiri refugees who returned to the relative safety of their ancestral land from other parts of Tajikistan to wait out the war, bringing the population to more than 200,000 souls.

Meanwhile, the Soviet state and its complex bureaucracy had stopped functioning, and what local institutional remnants remained were too weak to fill the vacuum. Only after living in the country for an extended period did I come to better understand the degree of shock that had descended on the society after the collapse of the Soviet Union and the ensuing civil war. Their rudder had been destroyed; the surety and security to which they had grown accustomed under Soviet rule had given way to an uncertain future. With the demise of communism, health care and education, once universally available throughout Tajikistan, became scarce. Where the government had once offered a code of ethics and a sense of stability, there was now only deprivation, civil war, and mass upheaval. The government itself had been so weakened by the collapse that in many areas it lacked the wherewithal to run even basic social services. Individuals raised in a world of adequate electricity and food were now forced to live hand to mouth.

In places like Badakhshan, which had survived on direct food and fuel shipments from Moscow during the Soviet period, the situation rapidly became dire. By 1993, the humanitarian crisis facing the region left almost the entire population at risk of death from starvation and exposure. It also led to the arrival of a number of international NGOs—including AKF—who, virtually overnight, had to provide the assistance to avert an even greater catastrophe.

NGOs stepped into Badakhshan's ravaged landscape with a remarkably expansive and varied mandate. Not only would they provide emergency assistance to citizens at risk of malnutrition and disease, but they were also, de facto, empowered to set up a system for providing Badakhshanis with the crucial social services once delivered by the Soviet state.

For me, an anthropology doctoral candidate having finished graduate work in public health, Dr. Claquin's invitation was a remarkable opportunity. AKF had received funding from the U.S. Agency for International Development (USAID) for their food assistance program, as well as an invitation to expand their health programs. USAID, he told me, had also provided funding for a social researcher to work with the foundation to better understand the effects of health care delivery interventions at the community level, specifically in providing pharmaceuticals. After spending two weeks together exploring the health situation in Badakhshan and discussing the pharmaceutical crisis, Dr. Claquin offered me the job.

At the time, I did not fully appreciate the extent to which the changes taking place in this small mountainous region at the far reaches of the recently dissolved Soviet empire would be a window onto global health policy. However, after spending time in Badakhshan, I realized that the rise of NGOs as major regional and global development actors, a social apparatus hitherto unknown in the Soviet world, was no accident. Their rise was linked to profound changes in economic and political thinking—what political scientist Mark Robinson (1993) refers to as the "new policy agenda" in the United States and the United Kingdom, which combined neoliberal economics (which at that time was being referred to as late twentieth-century capitalism but is now captured in the term *neoliberalism*) and, at least on paper, a commitment to liberal democratic theory and good governance.[15] It was part of an ideological agenda that saw participation in markets as an economic form of political democracy.[16] Its architects deliberately set out to re-engineer the role of government and the idea of the welfare state by arguing that private enterprise was more efficient in providing social services.[17] Under the new policy agenda, NGOs were conceived as instruments for fostering democracy and the creation of new markets, which, it was believed, would act as a bulwark against totalitarianism. Lester Salamon, founding director of Johns Hopkins University's Institute for Policy Studies, referred to this movement and the resulting social transformation as an "associational revolution" that "may constitute as significant a social and political development of the latter twentieth century as the rise of the nation state was for the nineteenth century."[18]

THE AFTERMATH OF EMPIRE

It is very difficult to sugarcoat the collapse of an empire, no matter how bad things may have been before. During moments of reflection, people would describe the hardship they had endured during Soviet times, but it paled in comparison to their post-Soviet predicament. As one woman in Khorog put it, "After the collapse . . . not many changes occurred. Everything is okay. The only problem is starvation."

The trauma of the people in Badakhshan, I would find, had implications that extended far beyond the borders of Tajikistan. Many of the changes brought on by the Soviet collapse were linked in subtle ways to broader processes associated with a sudden and relatively unbuffered immersion in the global economy. Using the lens of medical anthropology and combining ethnographic fieldwork, historical research, and social analysis, I hoped to capture a snapshot of rapid political-economic change, set against a back-drop of the collapse of empire, civil war, and the previously unimaginable local presence of NGOs. In the end I focused on pharmaceuticals but could just as easily have studied the distribution of food, clothing, housing, fuel, or other necessities of life, all of which became increasingly subject to larger global processes. For all its poverty and isolation, Badakhshan would yield a rich treasury of ethnographic material on the consequences of abrupt, radical privatization, supported by bilateral and multilateral institutions with mandates largely framed by the discourse of neoliberalism and imple-mented amid profound social upheaval and transformation.

Working with the Aga Khan Foundation placed me in a privileged ethno-graphic position. On the face of it, the organization was like any large international NGO in the region—a characteristic that ultimately allowed me to use this analysis of one of its many projects as a vehicle for under-standing how the ideology of neoliberalism managed to enter the isolated local world of Badakhshan. It is this general attribute of being a large international NGO—in a space where funding is dominated by large glo-bal institutions made up of many countries (multilateral funding) and donor agencies representing single countries (bilateral funding)—that I wish to highlight in the pages ahead, and that has allowed me to draw conclusions about how NGOs can inadvertently participate in expanding the penetration of neoliberal ideology globally.

It is also relevant to highlight two other significant attributes of the foundation that allowed me to bring into such stark relief the ideological aspect of the program discussed in this book. First, AKF is an organization with a sterling reputation; it operates hundreds of successful programs in many countries. Its efforts have saved many lives and without question have positively contributed to the well-being of many across the globe. The foundation is known for its close connection with the communities in which it operates, involving community members in decision making and modifying programs based on community feedback.[19] These characteris-tics are not only laudable but represent the best of what one imagines to be a strength of nongovernmental development organizations as institu-tions of civil society.

Second, although AKF is a secular organization, the population of

Badakhshan had links to Prince Karim Aga Khan IV, AKF's founder. Most people in Badakhshan are Isma'ili Muslims, a Shi'a denomination that recognizes the Aga Khan as its spiritual leader, or imam. In the final years of the Soviet period, the Badakhshani people reached out to the Aga Khan for assistance. In 1992, after the Soviet Union collapsed and the Tajik civil war started, AKF became involved in providing urgent humanitarian assistance to the region. Starting soon thereafter, and continuing until the late 1990s, the foundation provided three meals a day to Badakhshan's more than 200,000 inhabitants. As an observer midway through this critical period, I can attest that if not for AKF's humanitarian assistance—given in conjunction with efforts by the United Nations World Food Programme, Médecins Sans Frontières, the International Committee of the Red Cross, and the International Federation of the Red Cross—many thousands of Badakhshanis would surely have perished.

Together, these distinct attributes could be expected to render AKF's work in Badakhshan relatively immune to external ideological forces like neoliberalism. To expect this, however—to put any organization, no matter how exemplary, on a pedestal—would be to grossly underestimate the power of neoliberal discourse and its ascendant role in defining thought and practice in global health. In fact, my analysis of one particular program instituted in Badakhshan—a revolving drug fund used by numerous NGOs around the world to address shortages of high-quality pharmaceuticals in poor communities—is illustrative of the penetration of neoliberal ideology into the design and implementation of development programs. This penetration is all the more salient in the post-Soviet context, given the roots of neoliberalism as an ideology expressly designed—by individuals who had an open antipathy toward the overarching Soviet model of cradle-to-grave care for citizens—to act as a counterforce to socialism, communism, and totalitarianism.

In response to the health crisis—particularly the shortage of quality-assured pharmaceutical drugs in the region—in 1996 AKF applied to USAID for resources to create a revolving drug fund in Badakhshan. The fund's mission drew heavily from the Bamako Initiative, a set of principles developed under the auspices of the United Nations Children's Fund and adopted by the health ministers of the World Health Organization African

Region at Bamako, Mali, in September 1987.[20] The strategy defined at Bamako was a response to poor countries not having enough money to purchase medicines or provide much-needed basic primary health care. The solution, however, turned patients into "consumers," and sought to shift expenses for care from governments to individuals ("cost shifting"). Although Badakhshanis did not have a tradition of paying for medicines (which were essentially free to citizens during the Soviet period), the architects of the health strategy at AKF—like many who have turned to this scheme in other parts of the world—likely hoped that implementation of the Bamako Initiative would accelerate and strengthen the delivery of primary health care and improve access to essential medicines.[21] The initiative outlines three priorities: (1) decentralized community-based decision making; (2) user financing of health services under community control; and (3) limitation of programs to the delivery of the most essential drugs, as determined within the framework of a national drugs policy.[22] User fees, it was believed, would improve "internal efficiency" by making important health inputs such as medicines more readily available; would improve "allocative efficiency" by making sure that medicines reached people who really needed them and discouraging "trivial" consumption; and would provide revenue that would make possible the expansion of services.[23]

The Bamako Initiative reflected the priorities and worldview of the dominant state and parastatal actors involved in international aid and development, most notably the World Bank and USAID.[24] The stated reason for favoring the private sector in providing health care was the belief that "the market" is more efficient in distributing limited health resources.[25] Underlying this belief was an ideological commitment to replacing the state with "the market" in allocating essential services. Though the World Bank and USAID are hardly alone in determining health policy in developing countries, their influence—particularly in the newly independent states of the former Soviet Union—has been immense.

Having worked closely with AKF during the initial stages of the revolving drug fund in Badakhshan, I understood that this approach was viewed as the only viable means of delivering medicines at a time when humanitarian assistance programs were ending. My sense was that like many NGOs working in the region, the Geneva-based leadership of AKF felt it had to pursue "sustainable" options, especially within a context of great uncertainty, the threat of continued war, a collapsed economy, and reduced international donor funding.[26] The approach defined in the Bamako Initiative was seen as a tool that would help the health system transition from "humanitarian assistance" to long-term "development."

Nevertheless, as I describe in the chapters to follow, the story of the revolving drug fund is complex and had negative consequences in both the short and long term. This book argues that the very idea of a revolving drug fund in the immediate aftermath of the Soviet Union's collapse and in the midst of a civil war—a plan to sell medicines to a physically and economically vulnerable population—was the result of the permeation into international development of a specific set of ideas about the relationship between citizen and state. Each pillar of the plan—user fees and ideas about "sustainability," decentralized decision making and reliance on foreign donors and governments, and the relative exclusion of the state from the system— was part of an ideology transplanted into a setting where it was hitherto unknown. At issue was not so much the delivery of health care but the ideological framework within which health care should be delivered. So while certain policies may appear pragmatic or instrumental, their application can, in the words of social anthropologists Chris Shore and Susan Wright, "serve to cloak subjective, ideological, and arguably highly irrational goals in the guise of rational, collective, universalized objectives.[27]

Of particular interest in this discussion is the link between the transplantation of neoliberal ideology and the nature and mission of NGOs in the global system of international aid and development. Because NGOs are traditionally thought of as institutions of civil society distinct from the state, they are believed to have a privileged place at the vanguard of democracy. In fact, many sympathetic observers argue that this status gives them a comparative advantage over governments in efficiently reaching vulnerable communities.[28] Yet most NGOs are accountable to communities neither in their home country nor in the areas where they work. Furthermore, because some NGOs receive large grants from external governments or institutions—grants that are organized and structured in a manner designed to serve the donors' aims—they are at risk of representing more faithfully the goals and ideology of their donors rather than those of the local communities in which they work.[29]

Anthropologist James Ferguson (1994) has pointed out that the only way to understand such policies is to examine the ideas behind them and to ask what the policies do, what social effects they have, and how they are connected with larger social processes.[30] As remote and isolated as Badakhshan remains—geographically, historically, and ethnically—this book aims to show that in a globalized world, culture and space do not exist in isolation. Rather, outside forces decisively shape the cultural space.[31] By understanding how the discourse of neoliberalism defined behavior and action on the part of both international NGOs and local actors, we will see that this story about medicines in Badakhshan is not simply one about pharmaceuticals in the post-Soviet period. Rather, it is a story about international development and the dominant discourses that define it.

As this story unfolds, it will be clear to the reader that this analysis is a snapshot of a social moment that can lead to a better understanding of discursivity in culture—how a specific set of ideas can define the construction of institutions, programs, and practice.[32] Anthropologically, this is not simply an examination of the post-Soviet period and the "development" work that accompanied it. Rather, it is an attempt to appreciate the way external forces and processes become an integral part of the local cultural space (this refers to both local culture in places like Badakhshan and the culture and practice of NGOs);[33] to recognize that culture and the social world are shaped by a changing political and economic context; and to account for agency and responsibility in the formation and manipulation of social structures, especially during a period of massive social transition.[34]

The provision of medicines was a particularly fertile area of study because medicines are imbued with significant meaning.[35] Modern health care relies on a complex resource and supply base to function. In the absence of this base, the practice of medicine becomes ad hoc, improvised, and neglectful of those most in need. Nowhere is this reality more evident than in the distribution of pharmaceuticals.[36] During the Soviet era, medicines played an active, state-sponsored role in the alleviation of general suffering and an important ideological role because of their metonymic association with a "progressive rationality" fostered by the Soviet state.[37] Having access to medicines represented having the "best health care system in the world," emphasizing the consumption of medicines as integral to deriving and maintaining health.[38] When the communist state collapsed, however, medicines, as a commodity, came to represent a foothold for the creation of a market-based approach to health care delivery[39] and a way of changing the relationship between patients—now "consumers"— and the health system (previously run only by the state).[40]

UNDERSTANDING THE ENCOUNTER: AREAS OF NEOLIBERAL PROGRAMMATIC BLINDNESS

This ethnography is set in the aftermath of the collapse of the Soviet Union, the independence of the Central Asian republics, and the ascension of a world economic order defined by neoliberalism. Foreign NGOs did not create the crisis in Central Asia, Tajikistan, or Badakhshan; that was the product of large-scale social and political forces beyond the control of such institutions. Yet, because of their funding streams, many NGOs working in the region turned to strategies that were not apposite to the place or time. Although we are twenty years from the events of the mid-1990s, that historical moment provides a unique opportunity to study an encounter between a local world shaped by Soviet communism—a centralized economic and social system—and capitalism, which, in its harsh late twentieth-century manifestation as neoliberalism, leaves allocations of resources and services wholly to the market, with the government simply playing an enabling role.[41] In part, this encounter is epistemological—related to the nature of knowledge and understanding the world—and in part it is ontological, about the nature of existing or being. It is also moral and political. With the collapse of the Soviet Union, this encounter became one-sided, defined by processes of globalization and the terms and conditions of the regnant world economic order. The facets of this encounter are like pieces of a jigsaw puzzle that, when analyzed together, give us a richer understanding of this moment of transition and its defining features.

In part 1, I aim to understand better the first pieces of this puzzle, the milieu in which this encounter took place. Though isolated geographically, Badakhshan was certainly not an ideological wilderness. By the time the Soviet Union collapsed, Moscow had had more than a century of direct involvement in the region, which fell on the boundary of the "great game" between the Russian and British colonial empires. Like most of Central

Asia, Badakhshan was a site for Russia's—and later, for Bolshevism's— push for modernity, often manifested in the drive to bring the fruits of modern medicine to the masses. The socioeconomic and ideological structures underpinning these efforts provided a framework for Soviet medical practice, which shaped the delivery of health care in the region until the collapse. Chapter 2 examines health care delivery during the Soviet period, in order to better understand the social context and value system in which the revolving drug fund program was transplanted and implemented. Chapter 3 describes the people of Badakhshan and the arrival of NGOs, particularly AKF, into the region.

Part 2 (chapters 4 and 5) examines the impact of the collapse of the Soviet Union on the local Badakhshani population, with a focus on the health situation and the paucity of medicines. It then describes the revolving drug fund as the solution presented to address Badakhshan's pharmaceutical crisis.

Part 3 (chapters 6 and 7) examines the Bamako Initiative as the product of a particular social history. The initiative's roots can be found in the complicated dance between Cold War rivals and its ideological effects on global development institutions. This section explores the roots of the global approach that gave rise to the Bamako Initiative—the creation of a global neoliberal narrative divorced from the local world, both in Badakhshan and elsewhere. As these pieces of the jigsaw puzzle are laid down and the picture becomes clearer, I argue that even in the global, postmodern world in which we live, with all its micronarratives and multiple voices, a single metanarrative—a way of constructing the world— seems to emerge as a defining force in global health. This metanarrative, which had a dominant role in shaping the post-Soviet health transition in Badakhshan, is one of a disordering capitalism characteristic of the late twentieth century,[42] now commonly referred to as *neoliberalism*.[43] It is shaped and enforced by funding streams from large international donors, who codify practices through the projects that they support. This way of *forming* the way citizens—and by extension, institutions—and their activities are organized is what the French philosopher Michel Foucault has referred to as "governmentality."[44] Through this approach—defining the requirements for funding grant applications, allowable approaches to program implementation, and the metrics used for program evaluation—ideology is transmitted.[45] The power of this metanarrative cannot be under-estimated: it does not simply champion individualism; it threatens to act as a great solvent, remaking fundamental values and reconfiguring social relations.[46]

Part 4 (chapters 8 and 9) examines how the commodification of health care delivery transformed interpersonal relations as well as other sequelae of the revolving drug fund.

In the epilogue, I reflect on what ideological penetration of neoliberal-ism means for current practice in global health. In examining an ideologi-cal enterprise—and I hope that by the end of the book the reader will agree that the Bamako Initiative and its revolving drug fund were instruments of neoliberalism—success and failure can be difficult to ascertain. For exam-ple, Ferguson (1994) suggests that studying the side effects of a program allows us to speak about a logic that transcends the program being imple-mented, what many refer to as discourse.[47] Thus in Badakhshan what may appear to be a programmatic failure for a NGO (e.g., drugs not reaching patients who need them), may actually be an ideological success for a bilat-eral donor (e.g., the penetration of neoliberal ideas about the relationship between the citizen and the state into a distant locale).

On the flip side of side effects are the programmatic failures that somehow go unexamined. I argue that these are programmatic outcomes that fall into *realms of programmatic blindness* or, in the case of this analysis, *realms of neoliberal programmatic blindness*. These are the original aims of projects that get lost or ignored. In the case of global health, a commit-ment to health delivery—not to mention, as is often the case, a commit-ment to equity in access and outcomes—requires that we closely examine elements that have fallen into realms of neoliberal programmatic blind-ness and attempt to remediate such lapses. Describing and enumerating these programmatic elements allows us to examine how discourse has shaped and framed programmatic indicators and outcomes, and more importantly, is a critical first step in the moral and programmatic reorien-tation of global health interventions.

Attempting to describe and analyze any moment of massive social transi-tion—in which the simultaneous forces of nationalism, ethnicity, religious identity, and massive economic and social transformation are all occurring within local social structures increasingly defined by global economic modes of rationality—is difficult. These forces are not all bad: often, they take the form of well-meaning individuals, well-meaning organizations, charities, religious groups, and solidarity groups. Often decisions have been made for purely pragmatic reasons. By focusing on the very narrow program of the revolving drug fund, this ethnography's main aim is to examine how ideology and its instruments can infiltrate development programs and contribute to a situation where important local needs fall into the realms of neoliberal programmatic blindness.

It has been eighteen years since I conducted the ethnographic research for this book. In completing the manuscript over the last few years, I have had two worries. The first was a concern that publishing this work would impugn an organization that I both admire and respect. I was worried that it would detract from the hundreds of successful projects that AKF has implemented over the years in so many countries, improving the well-being of many. I also did not want it to minimize the difficulty of working in the immediate post-Soviet period in Tajikistan or to diminish in any way efforts that saved the lives of thousands of people in Badakhshan and continue to do so, worldwide, to this day.

Over the last decade I have had the opportunity to lead complex health delivery operations in difficult settings, and I know how hard it is to make decisions around funding and operations, especially in times of financial scarcity. In fact, my own feeling is that more than most NGOs, AKF and its partners in the Aga Khan Development Network are sensitive to the needs of the poorer and weaker members of the local population. The fact that they invited me to Badakhshan, funded part of my ethnographic work, and knowingly permitted me to conduct anthropological research from within their organization, with access to all aspects of its programs and projects, is a positive commentary on the desire of the organization for excellence. I learned a great deal from the highly trained local and international staff members working there, some of whom have remained friends over the years. More importantly, the network continued to subsidize pharmaceuticals in the face of the relative failure of the revolving drug fund and remains unstintingly committed to the people of Badakhshan, Tajikistan, and the region. My hope is that readers of this book will be judicious in their assessment of this particular organization—an NGO working in solidarity with a number of poor communities—and save their disapprobation for the main topic of this book, namely the discursive landscape that has led dogma to replace data in shaping and framing the activities of NGOs engaged in global health care delivery and development.

My second fear in publishing this book now was that an analysis of neoliberalism's penetration into the post-Soviet world would seem outdated. Sadly, this has not been the case; neoliberalism continues to play an important role in shaping global health care delivery even today. In fact, since the economic collapse of 2008, we have seen neoliberal policies shape the lives of millions around the world, including in Europe and North America, only to see the social, political, economic, and moral effects—and backlash—in real time.

Today, we have to be more vigilant than ever. As we think about global health care delivery, we must put those components that fall into realms of neoliberal programmatic blindness—those elements that are not simply about profit and loss but about social cohesion, equity, and a just society—at the forefront of decision making. This ethnography is a case study and a cautionary tale about the forces driving decision making in health and development policy today.

PART I **The Beginning of the Encounter**

THE SOVIET WORLD MEETS ITS
GLOBAL COUNTERPARTS

2 Health in the Time of the USSR

A WINDOW INTO THE COMMUNIST MORAL WORLD

ASTROV: During the third week of Lent, I went to the
epidemic at Malitskoi. It was eruptive typhoid. The peasants were all lying side by side in their huts, and the calves
and pigs were running about the floor among the sick. Such
dirt there was, and smoke! Unspeakable! I slaved among
those people all day, not a crumb passed my lips, but when
I got home there was still no rest for me; a switchman was
carried in from the railroad; I laid him on the operating
table and he went and died in my arms, under chloroform,
and then my feelings that should have been deadened
awoke again, my conscience tortured me as if I had killed
the man. I sat down and closed my eyes—like this—and
thought: will our descendants two hundred years from now,
for whom we are breaking the road, remember to give us a
kind word? No, nurse. They will forget.

Anton Chekhov, *Uncle Vanya*

Even a casual reader of Russian and Soviet literature is likely to be struck
by its frequent and detailed invocations of country doctors, epidemics,
surgery, sanitariums, infection, bloodletting, consumption, asylums, midwives, and madness. The works of Pasternak, Gogol, Dostoyevsky,
Pushkin, Turgenev, Solzhenitsyn, and Tolstoy reflect an interest in medical subjects that occasionally borders on the obsessive. Several of Russia's
greatest literary figures—notably Chekhov and Bulgakov—were themselves physicians. Perhaps it is fitting that a society at once so culturally
advanced and so linked to a history of rural poverty should be preoccupied

with medicine, which represents a kind of meeting point between modern science and the depths of human despair.

In this one area at least, Russia's political and literary histories converge. In addition to being the site of the world's first socialist revolution, Russia witnessed some of the earliest efforts to deliver health care to the general public on a national scale. To a degree little appreciated abroad, for well over a century and a half, reform-minded administrations in Moscow intermittently tried to direct the resources of the state to the provision of medical services. These efforts variously took the form of rural vaccination programs, factory- or farm-based clinics and dispensaries, the construction of urban sewer systems, as well as traveling caravans of physicians and midwives.

Though woefully inadequate in dealing with the vast health needs of the population—particularly the rural peasantry—such initiatives were nevertheless well ahead of established practice in many other European countries. In the Soviet era, health care became a national priority, a fundamental right of the proletariat, and access to doctors and medicine was radically expanded. The emphasis on health care and public health paid significant dividends for the population: life expectancy increased and infant mortality was reduced. The epidemics that had plagued the pre-Soviet period were largely contained.

However, most of Central Asia, which until Stalin's rise to power lay at the periphery of Russian settlement, still relied heavily on traditional healers and practitioners of folk medicine well into the twentieth century. Stalin's distrust of the largely Muslim peoples of the region—which led him to emphasize security concerns over social programs—coupled with the logistical challenge of building and supplying hospitals and dispensaries across a sprawling region, ensured that Central Asia lagged far behind the rest of the Soviet Union. But by the mid-1960s, even remote areas had their own health posts and simple pharmacies, and the local population began to reap the benefits of a modern health care apparatus.

For the Badakhshanis living in the Pamir Mountains, the Soviet health care system acquired a variety of complex and often contradictory associations and meanings. It offered some relief from the experience of disease and mortality that had shaped this population. No longer was a respiratory infection or complicated childbirth necessarily a death sentence for villagers, at least in places that had access to roads. And by providing free curative and preventive health care to populations where they lived, the Soviet state showed its benevolent side, giving tangible meaning to Lenin's dictum that "the fight for socialism is at the same time the fight for health."[1]

ZEMSTVO MEDICINE

According to sociologist Vicente Navarro, the first socialized health system anywhere in the world appeared in Russia following its defeat in the Crimean War (1853–1856). The system came to be called *zemstvo* medicine (district, or rural, medicine).[2] Tsar Alexander II realized that the backwardness of the Russian economy had contributed to battlefield losses, and thus embarked on a policy of state-directed industrialization funded by foreign capital.[3] The need for an industrial labor force led to the emancipation of the serfs in 1861 and the creation in 1864 of the *zemstvo*, a local authority structure responsible for central administration, taxation, and social services, including health care. *Zemstvo* medicine was the first attempt in the world to organize clinic- and hospital-based care in rural regions on a large scale.

Zemstvo health reforms were lent greater urgency by Russia's extremely high mortality and morbidity rates. A physician's report from a late nineteenth-century cholera epidemic reflects the suffering often encountered by *zemstvo* doctors. "I shall never be able to forget," the doctor writes. "In a cottage lay the bodies of a mother who had died of cholera and of her three-month-old infant, who had died of hunger, his body still warm. Outside lay the cholera-infected father and two frightened, starving, five- or six-year-old children."[4] Illnesses such as measles, whooping cough, scarlet fever, and dysentery contributed to a Russia-wide infant mortality rate estimated at 500 per 1,000 live births. Mortality rates for those afflicted by infectious diseases—usually cholera, smallpox, diphtheria, or typhoid—ranged from 30 to 70 percent.

Rural areas were especially hard hit, and medical care outside urban centers was virtually nonexistent. The doctor-patient ratio, which in 1862 stood at 1:7,000 for all of Russia, was only 1:33,000 in rural areas.[5] One of the primary goals of *zemstvo* medicine would be to bring free health care to patients in the mostly rural communities in which they lived.[6] In so doing, it explicitly linked the social roots of disease to illness and cure. One *zemstvo* authority at the time wrote, "If a physician wishes to prevent diseases, there is only one way—to cease to be a physician and to occupy himself with the improvement of the economic, material, and moral structure of our life."[7]

Ironically, much of the impetus for the *zemstvo* reforms in health care may have come from Russian elites, who feared that ill health among the poor threatened their own well-being. Historian Nancy Mandelker Frieden (1981) notes that after the emancipation of the serfs, some of the gentry ended up moving to the countryside to look after their estates. Their need for better health care and for control and prevention of disease, she argues, drove the reforms.[8] As one *zemstvo* physician wrote, syphilis was commonplace: "No family, whatever its estate, is safe; . . . no person, no matter how just or high-minded his life, can be guaranteed that this illness will not be carried into his home by a nurse, wet-nurse for his infants, or a housemaid for his mother, wife, or daughter."[9] This fear—that the nobility could not be insulated from the sea of epidemics facing the general population—led in some cases to increased funding for the *zemstvo* health system.[10]

The *zemstvo* system provided two forms of health care: a stationary form centered on the construction of village clinics and provincial hospitals, as well as a mobile system in which doctors, physicians' assistants (known as *feldshers*), and midwives traveled around the district.[11] Earning the same wage as factory workers, these health workers, most under thirty-five, became known as *narodniki* ("revolutionaries") because of their close association with the people and their belief that medicine was not just a trade but a public service.[12] Extant diaries and memoirs of the program's participants show an awareness of its far-reaching implications. As Ivan Ivanovich Molleson, known as the father of *zemstvo* medicine, wrote at the time, "We Russians have the prospect of taking a strong step forward and showing the way to others; as is known, nowhere abroad has an attempt ever been made to organize public medicine or make a systematic collective study of the causes of disease, with the aim of eradicating those diseases, ending human suffering, and raising the level of popular health, wealth and happiness."[13]

It was inevitable that bringing health care to the far-flung communities where patients lived would have a profound effect on the urban-trained *zemstvo* physicians. A few were inspired to inquire into the root causes of the suffering they witnessed. Over time, the work of the *zemstvo* physician became intimately linked to the need to modernize a "backwards" rural population and eradicate poverty, an impulse both humane and paternalistic. A leaflet published in 1905, following the Pirogov Cholera Congress, stated: "It is impossible to protect people against infectious disease with medicine alone. The point is that those who most frequently become infected are the poor, living half-starved, in wretched lodgings, exhausted by inordinate work. Moreover, ignorance greatly aids the spread of infectious disease."[14] This sensibility was internalized by the cadre of physicians, who themselves faced poverty and hardship while serving in the *zemstvo* system. As the famous Russian physician-turned-writer Mikhail Bulgakov wrote of his medical practice and the perceived ignorance of the rural masses in the early postrevolution period: "After a hard night, sweet sleep overtook me. Darkness, black as Egypt's night, descended, and in it I was standing alone, armed with something that might have been a sword or might have been a stethoscope. I was moving forward and fighting . . . somewhere at the back of beyond."[15]

For all the idealism of its architects and foot soldiers, *zemstvo* medicine would produce only modest results in the long term.[16] Despite being placed under the direction of the important Russian Ministry of Internal Affairs— headed between 1861 and 1868 by the Russian statesman and writer Pyotr Alexandrovich Valuyev—bureaucratic inertia, underfunding, and a chronic lack of political will in Moscow conspired to thwart the program's most ambitious goals.[17] By 1889, for example, only one third of the *zemstvo*s had medical facilities of any kind.[18] The number of physicians working in rural areas increased from 756 in 1870 to 1,805 in 1890;[19] however, by 1917, 92 percent of all doctors were still based in large urban areas.[20] Periodic epidemics continued to take a heavy toll among rural populations, and there were still millions of Russian and Central Asian peasants who would live out their days without ever laying eyes on a doctor, nurse, or *feldsher*.

The real contribution of *zemstvo* medicine lies in the foundation it provided for a later, much more sweeping effort to bring health care to the population. The Soviet system would borrow heavily from the medical organization and expertise built up in the *zemstvo* era, as well as from its modern notions of health and its sense of a civilizing mission.[21] Many *zemstvo* physicians—such as Nikolai Alexandrovich Semashko and his deputy, Zinovy Petrovich Soloviev—would go on to occupy key positions in the People's Commissariat of Health Protection, founded a year after the October 1917 Revolution.[22] There were also philosophical commonalities. As the famous nineteenth-century Russian surgeon Nikolay Ivanovich Pirogov is believed to have said, the work of *zemstvo* physicians was both medical and educational, "to fight the ignorance of the popular masses and to change the entire aspect of their world view," an attitude embraced wholeheartedly by many Soviet-era medical reformers.[23]

HEALTH CARE FOR THE MASSES

As is true of all medical systems, health care after the Bolshevik Revolution of 1917 was closely tied to the political-economic system under which it developed. In Europe, for example, public health, hygiene, and sanitation were in part responses to the massive ecological disturbances resulting from the Industrial Revolution,[24] while the field of tropical medicine arose from the need to treat colonial officers suffering from "tropical" diseases.[25] Soviet medicine can be seen as the product of rapid social and cultural change, involving a shift from an agrarian order to an industrialized and urban one. This transformation took place as the young Soviet Union confronted warfare, poverty, and underdevelopment, and yet was poised to become, in the span of very few years, an international power.[26]

Despite the achievements of more than fifty years of *zemstvo* medicine, health conditions were abysmal at the time of the revolution. In 1919 alone, over 7 million cases of typhus were recorded, as well as 2.8 million cases of tuberculosis or syphilis. Almost a quarter of all diseases were thought to be attributable to poor economic and living conditions.[27] Large territories, including Central Asia, had no formal system of health care provision.

Faced with these daunting realities, the new regime in Moscow resolved to learn from the mistakes of its predecessors and make medicine more accessible to the general population. The *zemstvo* reform program had failed, the Bolsheviks argued, because its priorities were decisively set by the bourgeoisie. According to the Russian doctor and writer Vikenty Vikentyevich Veressayev, in *Memoirs of a Physician,* the practice of medicine at the time of the October Revolution was "a science dealing with the treatment of the wealthy and leisured." For the rest, "it was merely a theoretical abstraction, which told us *how* one might cure people, if they were rich and free."[28] Though many Russian physicians who participated in the *zemstvo* medical system did so for idealistic reasons, medical anthropologist Gordon Hyde contends that there were in fact two dominant schools of thought:

> One defended the necessity of the physician's service to the population, despite all obstacles of lack of doctors, of hospitals and illiteracy. The other was content with fine phrases, considering the *feldsher* as in practice the peasant's doctor. The supporters of the first line of thought recognized the necessity for participation of the State and well-off social strata in the improvement of public health; those of the second hoped to put the whole burden of health care on the shoulders of the peasants themselves. Supporters of the first line saw the problem of health, or rather lack of it, as being due to the bad hygienic condition of the people, above all their serf-like condition, poverty, illiteracy, etc.; the supporters of the second—"in the lack of moral development of the common people, the diffusion of syphilis, drunkenness, etc."[29]

During the revolutionary period, the medical profession, represented by the Pirogov Society, supported the anti-Bolshevik provisional government. And in a precursor to privatization efforts at that time, the society fought to create a physician-run system paid for by insurance funds or private sources. Moreover, many physicians felt that a special focus on the poor would undermine the ethical universalism of medicine.[30]

The Bolsheviks viewed doctors—and the Pirogov Society, in particular—as an elite that not only catered to the upper classes but also explicitly opposed the egalitarian ideology of the new revolutionary state. In contrast to the guild mentality of the doctors, the Bolsheviks regarded medicine as political by its very nature: it invariably served the interests of the ruling class, helping the working classes only by enabling them to produce more.[31] Reducing the status of doctors to that of other medical workers (such as nurses, morgue attendants, ward sweepers, and other medical "proletarians") thus became a priority for the Bolsheviks. To improve popular participation in the everyday administration of the state, Lenin called for the "replacement of certain institutions by other institutions of a fundamentally different order."[32] His goal was not merely to transfer medicine from one class to another but rather to democratize and deprofessionalize it completely.[33]

One of the first decrees signed by the Bolsheviks after the revolution created a social security system, which included restructuring of the medical sector.[34] Citing the "morbidity, mortality, and the unsanitary living conditions of the broad masses of the population," the decree called for "comprehensive sanitary legislation governing clean water, sewerage, industrial enterprises and residential housing."[35] Another provision stated, "It is necessary to take pharmacies out of private hands and transfer them to the public institutions of self–government [obshchestvennoe samoupravlenie]" as a means of waging "the struggle against morbidity and mortality and, in particular, against child mortality, tuberculosis, syphilis, etc."[36] By December 1917, social insurance was expanded to include free medical care, sickness and disability insurance, and maternity benefits.[37]

The medical profession was dealt with soon thereafter. On July 1, 1918, all health facilities and personnel were placed under the authority of the People's Commissariat of Health Protection, a move that further neutralized the power of the Pirogov Society and that of physicians in general, who were required to join the state-run union. Doctors were classified as "bourgeois specialists" and made subject to fixed salary scales.[38] They were also compelled to swear to "work conscientiously in the place demanded by the interests of society," "to treat patients with attention and solicitude," and to guide themselves "by the principles of communist morality."[39] At the village and neighborhood level, day-to-day authority was shifted to local Soviets, which were led primarily by peasants and workers.[40] Meanwhile, the relative status of other health professionals, such as nurses and feldshers, whose unions had supported the Bolsheviks, was elevated.[41]

These moves, as well as outbreaks of typhus and cholera, provided the context for Lenin's famous 1919 remark that "either the louse will defeat socialism or socialism will defeat the louse."[42] Defeating the louse was no easy task, of course, for a young government facing civil war, an economic blockade organized by the major European powers, and widespread resistance to the collectivization of farms.[43] To complicate matters further, an ideological debate broke out within the revolutionary leadership on how best to deliver social services to the masses while preserving the state's economic viability. This debate would rage well beyond Lenin's life.

THE PUSH TO INDUSTRIALIZE

The First World War (1914–1918) and the Russian civil war (1917–1922) left the newly formed Union of Soviet Socialist Republics (USSR) exhausted. Industrial output had plummeted, agricultural production was stagnating, and in some remote areas, early signs of famine were appearing. To reverse the decline, Lenin sought to introduce state-controlled capitalism, which Marx had seen as a necessary precursor to true communism. In March 1921, the Tenth Congress of the Communist Party established the New Economic Policy, liberalizing the Soviet economy and granting concessions to private industry in the interest of stimulating industrial and agricultural growth.[44] Under this policy, the program of social security was scaled back.

The New Economic Policy's effect on health care was immediate and dramatic. The economic devastation of the war years convinced the Bolshevik government that it could not afford universal health coverage across such a large territory. The situation became so critical that some Politburo members even briefly considered abolishing the newly unified medical service and free medical care altogether.[45] Recently nationalized pharmacies were returned to their owners, and physicians were once again permitted to choose between public and private practice. Many public health services were converted to private facilities, with users either paying a fee or carrying private insurance.

Shocked by the New Economic Policy's betrayal of Bolshevik principles, officials at the Commissariat of Health Protection tried to preserve what they could of the revolutionary health care system. They decided to emphasize preventive medicine, using whatever resources they could muster. Health cadres were organized and dispatched to rural areas to staff farm-based clinics and address medical crises before they became epidemics.[46] Equally importantly, medical schools were for the first time opened to women and non-Russian ethnic groups, and more medical students were enrolled.[47] As Zinovy Petrovich Soloviev, the deputy commissar of health protection and an ideological force within the regime, wrote, "The basic difference between Soviet medicine and the medicine of capitalist countries is that the latter cannot, without impinging upon the very foundations of the capitalist system, embark on prevention; [the capitalist country] limits itself to so-called 'general' measures and becomes caught in the narrow circle of individual charity."[48] This ethos of prevention would become a trademark of the Soviet health care system for decades to come.

In the years following Lenin's death in 1924, Stalin scrapped the New Economic Policy and embarked on a program of rapid collectivization and industrialization.[49] "We are behind the capitalist countries by fifty to a hundred years," Stalin declared. "We must catch up with them in ten years. Either we bring this about or we are finished."[50] He recognized that social security, including health benefits, could be deployed to increase the discipline and productivity of the labor force.[51] The health sector was reshaped to supply services to critical areas of the economy, such as factories, mines, railroads, and collective farms.[52] The Communist Party Central Committee, meeting on December 18, 1929, passed a resolution concerning the Medical Services of Workers and Peasants, which stressed "providing health services on class proletarian lines [and] giving priority to those in leading branches of industry and in state and collective farms."[53]

In the words of Nikolai Shvernik, the commissar of labor, "We shall handle social insurance as a weapon in the struggle to attach workers to their enterprises and strike hard at loafers, malingerers, and disorganizers of work."[54] What resulted from these efforts was a multitiered system— consisting of separate hospitals, polyclinics, sanatoria, and so on—where workers in critical industries received better care than those in the general population and loyalty to the Communist Party was rewarded.[55] This was, of course, precisely the favoritism that Lenin, inspired by Marx, had tried to abolish.[56]

Stalin saw that preventive medicine, inaugurated under the New Economic Policy, could also serve his own purposes. In 1933, a Public Health Inspectorate *(sanitarnaia inspektsia)* was created to take more active preventive measures in protecting the public's health.[57] Investment in preventive medicine cut down on work days lost and enhanced the productivity of the work force. To meet the program's staffing needs, the number of physicians in the Soviet Union was increased sevenfold between 1920 and 1940, while the proportion of women grew from 10 percent in 1917 to 60 percent in 1940.[58]

During the Second World War, health services were directed toward the war effort, both at the front and in preventing epidemics of infectious disease at home. The results, in a country decimated by fighting, were remarkable. In 1945, the head of the army medical service, General Efim Ivanovich Smirnov, wrote: "All previous wars were accompanied by a significant increase of epidemic diseases. However, neither our army nor our country knew epidemics during these years. This is indeed the result of the heroic work of the communicable disease personnel of the Soviet Army and the public health workers of the rear."[59] While Smirnov's assertion was not entirely correct—in fact, there were epidemics during the war, including tuberculosis[60]—it is true that although the infrastructure had suffered extensive damage and destruction, by 1946 the number of physicians in the Soviet Union had increased.

One effect of industrialization was that the structure of the health sector became increasingly hierarchical, with the hospital eventually positioned at the fulcrum of both therapeutic and preventive health care. The system was further broken down into highly specialized areas of care, biased toward specialized hospital-based medicine.[61] The hierarchical framework of the system and the accentuation of a hospital-focused system hampered delivery systems for ambulatory and community-based care in both curative and preventive services.[62]

Despite a century-long battle to improve rural health—from *zemstvo* medicine to the efforts of the early Bolsheviks—by 1958, five years after Stalin's death, only 11 percent of the nation's physicians were working in rural areas, leaving a considerable proportion of the population, including most residents of Badakhshan, dependent on clinics staffed by *feldshers* or midwives.[63] The lack of effective logistic, budgetary, and technical support from local authorities—the local "soviets" or citizens' councils—contributed to this problem. As a senior health administration official in Kazakhstan complained in 1956, "During the past seven years, of the several thousand doctors coming in [to practice in the republic] more than one half have left. The main reason for this is the lack of normal housing conditions for public health workers."[64] Physicians saw assignment to the countryside—often referred to as the "periphery"—as a kind of exile.[65] In 1961, the number of physicians across the Soviet Union was 18.8 per 10,000 people, but while the urban average was 27.6, the average in the countryside was 5.4.[66] A 1964 article in *Sovetskoye Zdravookhranenie* (Soviet Health Care) found that fewer than 10 percent of doctors were serving about 50 percent of the population.[67] Moreover, the British medical journal *The Lancet* reported in 1954 that, despite the rhetoric and the well-deserved pride in early achievements of Soviet preventive medicine, most efforts were directed toward treatment, not prevention.[68]

Yet, despite these failings, by the late 1950s, the average Soviet citizen could expect to live 68.7 years, longer than the life expectancy in the United States.[69] In the mid-1960s—the height of Soviet economic, scientific, and political achievement—life expectancy in communist Europe (excluding Asia and Siberia) was equal to, or higher than, the average in Western countries. Many of these gains were attributable to the health ministry's success at vaccinating the population against common infectious diseases and making pharmaceuticals, including antibiotics, free and widely available.

Although health was a major state priority, the health budget began to shrink after the Second World War, evidenced by the dilapidated condition of medical facilities even during the Soviet era.[70] Field (1995) argues that allocations to the health system were dictated by one driving force: to spend the minimum required to maintain the level of health necessary to realizing the regime's objectives, without affecting needs of equal or higher importance. As a result of this policy, health care expenditures in the Soviet Union were a fraction of those in the industrialized West. Salaries of medical staff were so low that the system became completely corrupt: physicians and nurses began to demand money under the table for free services.[71] Thus it became necessary to pay the narcotics nurse "an extra ten rubles in order to have one's pain sufficiently alleviated, and an orderly to help one to the bathroom."[72]

MEDICINES DURING THE SOVIET ERA

The Soviet state saw itself as "the only state which undertakes to protect and continuously improve the health of the whole population."[73] One functional aspect of providing and improving health care for the population was that health care and allied services were to be made available at no direct cost.[74] All hospital stays were free of direct charges to patients, and sanatoria were either free of charge or highly subsidized.[75]

In general, pharmaceuticals were free. Although there was a small charge for outpatient medicines, since the system was largely hospital-oriented, the bulk of medicines, medical supplies, and medical equipment were not paid for directly by patients, and were, in theory, available to every citizen.[76] Even for outpatient medicines, whose price likely did not reflect the full production costs nor include any prescription charge, those with communicable diseases (e.g., tuberculosis, syphilis, dysentery, or leprosy) or chronic conditions (e.g., diabetes, cancer, schizophrenia, or epilepsy), children under one year of age, invalids of the Second World War, and pensioners were exempt from charge.[77] Dental and ophthalmic care, as well as the cost of prostheses, were without formal charge.[78]

In practice, however, the pharmaceutical industry was notoriously deficient, and medicines were often lacking. For example, in August 1970 the Soviet newspaper *Izvestiya* published a report stating that some Soviet pharmacies did not have essentials like potassium permanganate, tincture of iodine, and the most common painkiller used in the Soviet Union, Analgin.[79] In general, there were shortages of basic medical supplies.[80] Many doctors reported running out of antibiotics, rubber gloves, and even surgical sutures of various types.[81] Since the central government was responsible for production, all medicines and supplies were subject to the pitfalls of Soviet industrial distribution: poor distribution resulted in supplies not arriving on time and, when they did arrive, hoarding by desperate health providers created shortages.

Trading scarce supplies among Soviet medical institutions became commonplace: if by chance one hospital received its entire inflated requisition of a specific item, the excess could be traded for materials in short supply.[82] Because of the central budget's low allocation to health care, the eighty or so operating pharmaceutical factories could not maintain full production capacity.[83] As a result, the Soviet pharmaceutical industry was unable to supply required medicines, and medicines were imported from Eastern bloc countries. It was not uncommon for patients' families to be asked to purchase a formally unavailable drug at three to five times its normal price.[84]

HEALTH AT THE END OF EMPIRE

The final fifteen years of the Soviet Union witnessed a steady decline in the effectiveness of the health care system. In the early 1970s, both infant and adult mortality began to rise in the USSR, as they did in the satellite states of Czechoslovakia, Hungary, Poland, Romania, and Bulgaria. The shift in life expectancy was startling. In 1980, two American demographers, Christopher Davis and Murray Feshbach, analyzed data from various sources and published the conclusion that the Soviet Union was the first industrialized country to report a decline in life expectancy in peacetime (the Davis-Feshbach report).[85] It was clear that the Soviet Union, even two decades before its demise, was in the midst of a devastating health crisis. The matter became a state secret: the country stopped publishing data on life expectancy after 1972 and on infant mortality after 1974. On the rare occasion health officials spoke of these disturbing trends, they blamed them on improvements in data gathering, particularly from the Central Asian republics. Only in 1988 did the government of Mikhail Gorbachev finally admit that the reports had been correct.[86]

The causes for the decline were not hard to discern. First, alcohol consumption surged during this period, contributing to a precipitous rise in heart-disease-related deaths in men, while in some areas alcohol consumption by mothers was blamed for over half of all infant deaths.[87] The second culprit was pollution, both of the air—the direct result of rapid urbanization and industrialization—and the water, thanks to the overuse of chemical fertilizers and pesticides in large-scale agriculture, and the release of toxic industrial wastes directly into rivers and streams.[88] Another source of pollution was radiation leaking from poorly constructed nuclear reactors.[89]

The third and most damaging factor was inextricably linked to the Cold War itself: chronic lack of funding for social services, including the health sector.[90] Military expenditures rose steadily throughout the 1970s, accelerating with the ill-fated invasion of Afghanistan in 1979 and the armament program that coincided with the election of Ronald Reagan as U.S. president in 1980. Meanwhile, the share of GNP formally spent on medical care fell from 9.8 percent in 1955 to 7.5 percent in 1977.[91] By the end of the Soviet period, it was said to be close to 2 percent of GNP.[92]

As difficult as the situation was during the Soviet period, it became untenable with the collapse of the Soviet Union—most notably in the area of pharmaceutical drug supply. By the late 1980s, some pharmaceutical factories had closed due to poor environmental standards, and construction on twenty-three new ones was halted because of environmental protests. The distribution system deteriorated to the extent that the few medicines produced were not delivered. In December 1989, even Russia's state airline, Aeroflot, refused to ship freight from Moscow without payment in hard currency. As a result, medicines were increasingly distributed through the informal economy. Health sector employees started to sell medicines to speculators, who in turn sold them to desperate citizens.[93]

At various points after the collapse, even the informal sector was in short supply of medicines.[94] Part of the problem was that the Ministry of Medical Industry, which was separate from the Ministry of Health, ceased to exist. In addition, the central pharmacy system, controlled by the Ministry of Health, started to break down in the republics. Eventually, each republic had to make a qualitative and quantitative judgment about drugs based on its ability to pay in foreign currency, leaving many of the poorer ones, like Tajikistan, simply unable to afford them.[95] The collapse of the pharmaceutical industry occurred so rapidly that by 1992, it could barely meet 30 percent of Soviet need.[96] During that period, which a leading Soviet medical newspaper, *Meditsinskaya Gazeta*, called a "medical famine," doctors faced acute shortages of almost everything: disposable syringes, catgut, dressings, incubators, disinfectants, antibiotics, and even condoms and diaphragms.[97] To conserve supplies, disposable syringes were reused and old needles filed down, and pharmacies hoarded medicines to sell later.[98]

In the newly formed Republic of Tajikistan, the situation became critical. According to the World Health Organization, in 1991 pharmaceutical expenses constituted 10.3 percent of the Tajik national health budget (only 7.3 percent was actually spent), which dropped to 8.4 percent in 1992 (only 5.9 percent was actually spent). Overall, the Tajik state funded pharmaceutical consumption at a level of less than five cents per capita per annum.[99]

In 1996, the year that AKF conducted its planning for the revolving drug fund in Badakhshan, the situation there could only be described as dismal, despite the active participation of the Red Cross, Médecins Sans Frontières, and AKF itself.[100] While most essential medical supplies were available through humanitarian assistance channels, because of the leakage of these humanitarian assistance medicines, which were sold alongside other imported medicines in the informal market, medicines became unaffordable for the majority of the population.[101] In places like Badakhshan's capital, Khorog, people sold medicines in the general bazaar, often leaving drugs sitting in heat and direct sunlight. The sellers sometimes had no knowledge of the medicines they were peddling and could not answer questions about what these products contained, what diseases they were meant to treat, nor their contraindications.

It is difficult to sit in judgment over an ideology once it has collapsed and its nemesis has emerged victorious. But despite its failings in the latter part of the communist era, Soviet medicine brought health care to millions of people who had never before met a physician, nurse, or *feldsher* or set foot in a clinic or hospital. And as coercive and inefficient as the Soviet state often was, it rarely strayed from its remarkably humane commitment to equality of access for all citizens. In public health, equality of access often means equality of outcome. As medical historian Henry Sigerist points out, the Soviet leadership viewed medicine as a mission and a responsibility rather than a commodity to be purchased.[102] Although the system was by no means perfect, there was general recognition that health care services ought to depend on need.

In some ways, the neoliberal political-economic model that supplanted the Soviet system elevated economic efficiency and a patient's ability to pay above the health needs of the people. And though these values have their place in some sectors of the economy, their application in the health care arena would carry devastating consequences for the people of

Badakhshan and throughout the former Soviet Union.[103] The opportunity offered by the Soviet collapse—to wipe away a dying state and start again as if from nothing—was widely celebrated in the West as a chance to test free-market theories. But the grand experiment in market-driven health care would ultimately go awry in ways its unquestioning implementers never anticipated.

3 Seeking Help at the End of Empire

A TRANSNATIONAL LIFELINE FOR BADAKHSHAN

> After the collapse of the Soviet Union, we lost hope. We
> were waiting for our death.
>
> Jalal, *fifty-one-year-old farmer from Roshtqala District,*
> *Badakhshan, 1996*

It is nearly impossible to travel to Badakhshan without pausing to wonder
how anyone came to live there in the first place. Whether taking the long-
abandoned Silk Road route through the Murghab Desert from Osh in the
Kyrgyz Republic—a rugged thoroughfare once patrolled by leopards, vul-
tures, and the magnificent Turanian tiger—or the equally forbidding
mountain passes stretching east from the Tajik capital of Dushanbe, one
is forced to conclude that such a journey into the void would only be made
under duress. And indeed, the history of human settlement in the region
is a dismal catalogue of conquest, persecution, diaspora, and forced migra-
tion on a grand scale.

During Soviet times, the West saw Central Asia as a vast undifferenti-
ated land mass, remote from the centers of power and subject to the
whims of successive administrations in Moscow. But with the collapse of
communism, subtle shadings of geography, ethnicity, and historical context came into focus. Tajikistan is an island of Persian dialect speakers set
amid a linguistic ocean of Turkic dialects, including Turkoman, Kyrgyz,
Uzbek, and Kazakh.[1] Settlement in the region dates from at least the
fourth millennium B.C.E., and the land passed through many hands,
including Alexander the Great's, whose troops were said to have come east

of the Oxus River (now the Amu Darya River), with Alexander himself having come to the town of Qal'ai Khumb, along the Panj River (a tributary of the Oxus) in the Darvaz District of present-day Badakhshan.[2]

Since then, the region has been contested and controlled by successive waves of outside rulers and empires. In the middle of the seventh century A.D., the region was conquered by Arab Muslims.[3] It changed hands a number of times, but by the fourteenth century, the land that is now Badakhshan had fallen under the rule of Timur (Tamerlane) and, later, the first Moghul emperor, Babur. After many battles over a 150-year period, the land fell to the Uzbeks. Although sources vary as to the exact rulers of the region, the area was thereafter conquered by the Afghans and ultimately the Persian Emirate of Bukhara.[4] The region played an important role in the "great game" between the British and Russian colonial empires, and in 1891, Russia claimed the area around Badakhshan for itself. After much wrangling, the Pamir Agreement of 1895 was signed and the region officially became part of the Russian Empire. Although there was still an arrangement of shared sovereignty with the Bukhara Khanate (until 1924), the Russian military set up a base in Khorog in 1897, giving Russia full control over the area.[5]

THE PEOPLE OF BADAKHSHAN

A majority of Badakhshan's population adheres to the Shi'a Imami Nizari Isma'ili interpretation of Islam.[6] Currently, the Nizari Isma'ilis, said to number in the millions, are scattered over more than twenty-five countries in Asia, Africa, Europe, and North America.[7] They acknowledge Prince Karim Aga Khan al-Husayni IV (Aga Khan IV), who traces his descent directly from Muhammad through his daughter Fatima and son-in-law Ali ibn Abu Talib, as their forty-ninth imam, or spiritual leader.[8]

Although it is not completely clear how the Isma'ilis settled in Badakhshan, the region has had an Isma'ili influence since the ninth century. The Samanids, who ruled Bukhara (now in Uzbekistan) from 874 to 999, were a Shi'a Muslim dynasty. It is said that the Samanid ruler Nasr ibn Ahmad Samani publicly professed his faith in Isma'ilism, laying the foundation for the practice of the tradition in the region.[9] The Badakhshanis, locked as they were in the valleys and slopes of the high Pamir Mountains, have their own variations of this history. They trace their conversion from Zoroastrianism to the tenth century, when Nasir Khusrow, a Persian poet-philosopher and missionary, arrived in the region from the Isma'ili-led Fatimid Empire in North Africa.[10] Other historical accounts suggest that there was an influx of Isma'ilis and other Shi'a Muslims into the region after the Moghul conquest of present-day Iran in the twelfth century.[11]

Badakhshan's physical isolation served as a metaphor for the community's sense of separation from their neighbors, the majority of whom adhere to the Sunni interpretations of Islam. Although they were relatively safe in Badakhshan, over the years the Isma'ilis (and other Shi'a Muslims of the region) were persecuted intermittently by their neighbors, and they were targets of *jihad* (holy war) multiple times.[12] By the middle of the eighteenth century, Badakhshan was integrated into the Afghan domain under Ahmad Shah.[13] In the nineteenth century, people in the lower-lying regions of Badakhshan were sometimes burned to death by their neighbors in Afghanistan.[14] In 1893, prior to the arrival of the Russians, the Isma'ili lands in Afghanistan (what is today Afghan Badakhshan) had for the most part been overrun. Their property was confiscated, and they were sold as slaves. Villages were burned, and women were sexually violated.[15] So it is no surprise that Badakhshan's inhabitants welcomed the coming of the tsar's troops in the mid-1890s. In 1895, when Badakhshan was ceded to Russia as part of the Pamir Agreement with the British Empire, the local population immediately asked Russia's Tsar Nicholas II for protection.[16]

Under the Soviets, Badakhshan became an autonomous *oblast* (province) with close links to Moscow. Relations between the inhabitants of Badakhshan and the central government in Saint Petersburg and Moscow fluctuated depending on which minority the state was cultivating. The Soviet state knew full well the relationship between the Isma'ilis of Badakhshan and their Sunni neighbors and used this to its advantage.[17]

For most of rest of the twentieth century, the Isma'ili Muslims of the Pamir Mountains were largely cut off from the outside world.[18] In the final months of Soviet rule, as the state was crumbling from within and Badakhshan was facing an existential crisis, members of the local community contacted the Aga Khan to seek his guidance and assistance. In 1991, three emissaries from the Aga Khan arrived in Badakhshan.[19] The reconnection with the Isma'ili imam marked an important historical moment, for the Aga Khan was more than a link with tradition. During the time the Badakhshanis had been cut off from the outside world, the Aga Khan had become closely associated with a series of largely secular nongovernmental institutions that were quintessentially modern, through which his secular interaction with the people of Badakhshan would occur. He would not come alone, but would bring with him a network of globally imbedded NGOs and, through them, a link to a world unknown.

RECONNECTING WITH THE OUTSIDE

For many people, the name Aga Khan conjures up images of great wealth, ranging from tabloid photographs of the imam with Queen Elizabeth II at Ascot—horseracing is a family tradition the current imam inherited from his grandfather and great-grandfather—to historical accounts of the portly third Aga Khan, Sir Sultan Muhammad Shah Aga Khan III, being weighed first in gold and later diamonds by his followers on the occasions of the golden and diamond jubilees of his imamate.

But behind this façade of wealth and lore is a much more complex reality. For example, Aga Khan III, who was the president of the Assembly of the League of Nations in 1937 and 1938, used the gold and diamonds given to him by his followers, along with his own contributions, to fund long-term social development programs for his community.[20] Similarly, the current Aga Khan, building on his family's long tradition of public service,[21] has constructed a secular, transnational network of NGOs capable of "providing everything from schools, clinics, and roads" to rural development.[22] His institutions, which are not limited to the Isma'ili community—in fact, significant funds flow to activities assisting non-Isma'ilis—draw considerably from his followers' tradition of volunteerism.[23] Despite their isolation, the capabilities of these modern institutions had become known to the leaders of the Tajik Isma'ili community, driving them to turn to the Aga Khan for economic and social assistance at the twilight of Soviet rule.

The Aga Khan Foundation (AKF) arrived in Badakhshan in 1992, as life reached a nadir for the local population. As the Tajik civil war unfolded—

pitting Tajikistan's Kolab Province against the neighboring Qorghanteppa Province, and ultimately Tajikistan's eastern provinces of Gharm and Badakhshan—the Pamir region became even more isolated. Fighting blocked the only road between Dushanbe, the capital, and Badakhshan. This meant that the region's only access to goods and supplies was the 728-kilometer (452-mile) road from Osh in the Kyrgyz Republic to Khorog. This incompletely paved and, at that time, irregularly maintained road—winding over passes of up to 4,600 meters (15,092 feet) and running through one of the world's highest deserts, the Murghab Desert—made providing humanitarian assistance to Badakhshan's residents, some living in remote valleys up to 500 kilometers (310 miles) from Khorog, a significant logistical undertaking. The difficulties were exacerbated by Badakhshan's severe winters, with temperatures reaching 40 degrees below zero in some districts, and heavy snows and avalanches cutting off the upper parts of the valleys for months at a time.[24]

Delivering humanitarian assistance to Badakhshan would have been challenging enough without the large movements of people displaced by civil war. As a result of the violence, between 150,000 and 300,000 people were killed, including many of Pamiri origin.[25] An estimated 700,000 refugees of Pamiri and Gharmi origin (the province of Gharm neighbors Badakhshan) fled from Tajikistan into Afghanistan across the Amu-Darya River; a further 145,000 refugees went to Russia.[26] As people returned home, Badakhshan was faced with an influx of some 60,000 refugees from other parts of Tajikistan, bringing the population to an estimated 200,000. The Badakhshan government was unable to meet the demand and by mid-1992—with no direct food shipments from Moscow as in the Soviet days and the link to Dushanbe severed—the entire population was at risk of starvation. In the midst of this acute crisis, almost overnight AKF's team from Geneva had to put together a system capable of providing food and fuel to Badakhshan.[27]

The nerve center for many of the Aga Khan's formal social development activities is a dark, nondescript, low-rise glass building standing at the green, leafy corner of Avenue de la Paix and Rue de Lausanne in Geneva, Switzerland. Nestled beside the offices of the United Nations Children's Fund, a neighbor to the World Meteorological Organization and the

World Trade Organization, the building looks more like the home of a small multinational corporation or an agency of the United Nations. It is here that the modest head office of the AKF, the Swiss-based nonprofit organization created by the Aga Khan in 1967, is located.

AKF is part of the broader Aga Khan Development Network (AKDN), a nondenominational group of development agencies with 80,000 employees working in thirty countries spanning the globe from Afghanistan to Mali, and from Russia to Tanzania. In 2010, AKDN disbursed USD $625 million for its nonprofit development activities (which range from ensuring food security, access to health care and education, and access to financial services and economic opportunity, to promoting Islamic-influenced architecture and art). The AKDN also has a for-profit arm, the Aga Khan Fund for Economic Development (AKFED), which generates revenues of USD $2.3 billion, the surpluses of which are reinvested in its development activities.[28]

Others have studied the AKDN and other imamate institutions as forms of transnational civil society.[29] Their analyses highlight three salient characteristics. The first important observation is that, in framing the institutions of the AKDN, the Aga Khan has placed considerable emphasis on upholding the ethic and ethos of Islam. For example, in a convocation address at Peshawar University on November 30, 1967, the year AKF was created, the Aga Khan said, "It would be traumatic if those pillars of the Islamic way of life, social justice, equality, humility and generosity, enjoined upon us all, were to lose their force or wide application in our young society. It must never be said generations hence that . . . we have forsaken our responsibilities to the poor, to the orphans, to the traveler, to the single woman."[30]

The second defining feature of the Aga Khan's organizations is the emphasis on rigorous management. Political scientist Paul Kaiser reports that a corporate ethos permeates AKDN structures, which resemble those of a well-run multinational corporation or transnational enterprise.[31] This organizational form, Kaiser argues, is aimed at addressing how social service organizations can achieve increased organizational self-sufficiency and programmatic independence in light of continued dependence on external donors. This is achieved through the use of efficient management techniques while maintaining a strong commitment to the delivery of basic social services.[32] The Aga Khan has been very clear about the importance he places on managerial efficiency: "In neither commerce nor welfare should one put in substantial capital—and the capital required in welfare programs is substantial—without ensuring that management is capable of dealing with the investment fruitfully, although ways of measuring productivity will of course be different."[33]

Third is the importance the Aga Khan places on the role of private enterprise in fostering social and economic development. While the AKDN's institutions work closely with governments in areas ranging from health and education to the financing of large infrastructure projects, the Aga Khan has argued that the state "cannot do it all."[34] Private enterprise, he suggests, can introduce competition and stimulate growth, while developing managerial skills and organizational structures that are essential to economic growth. In the case of health and welfare, since they usually constitute a large part of most countries' budgets, "huge amounts of money can be wasted on them if management is poor."[35] This form of institutional endeavor and engagement with the private sector, the Aga Khan has been careful to point out, "is not to be confused with the less desirable aspects of unrestrained capitalism."[36]

A strong social ethic, robust management structures, and an emphasis on encouraging private-sector initiatives have helped make AKF and the institutions of the AKDN exemplary in the development world. These characteristics have also led to positive outcomes in the communities with whom they partner. The network has been lauded for its work in a number of areas, ranging from social, economic, and rural development and provision of health services in many poor- and middle-income communities, to promotion of education, architecture, and urban green spaces. It receives funding from individual donors, including the Aga Khan himself, as well as from large bilateral and multilateral funding organizations. In short, AKF and its partner organizations are often at the cutting edge of global development.[37]

These qualities make AKF an unusual candidate for a case study, since one would expect the organization's attributes to provide immunity of sorts to external ideological forces like neoliberalism. Yet to believe this would be to underestimate the profound and widespread institutional penetration of neoliberal ideas at the global level and, through this, neo-liberalism's power to define thought and practice in global health and development.

According to David Lewis, a political scientist at the London School of Economics, when NGOs adopt contractual service roles requiring closer relationships with both states and donors and management of large tranches of resources, they turn to the private sector for management concepts and practices.[38] Though this is not bad in and of itself, Lewis suggests that *management*—a way of improving an organization's structure and processes to achieve improvements in efficiency—when not closely guided by strong vision and values, can become confused with *managerialism*, an unwarranted and often ideological reliance on technical problem solving that is tied to *economically defined productivity*.[39] This focus, he argues, runs the risk of crowding out other organizational values. In situations requiring large amounts of donor funding—such as that needed to run large development projects—unchecked *managerialism* can result in important organizational risks: it reorients accountability upward rather than toward the grassroots;[40] it leads to a corporate management structure that, in the name of financial efficiency, can lead to short-term financial sustainability overriding long-term service goals (e.g., preventive health care);[41] and it can limit the voice of the local population by encouraging the growth of a managerial bourgeoisie that makes decisions and interprets data.[42]

Every NGO involved in large-scale international efforts is at risk of *managerialism*—and through this, neoliberalism—encroaching into its practices. Three factors add to this hazard. The first is the nature and scope of the interventions in which NGOs are participating as they increasingly replace certain state functions. The second is the funding required for large scale-interventions, which necessitates NGOs working closely with donors. The third is the global political and economic environment that allowed an idea like the Bamako Initiative to be accepted within the lexicon of development and that encourages managerialism. Together these create a perfect storm for a development blind spot.

PART II Life at the End of Empire

THE CRISIS AND THE RESPONSE

4 The Health Crisis in Badakhshan

SICKNESS AND MISERY AT THE END OF EMPIRE

I am afraid of starvation, cold and poverty.

Dental clinic survey respondent, *Badakhshan, Tajikistan, 1996*

If I cannot buy bread when it is being sold, how then will I
be able to pay for the treatment or for the medicines? And
what does it matter if they are available if I do not have
money to buy them?

Health survey respondent, *Badakhshan, Tajikistan, 1996*

My field assistant Ahmed and I sat with Moom, Rais's mother, in his traditional Pamiri house.[1] Soot covered the walls and ceiling, leaving a smoky
scent in the air, though no fire was burning. Rais and Rahmatekhudo, his
best friend from childhood, served us tea while Rais's children looked on
from behind one of the five posts holding up the roof. As we sat on cushions laid on the floor and sipped from our cups, Moom, Rais, and
Rahmatekhudo reminisced about the many ways Kuhdeh had changed
during their lifetimes—their recollections clouded, no doubt, by the tur-
bulent times they were living through.

The entire history of the region, they explained, could only be described as
one of hardship and survival. Kuhdeh was settled as early as 1780, Rais said,
but the village was promptly burned to the ground by the ruling Afghans.
Years later, Zulob, a grandson of one of the original settlers, despaired of
finding land elsewhere and was given permission by the emir of Bukhara to
resettle Kuhdeh. Others followed, but the conditions they encountered were
difficult. The unfortunate placement of the village, downwind from the

Murghab District in eastern Badakhshan—home to one of the highest deserts in the world—meant that even summers were cold and often the crops froze. Its location between two high mountains meant that the sun rose—or rather became visible—only after nine in the summer, and set around five. The little arable land was all farmed, every foot of it; the rest was rock.

People told us that Moom was at least ninety years old, but even she was unclear on when she was born. That afternoon, as we talked, Moom surprised us with her recollections of the arrival of the Russians. She recounted how as a young girl—perhaps in 1912 or 1915 or thereabouts—she saw the tsar's soldiers come to the village. They did not come often, she told us; the Russians hesitated to venture all the way up to Kuhdeh and would summon villagers to meetings in the lower areas. She fondly recalled occasions when some of the men from Kuhdeh went down the mountain to have their pictures taken with the soldiers.

Rais, one of Moom's younger children, was born in 1943, during the famine of the Great War, and knew only Soviet rule. His father was a *kolkhoznik* who worked in the state collective farm (the *kolkhoz*)—a man who in most parts of the world would be considered a peasant. Rais grew up in Kuhdeh, leaving to join the Soviet army in Kazakhstan, where he learned Russian (his local teachers spoke only Pamiri languages). When he left the army, he went to Dushanbe to train as a driver. In 1974, after returning to Kuhdeh, Rais joined the Communist Party to "have higher status in the community." He married a woman from a neighboring village, and together they had ten children; seven died soon after birth.

Seven out of ten children died soon after birth *during the Soviet era*. It was a gruesome number. I pressed Rais on this and was assured that it was not because the doctors were not working hard, but because "people didn't go to doctors much."

RAIS: Several of my children died because we didn't consult with the doctors; we
        didn't take the children to the doctors in time to consult with them. We
        didn't use those services, perhaps due to ignorance. We didn't care that
        much—we thought that way for all [seven] of them. No doctor or nurse
        ever came to teach us about hygiene or anything like that. Nobody ever
        came to tell us what to do when our children are sick. We would call an
        ambulance, and it would take our children to hospital. I remember when we
        used to call the ambulance in the middle of the night, they used to come.

Rahmatekhudo told a slightly different story, which seemed to fit the statistical evidence a bit better. Laughing, he told us about an operation that his mother had had where they forgot to remove the scalpel. I asked him about the emergency services and the use of health services. He told me that before the telephone came in the early 1970s, there was no way of phoning for assistance.

RAHMATEKHUDO: If somebody was sick, what could we do? We couldn't run to Roshtqala [the district center] with our sick people. There were many pregnant women who weren't given care, and they died. There were many such cases. After 1972 it became better, but as far as pregnancy, there was no place for that, no doctors for that. It all appeared recently. . . . Okay, while the Soviet Union existed, we built a road to Kuhdeh, and then cars came. One could call an ambulance, from Zanodj, to come from Roshtqala, or use the *kolkhoz* cars to take relatives to the hospital. There was never a doctor that lived here, at that time or now. When the health post opened here in 1991— after the Soviet Union ended—a nurse used to come from Laldeh in the mornings and leave in the evenings. There were times, mind you, when she stayed overnight. Then, one day, she went on a holiday, and the health post shut down. She never came back, and it stayed closed! She is my older sister's daughter. It doesn't matter who she was; it was a bad situation.

As Rais shifted to a more comfortable position on the cushions, the rest of us leaning against the cool wall of the house, I asked more about the Soviet period. Rais thought a bit, then remarked that the communist system had served Kuhdeh well. "During the former Soviet Union, shops were crammed with items," he said. "Those were really good times—everything was available. Kuhdeh always had enough food. There were a lot of supplies, and people had money to buy things. People used to get their salaries every month and could buy whatever they wanted."

Despite its reputation to the contrary, the Soviet Union, it seems, was fairly efficient in bringing goods to remote and forbidding destinations—a fact that made life possible in places like Kuhdeh. "All the things that we have now, like our fridge, are things from the Soviet era," Rais said. "We have not bought anything new since then. All the clothes that we have are remainders from the Soviet period. If we wear them out, we will be naked." He paused and added, "That time was different and won't ever come back."

More than material security, it seemed, Rais cherished his memory of an ethos of mutual aid that flourished during Soviet times and had all but disappeared. "Even if there was some inequality, the Soviet Union had the best system for poor people," he said. "It had a conscience. Food was brought in, piled up along the road—nobody would steal it. Electricity was brought in, even television. And now, there are many goods in [the stores], but nobody here can afford to buy them. There are even things that didn't exist in the Soviet Union—yet for now our children walk barefoot."

Two decades earlier, the *kolkhoz* had built the road and bridge that connect Kuhdeh to the outside world, so that cars and trucks could be used to transport the harvest. The government sent an engineer and contributed the dynamite. Though the road was initially built using shovels, a few years later a bulldozer was used to widen it to two lanes. "Trucks would go to upper Kuhdeh to get milk and deliver goods to Khorog," Rais told me. "It was a huge help to people because, before that, we used to carry goods on our backs." In the past, residents had used donkeys only for getting water from the mountain passes during the winter. But since the Soviet Union collapsed, inhabitants of Kuhdeh once again carried goods on their backs and brought supplies from Roshtqala on donkeys. At the dawn of the twenty-first century, severe gasoline shortages and poorly maintained roads had conspired to revive medieval modes of transportation. My hosts in Kuhdeh and elsewhere in Badakhshan invariably reached for the telling detail—*our children walk barefoot, we have to rely on donkeys*—to illustrate what had been lost since the Soviet collapse.

As the poorest republic during the Soviet era, Tajikistan had some of the USSR's worst health indicators in the years leading up to the collapse. Compared with ethnic Russian lands lying closer to the centers of government administration, Tajikistan lagged badly in such areas as infant mortality, life expectancy, nutrition, and the prevalence of infectious diseases. Quite often, basic food and clothing needs were not met.[2]

On the one hand, the Soviet state attributed the poor health of the peripheral populations, especially those in Central Asia, to their "national culture." For example, Poliakov (1992) pointed out that during the medical examinations for induction in the Soviet Army, doctors found many young men from Central Asia to be in ill health due to diseases caused by "their life style," which he described as "child labor practices" and families saving what little money they had for the observance of religious and "national" traditions. He made no mention of the relative poverty of these regions.[3]

On the other hand, Soviet authorities recognized that while health conditions in Soviet-ruled Tajikistan were better than those of neighboring Afghanistan or other developing countries in Asia, more needed to be done. And it seems that concerted efforts were made to improve the situation. For example, I was told by physicians in Badakhshan that during the Soviet period, when public health officials became aware that large numbers of Tajik children were underweight, milk was provided to their families without charge and inexpensive baby foods were made available in the state-run stores. How far this penetrated into Badakhshan is difficult to gauge. A nurse at the main health clinic in Khorog told me that children were chronically undernourished: "We would not have meat. Even if it could be bought, not everybody could get it. In general, our nutrition was worse than in Dushanbe. We had those dried milk packets, but they would be expired."

Yet when I discussed the matter with Rais—a man who had lived in some of the most difficult environmental conditions one would ever encounter—he put it quite plainly: "People were less sick during the Soviet period. Even if they were sick, they could easily get to a doctor. Children rarely died of diarrhea. People would die in any state. But if a person fell ill during under the Soviet Union, he could cure himself." I pushed him a little more, asking if he had access to modern antibiotics when he needed it, if they were always available. His response, again, was clear: "I don't know what an antibiotic is, but I used to take what the doctors gave me. I used to take a lot of medicines, mostly for my stomach; mostly Hungarian and Indian medicines. We didn't know whether the medicines were modern or not. We just took them. The best way to cure a disease is to go to a doctor."

In the health care sector, the disappearance of the state resulted in both physical and psychological distress for the people of the Pamir Mountains. Within weeks after the collapse, salary checks for medical staff at the clinic in Kuhdeh and the hospital in Roshtqala simply stopped arriving. Since doctors and nurses were no longer paid, they turned to their patients to give them money under the table, or else they packed up and moved back to urban areas. Eventually, the small staff at the Kuhdeh clinic wandered off, leaving the clinic empty and padlocked. Even though things had improved somewhat since 1992—salaries, though irregular, had restarted and essential medicines were available, albeit in short supply—visits to the district hospital in 1996 revealed a lack of even the most basic supplies, including pens and paper for birth certificates and patient charts. The doctor in Roshtqala responsible for monitoring the Kuhdeh clinic told me that the human resource crisis had again reached a critical level because of finances: "Our hospital should have twenty-three doctors, but we have only nine. The major difficulty we face is that the medical staff do not receive any salary. In fact, the medical staff . . . have not received any money for five months."

As supplies ran out, basics such as gasoline and spare ambulance parts became unavailable. "If we had gasoline," the doctor said, "we could send people to distant villages. But both the ambulance and emergency services don't work, and mostly, we operate on people with serious complications, because they come too late." Without fuel, the community clinics could not be staffed, medicines could not be delivered, and doctors could not visit patients who were too ill or elderly to come to the hospital. Administrative oversight of local clinics became impossible. Meanwhile, the skeleton medical staff that remained in rural clinics began to turn to their own needs and spend the daylight hours growing crops or searching for diminishing food supplies, as well as tending to aging and sick relatives. It was impossible for them to perform their official tasks without pay.

THE RETURN OF MALNUTRITION AND DISEASE

The summer of 1996 was particularly difficult for the people of Badakhshan. The road connecting the province with the rest of the country remained closed due to the civil war, and unpaid salaries and lack of fuel were taking their toll. Piles of garbage were collecting on the streets. The costs of even the most basic goods had skyrocketed. A bar of soap that had cost pennies during the Soviet period now cost over one U.S. dollar—one-sixth of the average monthly income at the time.[4] Theft had become rampant—a phenomenon relatively unknown during the Soviet period—and at one of the local bazaars in Khorog, a man had been killed in a fight over the price of a piece of meat. And in the midst of this, babies were dying of diarrhea. Not only in the periphery, but in Badakhshan's capital of Khorog, and all over Tajikistan. According to countrywide statistics, in 1995 infant mortality in Tajikistan due to infectious diseases, mostly diarrheal and respiratory infections, accounted for up to 72 percent of all infant deaths (under one year of age).[5]

Diarrheal diseases were not new to the people of Badakhshan, but there had been a marked increase since the collapse. Regional health experts attributed this to the breakdown in sewerage and sanitation throughout the region. The situation during the Soviet period may not have been perfect, but by all accounts the infrastructure had degraded. Lack of fuel for vehicles prevented maintenance workers from emptying public toilets, resulting in a public health danger. Many residents were suddenly forced to fetch water from rivers and canals because water no longer came out of the pipes in their homes. With the potential cross-contamination between drinking water and sewerage in many of the rural (and more recently, urban) areas of Badakhshan, waterborne transmission of infectious pathogens—along with fecal-oral transmission from unwashed hands—became a major concern.[6] Rates of laboratory-confirmed intestinal infections in Badakhshan jumped from less than 500 per 100,000 people in 1991 to almost 3,000 in 1996, a sixfold increase. Given the breakdown of the health system (including laboratory testing supplies) and the inability of patients to get to clinics due to lack of fuel, this was likely an underestimate.[7]

As a social researcher working in AKF's health department, one of my roles was to examine access to medicines and health services in the general population. In June 1996, when I returned from Kuhdeh to Khorog—whose population was only 10,000—I learned that fifteen babies had recently died there from diarrheal disease. I asked Dr. Claquin if I could explore the situation further by interviewing the families of the infants and children who had died. In most Western countries, infant mortality from diarrhea is almost nonexistent, so I wanted to find out what exactly had happened and what had led to these preventable deaths. Dr. Claquin, who himself had expressed concerns about the health crisis and misgivings about the ability of local people to pay for medicines, agreed.

The stories I heard from the families of the infants and children who had died were heartbreaking, especially since medicines that cost literally pennies could have saved the lives of their loved ones.[8] The plight faced by Maryam, a forty-year-old unemployed factory worker, was typical of the women who shared the stories of their loss with me. Arriving at Maryam's apartment in a dilapidated building in Khorog showed my field assistant Ahmed and me how poor even Badakhshan's urban population had become. Although her husband was still employed, Maryam's home had very few signs of comfort and looked destitute. Though it was summer, the day was cold, and a cool wind was blowing through her house. Her young daughter, sister to the five-month old baby who had just died of diarrheal disease, was not wearing warm clothes.

Life after the collapse of the Soviet Union had not been good for Maryam and her family, and the preceding year had been especially tough:

> The factory where I was working is not operating at the current time, due to a shortage of raw material. I am on a forced vacation. I recently had a baby, a girl, who died of diarrhea. In general, our family's support is from AKF assistance and the Red Cross's aid for children. My son, who is in the fifth grade, cannot go to school because he does not have warm clothes. We are living in a flat with two rooms, which is not enough for our family. We applied to the government for land to build a house, but they said it is impossible because there is no land available. My second son wants to get married, but because of the problem with housing, we cannot let him do it.

In the spring, one of Maryam's sons was hit by a car and had to undergo surgery to repair a broken leg. He was due for a second operation but had not returned to the hospital yet, because they had been unable to purchase the five meters of gauze that the surgeon had asked them to bring. When I asked Maryam whether it had been difficult to access care for her daughter, she recalled how hard it had been, and how even the doctors in the hospital did not have the necessary supplies and had asked her family to try and find them:

> We called the doctors, and they said that we needed to take her to the hospital. She was sick with diarrhea at home for two days. . . . [At the hospital] they took her to the pediatric medicine department. They started treating her and asked us to bring the following drugs: rheopolyglucine [dextran], ampicillin, and other drugs whose names I do not remember. They said that they would also treat her with everything they had. They gave her an oral medication whose name I do not know, and also injected her.

They put an intravenous of Ringer's solution and rheopolyglucine into her. My husband and son were looking for Ringer's solution [intravenous fluids] but could not find it, so the doctors said that they would find it themselves. I got the ampicillin from the commercial drugstore located in the hospital—I have a friend there who gave me the drugs for free. My son borrowed rheopolyglucine from our neighbor who works in the drug store. Each vial cost 2,500 Tajik rubles.

We still have not been able to pay back the money because we do not have it. In any case, we got the medicines too late because even after putting an intravenous line into her on the third day, some minutes later the doctors said that her kidneys had stopped functioning and that although they had tried, they could no longer help her. The doctor said that at this point her situation was hopeless, and asked me to call my close relatives to take her from the hospital. After a few minutes, she died.

Maryam's story was similar to those of the fourteen other families I interviewed. They all recounted that they had struggled to find medicines and raise money to pay for them. Maryam aptly summed up the pharmaceutical situation in Badakhshan: "We do not have money for medicines; we only take them when we are totally desperate." Though the families were willing to extend themselves financially, perhaps disastrously, lack of access to medicines and the delay inherent in finding them in the bazaar led to catastrophic outcomes. And diarrheal diseases were not the only killers of children in Badakhshan: the region also saw a marked rise in the incidence of upper respiratory infections and malaria, the latter essentially eradicated during the Soviet era and reintroduced after 1991.

Dr. Banoz Mahmadwafoeva, a pediatrician at Khorog Hospital, looked perplexed when I asked her why the mortality rate and infectious disease rates were so high among children. "They don't have enough food," she told me. "The solution for childhood infections, first and foremost, is . . . nutrition."

Food was hard to come by in Badakhshan. By 1992, the situation had become critical, and relief agencies stepped in with food supplies brought in by trucks from Osh in the Kyrgyz Republic, eventually providing three meals a day to almost all of Badakhshan's population. While this intervention undoubtedly staved off widespread starvation, even the phenomenal amounts of assistance provided by the Aga Khan Foundation, the Red Cross, and the United Nations' World Food Programme could only mildly mitigate the repercussions of the breakdown of Soviet supply lines. The result was that malnutrition in the region increased markedly. Rickets, a nutritional disease related to vitamin D deficiency—and preventable by fortifying packaged milk with vitamin D, standard in the USSR and in most middle- and high-income countries—tripled between 1991 and 1996.[9]

In July and August 1996, AKF brought in an expert on nutrition, Dr. Isabel Hemming, along with a team from Aga Khan University led by Dr. Aamir J. Khan, to assess the health situation in Badakhshan and follow up on a nutritional survey from 1994, two years after the Soviet collapse. During the summer of 1996 the team managed to survey households representing almost a quarter of Badakhshan's population. Their report, "Health and Nutrition Survey, Autonomous Oblast of Gorno Badakhshan (Tajikistan)," found that among children six to fifty-nine months old, rates of acute malnutrition, chronic malnutrition, and low weight for age had increased dramatically between 1994 and 1996 (see table 1).

The survey provided empiric evidence that despite ongoing food assistance, the percentage of children suffering from acute malnutrition had increased markedly, and almost half the children of Badakhshan continued to suffer from chronic malnourishment. This spoke not only to a nutritional crisis among Badakhshan's children, but also to a crisis of prenatal nutrition among mothers.[10]

The effects of these findings were potentially far reaching. As Dr. Mahmadwafoeva had noted, children who do not get enough food are vulnerable to stunting and wasting; malnutrition can also lead to impairment of the immune system, increasing the case fatality from diseases such as measles, upper respiratory infections, diarrheal diseases, and malaria.[11] The children Ahmed and I had seen in Kuhdeh—often sick, always thin, and always shorter than their age warranted—were testament to the lived experience of the statistics in AKF's report.

PAYING FOR HEALTH

Other than the food provided by AKF, the Red Cross, and the United Nations' World Food Programme, it was difficult for most families to purchase food in the market. Food prices in Tajikistan as a whole had quad-

Table 1   Indicators of Malnutrition among Children Age Six to Fifty-Nine Months

Year of survey	Weight for height (indicator for acute malnourishment)	Height for age (indicator for chronic malnourishment)	Weight for age (indicator for weight deficit)
1994 (n=818)	3%	40.3%	19.2%
1996 (n=5299)	5.8%	44.8%	27.4%

NOTE: These are the percentages in each category that are < -2 Z Scores (less than two standard deviations from the local mean, which is considered outside the normal range). See WHO 1997b: 50. This statistical approach means that 2.3 percent of the reference population will be classified as malnourished even if they have no growth impairment. For this reason, 2.3 percent can be regarded as the expected prevalence in any category. Note that the 2.3 percent is customarily not subtracted from the observed values.

SOURCE: Results from an AKF report, "Health and Nutrition Survey, Autonomous Oblast of Gorno Badakhshan (Tajikistan)," July–August 1996, revised February 1997.

rupled between January and September 1995, with the cost of meat and cheese increasing more than tenfold.[12]

As difficult as it was to find food, medicines were even more scarce. Despite the efforts of Médecins Sans Frontières, the Red Cross, and AKF, who over the previous three years had been bringing medicines to Badakhshan, there were shortages. Médecins Sans Frontières had been distributing medicines and supplies to the district health posts and hospitals, and along with the Red Cross had supplied the regional hospitals. This assistance was given for free. Yet when Ahmed and I led a survey of one thousand households in four districts for AKF, we found a disturbing situation: only 44 percent of respondents indicated that they had received prescribed medicines free of charge. Only 31 percent of respondents reported that they were able to afford medicines prescribed by the doctor but not made available free of charge, with the proportion as low as 14 percent in Ishkashim, one of Badakhshan's poorer districts.

The reason was clear: people did not have money, and the medicines available in the market were too expensive. In our small survey, more than 60 percent of households reported an income of less than US $6 per month in the preceding year.[13] In the larger health and nutrition survey, AKF had found that almost 23 percent of respondents had to sell household possessions in 1996 to purchase essentials such as food, shoes, and clothing.[14] Despite high levels of illness, less than 10 percent reported having enough money left to spend on medications.

Even for those who had some money, given their meager earnings and the markups in the pharmacies and bazaars of Khorog, the cost of medicines was beyond the reach of most people. For example, Médecins Sans Frontières estimated that a five-day course of benzyl penicillin, a drug given by injection or intravenously for pneumonia, cost around US $9.60 from a quality-assured manufacturer, well above the average monthly income.[15]

Using the relatively small amount of three hundred Tajik rubles (US $1) for a complete course of treatment as an example, Ahmed and I tested the idea of having to pay for medicines on a group of patients at the Central Dental Clinic in Khorog in a survey of their general health care needs and capacity to pay.[16] The responses were stark:

> It will certainly have adverse effects. For my family, for example, with eight hundred rubles as our monthly income and eleven people, how could we possibly pay for the services at such prices? We'll just not be able to use these services. The same will happen to the main mass of the population of Badakhshan. And it will bring adverse consequences for Badakhshanis' health. (Respondent 2)

> My income is around 1,500 or 1,600 rubles per month. I have three school-age children. I will just have to forget about medicines. It is the same for the majority of Badakhshanis. (Respondent 25)

> That would mean either complete ruin or our total refusal of medical services. You can judge for yourself. . . . There are families whose children are older, with more family members, but with less income. There are families with chronically diseased members who need long-term care. It would be a catastrophe for the health of Badakhshan. (Respondent 28)

> Such prices are unaffordable, even for well-off families. My family, even during the former Soviet Union, wasn't well off. And especially today [we remain poor]. We won't be able to pay for services. And then, you have to think about food, about clothes. (Respondent 32)

> That is impossible. It is destruction. It is a way to catastrophe. My family and I, and the whole of Badakhshan's population, will not be able to use the treatment. We'll have to forget the word *medicine*. (Respondent 39)

EXPLAINING THE FINDINGS

The lack of sufficient access for Badakhshan's population to even the most basic antibiotics—and the resulting high mortality from treatable diseases—became a crisis that vexed the Geneva-based leadership of AKF. They were desperately trying to find a solution and needed to explain to donors—and, undoubtedly, to the Aga Khan himself—how the nutritional and health crisis had worsened so quickly under their watch.

The logical approach would have been to ascribe the findings to the war and the influx of refugees, to generalized starvation (due to the breakdown in agriculture and external food deliveries), and to increased disease amid the breakdown of state health services and a "pharmaceutical famine" (which could not be mitigated even with the medical assistance provided by relief agencies). After all, the humanitarian assistance provided, though life-saving, was really the *minimum* needed to survive. It was likely that farmers and people without fuel were actually expending many calories beyond that provided by their food supplies. But instead, in a foreshadowing of the policy approach to come, the AKF leadership in Geneva cast blame for the poor health and nutritional outcomes on the people of Badakhshan, citing some local traditional practices[17] and the biomedical prescription practices of the Soviet-trained physicians.

To explain the high levels of malnutrition reported in the 1996 health and nutrition survey, AKF identified two local practices as major contributors to the nutrition crisis: the swaddling of infants and infant bloodletting. The report made a somewhat shocking claim: "The data may indicate that the cause of malnutrition is linked to the knowledge, attitudes and practices of the residents of GBAO [Badakhshan] *as much as* to the unavailability and inaccessibility of food and services needed to maintain good nutritional status."[18]

I was cited as their source for this information. When I saw this, I was horrified. The ethnographic findings that I had reported to my superiors at AKF's health division had been used out of context. This "immodest claim of causality"—described in the work of anthropologist, physician, and global health activist Paul Farmer as illustrative of how ethnographic information can be misused to mask the real causes of suffering—was the opposite of everything I had seen in Kuhdeh, Khorog, and the other villages.[19]

By the time the final report came out in early 1997, Dr. Pierre Claquin had left AKF. At this point, I had also left Badakhshan. I wrote to Dr. Claquin's successor, Dr. John Tomaro, a physician who had moved from the U.S. Agency for International Development (USAID) to Geneva to become the director of AKF's health programs. In my letter to him, I expressed my concern that this claim was not an accurate reflection of the minimal role these practices played in the nutritional crisis in Badakhshan.[20]

It was true that almost every baby in Badakhshan was kept swaddled in blankets most of time. The reason was obvious to an outsider: in the high mountain air of Badakhshan, even in the summer, it was often cold, especially in places like Kuhdeh. From a medical perspective, swaddling could contribute to a deficiency in vitamin D, since the body's synthesis of the active form of vitamin D requires sunlight hitting the skin. Local doctors told us that even during the Soviet period they would tell families to make sure that children had enough time in the sunlight to prevent nutritional diseases like rickets. Though the practice of infant swaddling had not changed—what had changed was the loss of milk fortified with vitamin D and greater general malnutrition—this practice was now being blamed for the observed rise in childhood malnutrition. To me, this constituted what Paul Farmer has referred to as the conflation of structural violence—a term coined by Johan Galtung in 1969 to describe the violence that results from the avoidable impairment of fundamental human needs or human life due to economic, political, legal, religious, and cultural structures— and cultural difference.[21]

Blaming acute and chronic malnutrition and high rates of infant and child death on the practice of infant bloodletting put AKF's report on even shakier ground. This practice was said to stem from the medicine of Galen and Avicenna. Families of sick children—those with diarrheal diseases and severe respiratory infections—sometimes used this approach when they could not find medicines, as a way of preventing their children from dying.[22] Ahmed and I had seen it performed, and although upsetting to watch, it was for the most part nothing more than a few cuts made on a baby's back. Little blood was let, and the infections one would associate with such a practice, such as bacteremia (bacteria in the blood), could not be found in any statistical reports from the Soviet period or afterward. While local doctors were not supportive of the practice, they felt that the superficial cuts did not cause grave harm, and in fact, some of their own children had had the procedure performed. Moreover, since infant blood-letting was not practiced throughout Badakhshan—it was used commonly in only two of Badakhshan's seven districts (Roshtqala and Shugnan)—it could not explain the widespread child malnutrition that was observed. In fact, the health and nutrition survey indicated that acute malnutrition, chronic malnutrition, and severe weight deficit were also high in regions where this practice was not performed, making it highly unlikely that it was the cause. The only common factors faced by all of these places were poverty, a shortage of appropriate food, and an increase in childhood ill-nesses that could have been ameliorated with medical care, including the use of antibiotics.

I suggested to Dr. Tomaro that the report be corrected, saying that as it stood, it constituted blaming the victim. He responded:

> Suggesting that appropriate traditional practices contribute to nutritional and health problems in GBAO [Badakhshan] is not, in my estimation, "blaming the victim." It is in some part a recognition, however painful, that individuals have some degree of responsibility for maintaining their health and well-being. *This position supports one of the policies that separates those in the West from the old Soviet system, a system that the Foundation is committed to reforming.* In my opinion, the sooner we can determine the extent to which individuals can practice effective health promotion and protection measures, the sooner we will be able to determine what the reformed health system needs to provide and what can be left to individual initiative.[23]

While I understood the many ways individuals could play an important role in protecting their own health, I could not help but think of the hardship being endured in Kuhdeh and the hundreds of other villages just like it in Badakhshan and Tajikistan. How would Rais and his family, now carrying hay on their backs because they had no fuel for their tractors, manage to protect their own health? How would his children, running barefoot along the stones of the ridge by their house, not require medical interventions at some point?

One thing seemed clear enough. Given the limited material choices available to poor people whose children are hungry and dying, health promotion and protection alone—based on the belief that lack of knowledge or cultural difference needs to be addressed before people will seek appropriate care—

would not alter the fact that families did not have fuel to visit doctors. Nor does it address the fact that even if they made it to a doctor, they would likely lack the capacity to purchase necessary medicines. Dr. Tomaro's response did not address my concern that in the midst of this crisis—with its hunger, suffering, and death—local practices were being misconstrued as an explanation for the gaps and challenges that any service organization would face in the midst of a brutal civil war following the sudden collapse of an empire. As for practices like bloodletting, I doubted that they would change unless poverty was ameliorated. The imperative to ensure that one's child does not die is strong, and people will turn to any care they can access to prevent the death of a child.

A HEALTH TRANSITION IN REVERSE

The collapse of the Soviet state resulted directly in increased poverty and malnutrition, and impeded access to health care, including medicines. Given the close association between childhood mortality and poverty, between childhood morbidity and poverty, and between childhood living conditions and adult mortality and morbidity, the long-term implications of the health and nutrition crisis were truly frightening.[24] Household income is the greatest determinant of living standards, affecting every part of family life: living conditions, exposure to environmental hazards, access to space, leisure, work, educational facilities, and health care resources. Income also influences a family's exposure to dampness and cold, to food, fuel, and clothing—all variables in the body's capacity to regenerate and to resist infection.[25] The psychological stress and depressive illnesses associated with living at the brink of starvation are additional risk factors.[26] For Badakhshan, the dissolution of the Soviet Union came on top of what was already a tenuous health situation.[27]

Readers should not be left with the impression that the disappearance of the Soviet system left nothing in its place. In fact, what replaced it—a hodgepodge that included free pharmaceuticals distributed by foreign NGOs, a thriving informal market, and later the revolving drug fund— constituted an alternative system, one with its own rules, expectations, and underlying assumptions about how health care should be distributed to poor people. It is clear, however, that there was considerable need for health care, especially access to antibiotics for the treatment of childhood infectious diseases. People were desperate, selling household goods to procure items essential to their survival: food, shoes, clothing, and sometimes pharmaceuticals. At the same time, the availability of medicines had decreased in the absolute, which meant little or no access for many.

At this juncture, in the midst of a crisis of considerable magnitude, it is appropriate to ask how exactly it was that public health authorities in a former Soviet republic and their well-meaning benefactors in a foreign NGO arrived at the startling decision to sell pharmaceutical drugs to people who barely had enough food to eat.

Figure 1. The washed away road to Kuhdeh, Roshtqala District, Badakhshan. Photograph by the author, 1996.

Figure 2. Rais, leader of Kuhdeh, with his granddaughter, Roshtqala District, Badakhshan. Photograph by the author, 1996.

Figure 3. Barefoot and stunted children in the village of Kuhdeh, Roshtqala District, Badakhshan. Photograph by the author, 1996.

Figure 4. Children on a neighboring peak, Roshtqala District, Badakhshan. Photograph by the author, 1996.

Figure 5. Typical Pamiri-style house, Roshtqala District, Badakhshan. Photograph by the author, 1996.

Figure 6. Children waiting for vaccination outside a health clinic, Roshtqala District, Badakhshan. Photograph by the author, 1996.

Figure 7. Boy dressed in rags, Roshtqala District, Badakhshan. Photograph by the author, 1996.

Figure 8. Physician at Khorog Central Hospital, Khorog, Badakhshan. Photograph by the author, 1996.

5 Minding the Gap?

THE REVOLVING DRUG FUND

Afterwards I could not help admiring the wisdom of our
hosts in the distribution of the children's presents. The little
girl who already had a portion of three hundred thousand
roubles received the most expensive doll. There followed
presents which decreased in value in accordance with the
decrease in the social rank of the parents of all these happy
children. Finally, the last child to receive a present, a small,
thin, freckled, red-haired little boy of ten, got nothing but a
book of stories with descriptions of the grandeur of nature,
the tears shed under the influence of strong emotion, etc.,
without pictures or even a tail-piece. He was the son of a
poor widow, the governess of our host's children, a completely cowed and scared boy. He was dressed in a jacket of
cheap material. Having received his book, he wanted terri-
bly to play with the other children, but he did not dare: one
could see that he already felt and understood his position.

Fyodor Dostoyevsky, *The Christmas Tree and a Wedding*

As we walked out of a meeting with the team from the Canadian
International Development Agency in the summer of 1996, Robert
Middleton, the architect of AKF's humanitarian assistance program in
Badakhshan and a senior member of AKF's Geneva office, patted me on
the back. "That went well," he said.

I was not sure what to think. The meeting, held at the Pamir Relief and
Development Programme (PRDP) guesthouse—set along the shore of the

Ghund River, its green waters providing a low rushing sound in the background as it flowed into the much bigger Panj River—was the culmination of a plan that had been put in place a few months before. PRDP was AKF's local affiliate, and the Canadians had come to talk about funding for medicines. We sat with them on the back porch of the main building, looking over a tree-filled garden that led down to a smaller guesthouse which abutted the river. The beauty of the surroundings, the sense of complete peace in this idyllic mountain setting, stood in sharp contrast to the gravity of our conversation.

As Dr. Pierre Claquin had explained to me months before, at a strategy discussion in mid-March 1996, Badakhshan was going to go through another major transition. Many of the organizations that had been working there since 1992 would likely reduce their footprint in the region. Funding was becoming tighter, and since the civil war was at a much lower pitch, it was likely that the Red Cross would reduce some of its efforts. Médecins Sans Frontières had already announced that it would work only in two or three regions. This meant that organizations would stop providing essential medicines for the hospitals and clinics in some of Badakhshan's districts. The leadership in Geneva, Claquin said, felt that the time had come to begin thinking about the shift from the "humanitarian assistance" phase—when goods and service were provided in an emergency situation—to the "development phase", when options believed to be more sustainable would be deployed. And here, "sustainable" meant that "the community" would begin paying directly for goods and services without "external financial inputs."

The call for reform in the social service sector was heard in a number of Central Asian states. In 1994, USAID had started a program called ZdravReform in the Central Asian region (*zdrav* is the Russian word for "health"). According to USAID, the purpose of the program was to "help governments implement and test new organizational, management and financing structures for health services delivery systems as the NIS [newly independent states] move to market-oriented economies."[1] With the aim of finding "long-term solutions to problems inherent in the health systems as they were organized and financed during the Soviet era," the program also called for "preserving relative equity of access." Writing in their

Strategic Plan for Tajikistan that "the overall goal of USAID involvement in Tajikistan is sustainable economic growth," the USAID Regional Mission for Central Asia listed as one of three major goals to "promote economic reform and, ultimately, American trade and investment."[2] In language that recalled discussions I was having with AKF's Geneva staff about the revolving drug fund, the USAID Regional Mission wrote that "in accordance with US Embassy Dushanbe priorities," it wanted to focus "its technical assistance on moving from the humanitarian relief efforts which have dominated the USG [United States Government] assistance to Tajikistan since independence towards technical assistance and development assistance."[3]

USAID's ability to influence regional policy was supported by large amounts of economic assistance provided by the U.S. government to the Eurasia region,[4] which totaled approximately US $20 billion between 1992 and 2002.[5] A large USAID contractor, Massachusetts-based Abt Associates, had been selected to carry out the ZdravReform program from their regional office in Kazakhstan's capital, Almaty.[6] Because of the political instability and security issues in Tajikistan, the program worked only in Kazakhstan, Uzbekistan, the Kyrgyz Republic, and Turkmenistan. In a keynote speech, "The Role of Consumers in Health Reform," given at a regional technical conference in 1995, Abt Associates' program vice president for health, Mr. Gary Gaumer, identified "elevating the role of consumers in the health system" as a universal belief. This, he argued, had to be tied to improved efficiency in delivering care to patients—whom he referred to as "consumers"—and decreased administration costs. And what would an increased role for "consumers" mean? According to Gaumer, "payments by users for services are important to involving the consumer financially," in part because paying "makes them financially responsible for their actions, makes them allies in increasing efficiency." While this would "mean a loss of traditional administrative control in NIS [newly independent states] countries," Gaumer posited that it would lead to "better overall outcomes."[7]

By "traditional administrative control," it seems Gaumer was referring to state control of the health system. In a document describing ZdravReform program strategies that Abt Associates submitted to USAID, the authors argued that "health may be a good vehicle to push the development of civil society as people cared about health issues." According to the report, "the health sector is a large monopoly, which needs to be decentralized to create competition and allocate limited resources more efficiently."[8] For this reason, the ZdravReform project had begun to "establish NGOs to facilitate the development of new primary care practices and to *contribute to democratic transition*."[9] According to the ZdravReform documentation, patient involvement in health care decisions as they chose their health providers—those in the new primary care practices rather than the government clinics—could "become a mechanism to shift power from health sector authorities to the population."[10] According to classic neoliberal doctrine, where an individual's participation in the market is viewed as a form of political democracy,[11] this type of health reform was viewed as having "an important and synergistic relationship" with democratic transition.[12] As to whether people could afford health services, especially medicines, the architects of the ZdravReform program argued, "The reality is that patients entitled to free drugs often end up paying 100% out of pocket, instead of being part of an equitable cost sharing arrangement."[13] Instead of allowing what they describe as the Soviet Union's "legacy of entitlement" to limit discussions about user fees—essentially, patients paying for services— ZdravReform's architects argued that "it may be useful to consider pilots in user fees in the future, in order to help balance some of the public drug budgets."[14]

The idea of Badakhshan's revolving drug fund, based on what became known as the Bamako Initiative, was simple. An initial sum of money would be given by a donor to purchase a stock of essential medications. Patients would buy the medicines they needed from this stock at a small markup, and the money would go into a fund to be used for more medicines. Thus the fund would "self-replenish," or "revolve." Some patients would not be able to pay for the medicines, and this would be subsidized by AKF. It would be a "win-win strategy." The local population would get high-quality medicines at a reasonable price—better than the local market, where quality was unknown and prices high—and the system would be "sustainable." "Sustainability," Claquin had told me, was very important to AKF's management team in Geneva. And most important, USAID, at that time the foundation's largest donor for humanitarian assistance in Tajikistan, was willing to fund a program that could achieve such a result.[15]

At first blush the idea of a revolving drug fund could make sense. Upon deeper exploration, however, significant questions arise. I asked Dr. Claquin what would happen to the current system, where the central government purchases medicines through a pooled procurement mechanism designed to bring down prices based on bids from suppliers? The central pharmacy had a network that could reach every rural health clinic. Would this network be part of that system? Would it not be better to help the government rebuild and strengthen its network? According to the Bamako approach, the answer was no. In fact, the premise behind the revolving drug fund, Claquin explained, was to bring health care closer to communities. The system would require village health committees to look after the medicines and make decisions about who deserved a waiver, allowing "the community" to "participate" in their own health. And per USAID rules at the time, the drugs would have to be purchased from U.S. manufacturers.

These were not our biggest problems, however. Our biggest challenge, Dr. Claquin told me, would be to change the mindset around medicines. Having himself had concerns about the viability of this strategy in Badakhshan, Claquin tasked me with finding out how people felt about paying for medicines and whether they would be willing and able to do so. How would they pay for the drugs? What percentage of the cost would they be able to pay? How much of the cost would AKF have to subsidize initially? How would communities decide who paid? Also, he foresaw that local doctors would not be happy with having to prescribe using "global standards." The World Health Organization, he said, had written a report that highlighted the "irrational use" of medicines in Tajikistan, with doctors prescribing what appeared (to the Western eye) to be inappropriately prolonged medication courses and multiple medications for illnesses where one medication would suffice.[16] Part of the Bamako strategy was to "rationalize" the use of pharmaceuticals, encouraging physicians to prescribe drugs found on the World Health Organization's Essential Drugs List, at the dosages recommended.

I was to spend time in the villages to find out what was going on and what would be possible; I would talk to the doctors and learn about their position on prescription practices and what they thought of Médecins

Sans Frontières's practice guidelines. This would help AKF answer some critical questions that it needed to address to implement the program. This was how I ended up in Kuhdeh and the other villages where Ahmed and I spent time. And this is how I ended up at PRDP's riverside guest-house that day, in the meeting with the Canadians.

THE BAMAKO INITIATIVE

The notion of the revolving drug fund, commonly known as the Bamako Initiative, arose from a meeting of African ministers of health in September 1987 in Bamako, Mali. The 1980s were a period of financial crisis for many poor countries, in part because of the lending policies of the World Bank and the International Monetary Fund. Health advocates were concerned that it would be impossible for cash-strapped governments to achieve the expansion of primary health care services that had been outlined at the 1978 health conference in Alma Ata, Kazakhstan, almost a decade earlier.[17]

The meeting in Bamako was cohosted by the United Nations Children's Fund (UNICEF) and the World Health Organization (WHO), and attended by WHO's director general, Dr. Halfdan Mahler, and UNICEF director James Grant. As a solution to the challenges faced by many African countries in maintaining a drug supply for their maternal and child health programs, Grant proposed what became known as the Bamako Initiative: "Drugs provided by donors and international agencies would be sold to communities at marked-up prices. The money thus raised would be used for strengthening primary level mother and child health care programmes and for paying health workers' salaries."[18] The markup—perhaps two or three times the actual cost of the drugs—would contribute to the revolving fund, which would then be used to purchase more drugs.

The initiative, inspired by the World Bank's advocacy of user fees in 1987,[19] combined decentralized community-based decision making, user financing of health services under community control, and a national policy to oversee the distribution of essential drugs.[20] By seeking input from "consumers," and requiring that they pay for drugs, the Bamako framework sought to curb the "frivolous" use of pharmaceuticals, ensure adequate supplies, and expand services to all residents, even the poorest.[21]

Despite the paucity of data to support its efficacy—the idea had been tested in a pilot project in Benin (covering a population of 12,000 people) and another in Ghana (for 30,000 people)—the resolution was adopted by the African health ministers. On March 15, 1988, the initiative was approved by UNICEF's executive board with a recommendation of $1 million funding for 1988 and 1989, and supplementary funding of $180 million for 1989 to 1991.[22] The program was backed by the World Bank and, ultimately, by USAID.[23] On slender evidence, the Bamako Initiative became a signature effort in public health.

From the outset, the Bamako Initiative had been controversial. It was received skeptically by researchers and practitioners alike.[24] According to Najmi Kanji, an expert on pharmaceutical policies in poor countries who was brought in by AKF in the middle of 1996 to lead their revolving drug fund initiative, UNICEF's alignment with the World Bank was not surprising, "as World Bank and donor support is crucial to UNICEF." "It is therefore no coincidence," he pointed out, "that, in the Bamako document, UNICEF identifies the role of health delivery systems as being responsive to demands. Need no longer appears to be the criterion."[25] Calling the underlying premise of the mechanism into question, Kanji argued:

> The Bamako Initiative rests on the belief that people will pay for drugs. The most powerful argument used by proponents of user charges for health services is that there is a "willingness to pay" on the part of the consumer. It is argued that people already pay for traditional and private services. However, payment to traditional healers may be in kind and over a longer period so as not to bankrupt a family. . . . If a family spends most of its savings or incurs large debts in the hope of saving a family member's life, it is because there is no choice.[26]

While "willingness to pay" may be demonstrated in a variety of settings, Kanji argued, "whether this reflects ability to pay is highly questionable."[27]

Critics pointed out that the policy had never been evaluated in the context of dire poverty.[28] Most realized that "community financing" meant that the care received in poor communities would be based on their place in the global economy rather than the hierarchy of need. In fact, several studies at the time suggested that when user fees were introduced in poor communities, utilization of health services actually went down, worsening "allocative efficiency."[29] As Kanji put it, "If families are stretched to pay for food, how are they going to pay for drugs?"[30]

Soon after the approval of the Bamako Initiative, the British medical journal *The Lancet* questioned the logic of the policy in a scathing editorial:

> Any cost recovery system would disqualify a considerable proportion of poor inhabitants of rural areas. A World Bank study in Kenya showed that any fee would exclude 40% of the population, and these are the people who most need access to the services. Charging the sick to pay for preventive services is also open to criticism. Management difficulties fall into two main categories. First, the management capacity of rural people in these poor countries is undeveloped. Secondly, the fees that would need to be set might have to be prohibitively high—perhaps four to six times the cost price of drugs—if basic MCH [maternal child health] preventive services and very poor inhabitants were exempted from payment. . . . Almost all African countries face a severe shortage of foreign currency for the purchase of drugs; the Bamako initiative may generate local funds, but this money cannot be converted into foreign currency. Even if donors supply the essential drugs for three to five years, this policy will maintain a state of dependence. And how could one ensure the rational use of drugs under such a system? If the nurse at the health centre depends on drug sales for her salary or maintenance of the centre she will be likely to overprescribe.
>
> . . . *It is dangerous to jump from two small projects to a multimillion dollar enterprise. The two pilot studies have been criticised as being exceptional, and it has been suggested that if they had been fully costed they would not have been economic.* Nevertheless, UNICEF is putting its considerable political weight behind the Bamako initiative, and the African ministers of health have supported it, so this scheme will not go away. There is a grave risk that the initiative will be implemented in a few countries; such hasty action is likely to hinder the development of rational drug policies for a long time. Before any country accepts or a donor pledges drugs, detailed plans must be made and no effort spared to establish an effective management system. *Development aid organisations and governments need to think deeply about the initiative to ensure that equity is served and the poorest people are protected.*[31]

THE RESPONSE TO BADAKHSHAN'S HEALTH CRISIS

In 1995, the Ministry of Health of Badakhshan formally requested assistance from AKF in addressing the pharmaceutical crisis. This request coincided with a significant push by the World Bank, USAID, and other donors to "reform" health care in the newly independent states of the former Soviet Union and its satellites.

By the time AKF began working with USAID on a proposal to create a revolving drug fund for Badakhshan, early data suggested that the editors of *The Lancet* were justified in their concern about Bamako. Where the initiative had been implemented, it failed to have a significant impact on the availability of medicines and other important supplies[32] and did not raise significant amounts of money.[33] In a context of widespread poverty, waivers did not seem effective in ensuring access.[34] Even the World Health Organization, which had cohosted the meeting in Bamako with UNICEF, had concerns about the approach, especially in settings without sufficient institutional capacity.[35] It seemed that the program was not appropriately designed to address the need for which it was created. Moreover, there were many system issues—namely, whether the target population had previously paid for such services and the expectations citizens had of the state—that had a bearing on the potential success of the endeavor.[36]

I knew from the research assignment given me by Dr. Claquin that AKF's leadership in Geneva understood well the potential shortcomings of the strategy and, as a result, the potential challenges in gaining popular acceptance of the plan. In fact, in their written funding proposal to USAID, the foundation acknowledged that "policies that propose user charges for social services are politically sensitive and require a supportive context."[37] Their application suggested that the new policies be publicly debated to "raise awareness and encourage acceptance."

In their proposal to USAID, AKF's Geneva office was clear about the role of pharmaceuticals in the health system: "It must be also recognized that unless essential drugs are available regularly at the primary level of care, morbidity and/or mortality is likely to increase, and the present health system is likely to lose its credibility with health cadres leaving the profession and the use of health units decreasing."[38] Yet, using language that mirrored the approach of USAID's signature ZdravReform regional initiative, AKF justified adopting the approach laid out in Bamako as a way of addressing what they identified as three constraints to the effectiveness of Badakhshan's health system and its "sustainability": (1) a shortage of good-quality, essential, low-cost pharmaceuticals; (2) inefficiencies in use of pharmaceuticals; and (3) lack of involvement of health care users in the management of health resources. The ultimate aim of the project, AKF said, was to create a model for pharmaceutical procurement, prescription, and distribution that would involve an element of cost recovery, rational drug policy, and community participation, and that could ultimately be replicated on a national scale.[39] It would also give AKF a defined period of participation in the provision of basic primary health care, which, Dr. Claquin had told me, the foundation's Geneva-based leadership believed to be the role of national governments.[40]

As in the broader ZdravReform project, part of the process of implementing the revolving drug fund was the (re)training of health care providers and managers to ensure that prescribing practices were in keeping with "international guidelines."[41] AKF, Médecins Sans Frontières, and the Red Cross were all concerned that local prescribing practices—based on years of Soviet training, scientific discourse, practice, and guidelines—were not in line with those in the West: more drugs were often prescribed and for longer periods. This was reinforced by a report from the World Health Organization. Thus the foundation felt that these types of "wasteful" prescribing practices contributed to drugs being in short supply.

With the view that "health professionals often resist change," AKF set out to obtain a technical consensus for the implementation of the revolving drug fund by working with the local government to establish an Oblast Committee on the Rational Use of Essential Drugs. Although decisions about medicines and their optimal prescribed dosages are ostensibly scientific and clinically based, in addition to senior officials from the Health Ministry, this committee would include senior officials from the Planning and Finance Ministries, nongovernmental organizations and donors active in the health sector, and one lay community representative from each district.[42] The committee would create a list of essential drugs adapted to the needs of Badakhshan and establish therapeutic protocols based on the Médecins Sans Frontières treatment manual (which followed World Health Organization guidelines and was available in Russian) and the assistance of a therapeutics consultant. Certificates would be issued to the health staff to "motivate them to adopt new prescribing procedures," and "only health units whose staff have successfully completed the course will be included in the project." Thus accessing medicines purchased through the revolving drug fund, envisioned to be the major if not the only source of medicines for Badakhshanis, would require compliance with the new therapeutic protocols.

According to what I was told, AKF's Geneva staff believed that the revolving fund would be more palatable to both USAID and the residents of Badakhshan if it was combined with "community involvement" in decision making. In what appeared to be a nod to USAID's mandate to shift decision making to "consumers"—often conflated in neoliberal political philosophy with "promoting democracy"—the application was rife with buzzwords such as "community," "empowerment," and "participation." A representative from each of Badakhshan's regions would be charged with ensuring that local communities—villages like Kuhdeh—were "encouraged and enabled to participate in the actual management of the pharmaceutical supply." The price list for the medicines would be defined by district management committees who would also identify and create a mechanism to assist patients who were too poor to pay. "Community participation" also offered other advantages: since funds from the sales of medicines would have to be collected at the community level and pooled at the central level, cooperation from local residents was key.

The proposal for the revolving drug fund submitted to USAID by AKF—a largely apolitical organization known for its efforts in some of the world's poorest communities—was aligned with USAID's broader mission of economic and political "reform." This was largely, I believe, to win funds from their chief donor for the humanitarian assistance they were providing in Tajikistan. Although AKF said in their application to USAID that they planned to subsidize the revolving drug fund in its initial years, the foundation, in line with the ZdravReform project, explicitly depicted the drug fund as more than just a means of providing pharmaceuticals or a solution to the current health crisis. Indeed, similar to the language used in USAID's mission reports and the ZdravReform documents, officials from AKF's office in Geneva wrote:

[If] the people of GBAO [Badakhshan] are to have an efficient, effective, equitable and sustainable health system, wider reaching reforms in the current system are necessary. *The strategic use of essential drugs to catalyse the start of these reforms is an opportunity that perhaps should not be missed.* In many ways, the timing for such an initiative seems right, and if the RDF [revolving drug fund] project can serve to change the old ways of thinking at the many levels of this society, then the project will have made a significant contribution. . . .

Although it is unlikely that the project will ever recover more than 50–60% of the actual drug costs, *it is imperative that both government and communities make the mental switch that the old system is not coming back, and that any new, viable system will require more community involvement in management as well as in contribution.*[43]

Thus the solution to Badakhshan's health crisis was couched in a project with a broader underlying mandate—namely, to "change the old ways of thinking." This echoed USAID's strategy for ZdravReform and was similar to what Dr. Tomaro, USAID's former employee, had written in his letter to me.

VOICES FROM THE VILLAGE

I am not sure when exactly the revolving drug fund was planned and the application to USAID written at AKF's offices in Geneva, but in my mind's eye, I think of it as having happened at the same time that Ahmed and I were living in Kuhdeh with Rais and his family, chatting with him and Rahmatekhudoh about his life and what would happen in the future if medicines were sold, visits to a health post cost money, or one had to pay fees for social services.

Rais was always hospitable to us, treating us like long-lost family that he was trying to orient. Even his most staccato answers had nuggets of a deep truth that made me feel like we were in the presence a very wise man. I remember the day I asked him how he felt when Brezhnev died:

RAIS: When Brezhnev died, I felt nothing. He died; everybody dies. I was sad when he died, but I only felt real sadness for the death of Brezhnev after Yeltsin started ruling. What would you do if you were in my position? I told you my life and our standard of living. Our ancestors used to live in poverty before the Soviets came. Would you be sad when Brezhnev died?

> If the whole state collapsed, what would you feel? When we served in the army, our officers were fostering us better than fathers and mothers, and everybody was like a brother. . . . It was sad when the Soviet Union collapsed as it was providing us with everything, just like AKF provides for us now.

As if on cue, his friend Rahmatekhudo chimed in: "We are scared that some good things will be lost from the Soviet period. In the past, everybody could have education; now they want money."

Whenever I spoke to Rais, I had the sense that suffering was an integral part of his existence. He had already told me that seven of his children had died in infancy and that his older brother had fallen to his death in a nearby gorge. I subsequently found out more. His father had died from cancer in 1991, the year the Soviet Union collapsed. His younger brother had died of heart problems, and his younger sister had died in childbirth. Rais himself had a serious stomach ulcer and had been hospitalized for an extended period.

Life was certainly not easy in Kuhdeh. Basic survival consumed most of the day, and even the few luxuries offered by the Soviet state could not have been enough to ameliorate the rough living. The only toilet in the village was two and a half kilometers away at the school, and it was only built in 1993. There was no piped water, and people had to walk down steep rocks to the river in the winter to fetch water in buckets. During the Soviet period, the collective farm had provided feed for the animals and other supplies, but now there was nothing. As Rais often told us, living in Kuhdeh was an exercise in survival.

RAIS: People here work hard to survive, but what can they do about the weather, about the lack of land? Last year we had no harvest—our crops were frozen because it was so cold. We work from morning to night, but the harvest is too little, and our weather is bad, and we don't have enough sunlight—it rises at ten and sets at five. You can feel how cold it is now. This is the most difficult thing.

And cold it was in Kuhdeh. Even in the summer, the water was so cold our hands became numb while we washed them. One night in mid-August it was so cold that the potatoes froze.

I once asked Rais why they had not built more toilets and other amenities during the Soviet period. He told me that it was because they never imagined the Soviet Union could end. When I asked if it was not too late to plan for the future, he gave me a very tired look: "People now have to think of ways to escape hunger."

When we first arrived in Kuhdeh, Ahmed and I had asked a lot of questions about illnesses and the use of medicines, only to find that many people, for lack of money, had not been able to purchase drugs. Because of distribution problems, the free medicines from Médecins Sans Frontières designated for Kuhdeh had never reached the health post.[44] People rarely smoked, pointing out that they did not even have money for soap. Scabies and lice were endemic, and most people wore the same clothes they had owned during Soviet times. New goods could be had infrequently via the *kommersant,* a trader who came on foot to Kuhdeh once every three months selling juice packets, shoes, hats, scarves, thread, and other such items. He told us that he did not bother to sell vodka and cigarettes in Kuhdeh because he knew nobody there had money for that.

In fact there was so little money in Kuhdeh that it was difficult for people to buy anything. The residents had livestock, but to sell their animals, they had to go on foot to Khorog, seventy kilometers away, to Badakhshan's central bazaar. When the government started selling notebooks for children through the schools, people said they were grateful to have access to them, but very few had money to actually buy them. Interestingly, AKF had cited the sale of education material in their application to USAID as a sign that the revolving drug fund could be successful.[45]

Even in the surveys we conducted, respondents often told us that, in principle, they were not against the idea of paying for medicines. The only problem was that with the economic crisis, they could not imagine such a scenario because it did not make sense. One respondent to the survey we conducted at the dental clinic commented, "If there were normal services and patients had proper incomes, then they would pay for their health care. But today, people are not able to pay, and that means the transition to fee-for-service in the current conditions will surely affect people's health."

Some of the poorest people brought up a classically Marxist argument for why it made sense for medicines to be sold. In the words of a nineteen-year-old farmer in upper Roshtqala Valley, far from Khorog and even beyond Kuhdeh, "Should pharmaceuticals be sold? Of course, because they are so vital to people; it is the first thing one needs if one gets ill. We have to think that they must be sold and not just given out for free. People need to receive money for the medicines. They are the product of somebody's labor and we should pay for them." However, willingness to pay for medicines meant little in the face of being completely unable to pay. With household goods that could be sold to traders dwindling and people beginning to sell livestock—their only asset base—the situation was perilous.

THE MEETING AT PRDP

We sat on the porch of the PRDP guesthouse around a big table listening to our colleagues from Canada, the rush of the Ghund River a distant hum. The Canadians had come to Badakhshan on a monitoring visit to discuss future funding. They wanted to give money for continued provision of humanitarian assistance, an offer that included funding pharmaceuticals for the region for one year.

Before the meeting, we had had a strategy session at the health office. AKF's revolving drug fund proposal was already with USAID, and it looked like they would fund it. Of course, it was clear that the population would not be able to immediately cover the full cost of medicines, and their sale would have to be highly subsidized. The Canadians wanted to give money, but not as part of a program that was selling medicines. They wanted the medicines to be provided for free since Badakhshan was facing a humanitarian crisis. The senior team from AKF's Geneva office reasoned that since the Canadian funding would not be enough to purchase all the needed medicines, if it could go toward supporting a subsidy for patients who could not afford to pay; this would ensure that the revolving drug fund program would work. That is where I came into the picture. My role in the meeting was to talk about the villages and the fact that there were no pharmaceuticals at the health points, highlighting how much the traders charged for medicines in the villages and at the bazaar. So when Robert Middleton patted me on the back as we left the PRDP guesthouse, it meant that I had done a good job. The Canadians had agreed to support the gap in the revolving drug fund. But for some reason I had mixed feelings.

In truth, I was confused. I was in my midtwenties and had been convinced by seasoned development experts that this approach was an integral part of the transition from "humanitarian assistance" to "long-term development." Of course, as a graduate student somewhat versed in development theory, I knew that something was not right about planning a strategy with people from France and Switzerland, whose medicines were paid for by health insurance, to convince the Canadians, whose medicines were paid for by health insurance, that the Badakhshanis, whose entire life-world had collapsed, who had no access to pooled-risk insurance schemes, and who were now living in poverty, should finance medicines from their destitute communities; that they should "participate in their own health" by joining committees that defined what doctors could prescribe for them; and that their system of curative care—with hospitals, clinics, and experts trained over seventy years of Soviet rule—should move toward a more "preventive" medical system in the midst of epidemic disease and hunger. But I participated in moving the strategy forward because I saw it as a means of protecting the most vulnerable (as did, undoubtedly, Robert Middleton and Pierre Claquin).

So walking out of the meeting that afternoon with Robert Middleton, I was not sure what to feel as an anthropologist and a participant-observer. But I did have one question that shaped my thinking for the rest of my time in Badakhshan and beyond: how did the revolving drug fund become the only way forward in responding to the health crisis in Badakhshan?

PART III Transplanting Ideology

VILLAGE HEALTH MEETS
THE GLOBAL ECONOMY

6 Bretton Woods to Bamako

HOW FREE-MARKET ORTHODOXY INFILTRATED THE INTERNATIONAL AID MOVEMENT

Only a crisis—actual or perceived—produces real change.
When that crisis occurs, the actions that are taken depend
on the ideas that are lying around. That, I believe, is our
basic function: to develop alternatives to existing policies,
to keep them alive and available until the politically impossible becomes politically inevitable.

Milton Friedman, *Capitalism and Freedom*

Bretton Woods, New Hampshire, is far from Bamako and even farther
from Badakhshan. Yet it was there, ensconced amid the beautiful views
and craggy ridges of the White Mountains of the northeastern United
States, that the seeds were planted for what emerged in the revolving drug
fund proposal more than fifty years later.

The United Nations Monetary and Financial Conference, held at
Bretton Wood's regal Mount Washington Hotel—a Spanish Renaissance-
style building whose interior was said to have taken 250 master craftsmen
two years to complete—was no small event, drawing together 730 delegates from 44 nations for the first three weeks of July 1944.[1] These delegates—men of power from government, academia, and large financial
institutions—discussed Europe's postwar recovery, paying particular
attention to monetary issues such as unstable exchange rates and protec-
tionist trade policies. The compact that emerged, known as the Bretton
Woods Agreement, established a postwar international monetary system
of convertible currencies, fixed exchange rates, and free trade. To realize
these objectives, two new international institutions were created: the

International Stabilization Fund (which later became the International Monetary Fund, IMF) and the International Bank for Reconstruction and Development (IBRD). The aim of the latter institution, which became a core institution of the World Bank Group, was to provide economic aid for the reconstruction of postwar Europe. A loan of $250 million to France in 1947 was the IBRD's first.

The discussion in Bretton Woods was about stabilizing the international monetary system and setting up economic structures that would expand the production, exchange, and consumption of goods[2]—a subject that seems remote from Kuhdeh in 1996 and from the travails of Rais and the people of Badakhshan. The conversation at Bretton Woods took place toward the end of the Second World War, in the context of a battle between fascism and democracy. This was more than two decades into Joseph Stalin's rule of the Soviet Union, amid a growing realization that Soviet and American visions for a postwar world were very different. The deep fear of communism had not yet reached a fever pitch. That happened with the 1946 communist uprising in Greece, and the United States' Truman Doctrine of 1947, which hardened American policy on the containment of Soviet communism. But fear of totalitarianism—an authoritarian state seen as anathema by those espousing the idea of freedom—was very real in Bretton Woods, and the discussion there was about significantly more than fixed exchange rates and monetary policy: it was a much broader debate about the relationship between the citizen and the state, and the role government should play in furthering social and economic life.

Some delegates, like the British economist John Maynard Keynes— whose theories rose to prominence during the Great Depression—argued that totally free markets were not ideal: sometimes the market failed to properly allocate resources, which could be corrected through appropriate intervention by the state.[3] The market, Keynes argued, was made of individuals acting in their own self-interest, while society and the state needed a broader and longer vision to achieve important societal goals. Keynes maintained that "not only does government have a role to play in remedying market failure, but it is also a provider of essential services related to education and health."[4]

Others disagreed. They called for laissez-faire economics, free trade, and the repeal of restrictive trade laws.[5] Their argument drew from the intellectual lineage of classical eighteenth- and nineteenth-century liberal thinkers like Adam Smith and John Stuart Mill, who, in the most general and unnuanced interpretation, saw liberty as the absence of interference from government and other political institutions. This argument linked Smith and Mill's ideas of liberty to nineteenth-century neoclassical economists such as Alfred Marshall, William Stanley Jevons, and Léon Walras, who emphasized the efficiency of market competition and the role of individual consumers in determining economic outcomes. In its simplest form, the argument was a repudiation of Keynesian economics. It maintained that state intervention caused "distortions" that led to market failures: the state, therefore, should have no role in production, services, and industrial policies, and should leave the market alone so that it could work efficiently.[6] This school of thought became known as neoliberalism, most often associated with thinkers such as Friedrich von Hayek and Milton Friedman, known as the Chicago school.[7]

Although Keynes is seen as one of the main architects of the Bretton Woods Agreement, and the IMF and World Bank are sometimes referred to as Keynes's twins—their creation is often attributed to Keynes and Harry Dexter White, one of Franklin Roosevelt's closest advisors—Keynes and his ilk lost the bigger argument at Bretton Woods.[8] What emerged was an institutional framework that supported an economic model based primarily on supply and demand, with minimal state intervention.[9] The International Stabilization Fund, more than its sister organization, was explicitly created to operate using this neoliberal framework. The IBRD took some years to fully adopt the neoliberal perspective; its political orientation, however, was clear from the start. The very first loan from the IBRD to France was delayed until the French agreed to remove "communist elements" from within the cabinet.[10]

As Soviet influence grew, the United States pushed for a sister organization to the IBRD to provide loans to poor countries. This led to the creation of the International Development Association (IDA) in 1960.[11] The combination of IBRD and IDA became known as the World Bank. World Bank president Eugene Black and his senior staff, along with some countries like West Germany and the Netherlands, opposed lending for social programs because they were too risky and would affect the bank's creditworthiness in the bond market (its bond credit rating).[12] Douglas Dillon, the U.S. undersecretary of state from 1959 to 1961, supported IDA lending for social overhead (specifically referring to non-revenue-producing areas such as sanitation, water supply, and housing).[13] These loans were seen as a way to reward loyalty in the face of perceived Soviet aggression and expansion. For example, Jordan, which had previously been turned down on loans for water and sanitation in 1958, was given a loan in 1960 after the pro-Nasser coup in Iraq.[14] Not only did this approach serve to reward states that had resisted becoming allied with the Soviet Union, but since the IDA required regular funding replenishment, this gave the government of the United States, the largest donor, significant influence over recipient countries and the bank.[15]

NEOLIBERALISM AS A "BULWARK" AGAINST COMMUNISM

Intellectually, the roots of neoliberal philosophy are mostly associated with the Austrian-born Nobel Prize–winning philosopher and economist, Friedrich von Hayek, who taught at the London School of Economics, the University of Chicago, and the University of Freiberg. Hayek was mentored by the Austrian economist Ludwig von Mises, a friend of the German sociologist Max Weber. Mises predicted the failure of socialism and championed the "sovereignty of the consumer."[16] Mises, who had moved to Switzerland, fled Europe for the United States in 1940, fearing a fascist takeover of Europe.

The rise of socialism and fascism in the 1930s, coupled with the implementation of New Deal economic programs by President Franklin Roosevelt in the United States, caused Hayek, Mises, and others a great deal of concern about the reach of the state and the liberty of the individual.[17] They saw economics as embedded in politics and, hence, saw the "free market" as an economic form of political democracy.[18] For them, state regulation of the market—which they termed "interference"—mirrored the state restraining political life, and was a harbinger for forms of the state that would limit individual liberty, such as fascism and communism.

Questioning the role of the state in the market, and in the lives of citizens, was a bold challenge to the prevailing social and economic orthodoxy of the day and would require an organized intellectual response.[19] According to political scientist Rick Rowden, thinkers like Hayek took a page from an unlikely source, the Italian Marxist philosopher Antonio Gramsci: "They realized that to transform the economic, political and social landscape, they first had to change the dominant intellectual and psychological landscape; they had to make their ideas part of daily life and propagated through books, journals, conferences, universities, research institutes, professional associations, etc."[20] They had to make them "common sense." To this end, Hayek—along with Mises, Karl Popper, George Stigler, Milton Friedman, and thirty-one other economists, historians, philosophers, and thinkers— founded the Mont Pèlerin Society in 1947, as a means of bringing American and European conservatives together for this project of social change.[21]

On April 2, 1947, the founders met at the Hotel du Parc in the Swiss village of Mont Pèlerin, about two hours' drive along Lake Leman from Geneva. Economics was discussed, of course, but in the context of the dangers faced by "civilization" from government encroachment into the lives of its citizens.[22] In the Mont Pèlerin Society's statement of aims, signed on April 8, 1947, they wrote that the "central values of civilization are in danger" and that "the position of the individual and the voluntary group are progressively undermined by extensions of arbitrary power." These and other changes, it contended, "have been fostered by a decline of belief in private property and the competitive market; for without the diffused power and initiative associated with these institutions it is difficult to imagine a society in which freedom may be effectively preserved." The group was very clear about their path forward, stating that a priority area of study would be "the redefinition of the functions of the state so as to distinguish more clearly between the totalitarian and the liberal order."[23]

At the meeting in April 1947, Hayek was said to have remarked that the battle for ideas would not occur overnight, that in fact it would take a generation to win, but it would be successful because such an intellectual army as the Mont Pelerin Society would attract powerful backers.[24] And it did. By the end of the 1970s, neoliberal ideas had come to dominate a number of major global institutions.[25]

The economic precepts of neoliberalism went much farther than the nineteenth-century liberalism and classical economics drawn from the ideas of

Smith and Mill.[26] In broad strokes, one can outline three core economic principles. First, that the mechanisms of the market, of supply and demand operating free of government interference, would lead to "equilibrium," where resources are allocated efficiently.[27] Government participation, even regulation, would "distort" the market. Any form of central planning was, of course, out of the question. The role of the state was simply to facilitate the market and otherwise stand back. Second, individual actors, regardless of social, institutional, and political context, always made choices that satisfied their individual objectives, and were "rational, utility-maximizing agents" with fixed preferences.[28] Accepting this premise, it was believed, would put decision making in the hands of citizens, not the state. And third, individuals have full knowledge of "the market" and all "externalities" and can always make the correct informed decision.

Critics of neoliberalism often view these core economic precepts as unrealistic, economically unsound, and empirically unsupported and unsupportable. This, suggests the economist Simon Clarke, misses the point. As the Mont Pèlerin Society's aims indicate, the philosophy behind neoliberalism is not so much economic theory as it is political theory. Clarke argues that "the neoliberal model does not purport so much to describe the world as it is, but the world as it should be. The point for [those who espouse] neoliberalism is not to make a model that is more adequate to the real world, but to make the real world more adequate to its model."[29]

Similarly, Wendy Brown, a political scientist at the University of California, Berkeley, has argued that neoliberalism is a form of "rationality," a way of understanding and organizing society that aims to reconstruct citizenship and the relationship between the citizen and the state.[30] "Neoliberal rationality," Brown argues, "while foregrounding the market, is not only or even primarily focused on the economy." "Rather it involves *extending and disseminating market values to all institutions and social action,* even as the market itself remains a distinctive player."[31] Drawing on the ideas of French philosopher Michel Foucault, Brown argues that neoliberalism defines and reconstructs fundamental relationships and reorganizes the world through "governmentality"—"a mode of governance encompassing but not limited to the state . . . which produces subjects, forms of citizenship and behavior, and a new organization of the social."[32] Thus subjects are *formed* and *organized* by the creation of certain structures and norms.

Not only do we have *Homo economicus*, as neoliberalism's "rational" individual is called but, as Brown puts it, "every action and policy" is submitted "to considerations of profitability." All institutional action, she says, is framed "as rational entrepreneurial action, conducted according to a calculus of utility, benefit, or satisfaction against a micro-economic grid of scarcity, supply and demand, and moral value-neutrality." This is at the core of neoliberalism as a political theory: "[Neoliberalism] does not simply assume that all aspects of social, cultural and political life can be reduced to such a calculus, *rather it develops institutional practices and rewards for enacting this vision.*"[33]

And it is in the development of institutional practices and rewards, the constructivist project that Clarke alludes to when he talks about "making the real world more adequate to the model," that neoliberalism makes its strongest contribution to an antitotalitarian utopian vision. If the neoliberal *Homo economicus* does not exist, as in Badakhshan and a number of other settings, then structures have to be put in place to *create* actors and impose market rationales for decision making in all spheres; this is part of what Brown describes as the "development, dissemination, and institutionalization of such rationality."[34]

The goal of such a project is to ensure that the market becomes "the organizing and regulative principle of the state and society."[35] And the role of the state? Michel Foucault suggests that, in such a paradigm, the role of the state is that of leading and controlling subjects or citizens, *but without being responsible for them.*[36] It becomes a facilitator for the market. Whereas state intervention in the social sector (e.g., by providing health and education services) is eschewed by neoliberals, a strong and coercive state is allowed and expected to defend the rights of private property, individual liberties, and entrepreneurial freedoms.[37] And in the end, as anthropologist Aihwa Ong describes, people are organized—and benefits and rights distributed to them—according to their ability to participate in the market rather than some other status (e.g., citizenship or residence) within nation-states. It is questionable, she argues, whether the possibility of the totalitarian state is vastly diminished, but what certainly will not emerge is a socialist or even caring one. Also weakened in this process are the bonds that bind community and nation.[38] In a book about the birth of neoliberal politics, historian Daniel Stedman Jones puts it this way: "The language of profit, efficiency, and consumption replaced that of citizenship, solidarity and service."[39]

NEOLIBERALISM AND GLOBAL HEALTH

In 1968, U.S. president Lyndon B. Johnson appointed Robert McNamara—defense secretary during the Vietnam War and a former president of the Ford Motor Company—as World Bank president. McNamara focused the bank's work on improving the situation in the developing world.[40] After attending a USAID-sponsored meeting on international nutrition at the Massachusetts Institute of Technology in 1972, McNamara became interested in nutrition and health and wanted the bank to become more involved in these areas.[41]

In 1973, McNamara requested a health policy paper from the scientists at the bank to guide its approach to the health sector. As if to rebuke the idea of a *Homo economicus* able to function "rationally" in all contexts, the *Health Sector Policy Report 1975* warned "about relying too narrowly on cost-benefit analysis and on the private sector to deliver health goods," because of "fundamental market failures."[42] The report outlined four points regarding the understanding of health care: "[First], consumers of health care will not have sufficient understanding to always make sensible choices. Second, there are too many externalities associated with disease for the responsibility for rational decision making to be given to the individual alone. Third, there is likely to be little competition in the health sector because hospitals require very large investment to provide any service and are therefore more like a public utility than a private good. Finally, maldistribution of income is also likely to limit the ability of the poor to gain access to health care through the market."[43] In 1979, soon after the International Conference on Primary Health Care in the Soviet city of Alma Ata (now Almaty, Kazakhstan), McNamara created the Health, Nutrition and Population unit at the World Bank.

In 1980, the main background paper for the World Bank's *World Development Report 1980* argued that health was a basic human right; that reduction of morbidity and mortality in the population was at the core of the development process; and that health care planning should incorporate all possible activities to improve health outcomes.[44] As for how health should be distributed, the authors echoed the 1975 health sector report. Not only did the report's authors state that "the use of prices and markets to allocate health care is generally not desirable," but they went on to argue that "incomes are not distributed in a manner that corresponds to health care needs of the population; consumers are not well qualified to select the best health services and thus cost is not a sound basis for choice; many people may be too ill to make health care choices and may rely on family members instead; eradication of disease has many social benefits that exceed private benefits; and finally, because health crises are frequently random and catastrophic, individuals cannot budget adequately to protect themselves."[45] The report itself ultimately identified user fees for health care, education, and water as major barriers to access. Taking the example of Malaysia, the report referred to the strong disincentive that user fees had on the utilization of clean piped water for the poorest 40 percent of the population.[46]

By the early 1980s, the language of some within the World Bank began to change. Over the decade when these reports emerged, there had been growing criticism of state-led development models. Development economist Howard Stein argues that the World Bank really began to move in the direction of neoliberal economics in the latter part of McNamara's tenure as bank president, after Ernest Stern, a managing director at the commercial and investment bank J. P. Morgan, became the vice president of operations and chair of the bank's loan committee in 1978.[47] Stern championed the idea of "structural adjustment" and brought the bank's ideological position much more in line with that of the more neoliberal IMF.

Structural adjustment policies, at their root a fundamentally neoliberal approach, were a game changer for the developing world. These gained traction after the oil price shocks following the 1973 oil embargo, during which the global economy faced a serious downturn, and many poor countries were forced to borrow from private lenders to remain solvent. At the beginning of the 1980s, it became clear that countries were not going to be able to pay the money back. In 1982, Mexico announced that it would stop servicing its debt. Private lenders panicked and withdrew credit.[48] Backed by the United States, the IMF—which had recreated itself as a lender of last resort in the mid-1970s—made it clear that it would lend money only to countries that undertook "structural adjustments" to their economies. These adjustments were based on the premise that fixing the "structural" causes of macroeconomic imbalances—through "stabilization," "liberalization," and "privatization" of economies—would lead to growth and development.[49]

In simple terms, "stabilization" meant not allowing excessive fluctuations in the macroeconomy (the economy as a whole). This is traditionally achieved by constraining monetary growth through the control of interest rates and cutting government spending to reduce inflation. For many countries, this often meant cuts in the areas of health, education, and social welfare. "Liberalization" meant removing the "distortions" and "inefficiencies" created by government participation in the economy by removing state intervention in the markets. For many poor countries, this meant "freeing prices" by removing government subsidies for such necessities as food or fertilizer for poor farmers. User fees, or charges to individuals for utilizing public goods such as education and health care, were introduced to promote "efficiency" in their allocation. And "privatization" meant selling state assets to the private sector, based on the idea that private ownership of such assets would be "more efficient."[50] For governments of poor countries, these requirements markedly reduced their control over their own macroeconomic and financial policies, limiting their ability to define development priorities; they also became a precondition for accessing subsequent loans and much foreign aid.[51]

Robert McNamara retired from the presidency of the World Bank in July 1981 and was replaced by Alden Winship Clausen, who left the posts of president and chief executive officer of Bank of America to take the job. Clausen was a believer in free markets and private sector institutions. In response to the debt crisis, he expanded the structural adjustment activities undertaken in the latter part of McNamara's tenure.

NEOLIBERALISM ENTERS THE WORLD OF INTERNATIONAL HEALTH POLICY

In 1981, the World Bank published the Berg Report—named after its lead author, economist Elliot Berg. Titled "Accelerated Development in

Sub-Saharan Africa: A Plan for Action," the report blamed government economic policies for the poor economic performance observed in the region. It was considered a turning point in the bank's thinking from Keynesian economics toward a market-oriented approach. The report made a case for structural adjustment and argued for user fees at public health clinics, layoffs of staff, liberalization of the pharmaceutical trade, and contracting out of most activities to private firms.[52]

Stein credits Princeton-trained economist David de Ferranti for the shift to neoliberal thinking in the health group at the World Bank. He points to ten papers that de Ferranti and his colleagues wrote for the bank's Health, Nutrition and Population Unit between 1981 and 1985—on Malawi, Nigeria, Argentina, and Peru—where ideas such as "affordability" and "effectiveness" were introduced into health care decision making. Their basic argument was that "a health program is affordable if and only if each of the parties that must contribute to financing its operation at its design scale are able and willing to do so . . . [and] affordability is a necessary condition for achieving an efficient balance of resource use."[53] In response to the gap between resources and recurrent costs, de Ferranti and his colleagues focused on the need for policy adjustments to restrain public sector involvement in health while increasing user fees. Calling for "cost-effectiveness analysis" to identify interventions that would yield the greatest improvement in health status, he wanted to get rid of "needless" usage and waste in the system.[54]

Although de Ferranti has since changed his approach and is now an advocate of universal health coverage,[55] at that time, Stein argues, de Ferranti and colleagues worked to create a consensus that "efficiency of the public health sector could be improved by the introduction of user fees, which would raise the revenues necessary to make the health sector financially viable."[56] In 1985 de Ferranti wrote a working paper, "Paying for Health Services in Developing Countries," which argues that efficiency is maximized by competitive market prices.[57] He argued that user fees generated revenues, created efficiency in allocation, and enhanced equity through improvement in both supply and quantity of services. With scant evidence, he asserted that user fees were not likely to have an impact on the ability of sick people to access care and, in fact, would be better for the poor because the fees would lead to improved quality of medicines and clinics ("the supply side"). As far as providing preventive care, de Ferranti argued that people knew enough about their health status and would seek out care when they needed it. In 1987, de Ferranti, Nancy Birdsall, and John Akin published "Financing Health Services in Developing Countries," which called for decentralization of services. The aim of this paper was to encourage collection of revenues "as close to the point of service" as possible.[58]

By 1987, the World Bank's language had shifted completely from that used in 1975, as the bank adopted the dictum that "the use of prices and markets to allocate health care is [highly] desirable."[59] The decisions were not based on data from studies evaluating the effects of imposing user fees on target communities.[60] The economist Gunnar Myrdal—who shared the Nobel Prize with Hayek in 1974, "for their pioneering work in the theory of money and economic fluctuations and for their penetrating analysis of the interdependence of economic, social and institutional phenomena"[61]—is said to have commented that "neither definitional difficulties nor a lack of empirical data" impeded de Ferranti from advocating user fees and privatization of health care.[62]

THE EMERGENCE OF THE BAMAKO INITIATIVE

By the time the WHO and UNICEF convened the meeting of the African ministers of health in Bamako, Mali, in September 1987, the effects of the economic downturn and the debt crisis, exacerbated by neoliberal structural adjustment policies, had taken their toll.[63] Sub-Saharan African countries, which received about 50 percent of structural adjustment loans between 1980 and 1990, did not benefit from "the market" distributing key social goods and regulating the allocation of resources.[64] In fact, after having seen growth rates of 4 percent per year between 1973 and 1980, these countries now saw an annual *decline* in economic growth of 3.9 percent. After having grown by 0.6 percent each year between 1973 and 1980, real per capita income fell by 1.2 percent per annum between 1980 and 1989. Per capita food production fell by 6 percent over the decade. At the same time, debt increased by an annual compound rate of 12 percent; by 1989, debt relative to gross national product (GNP) was 98.3 percent, up from 27.4 percent in 1980.[65] Despite the dismally low per capita health expenditures in these countries at the beginning of the 1980s, per capita expenditures continued to drop over the decade.[66] As far as health care, in twelve sub-Saharan African countries, per capita expenditures went down. In several of these countries, child mortality rates were over 200 per 1,000 live births.[67] The only notable increase in expenditures in these countries was in the area of defense.[68] In sum, much of the progress made in economic development in the 1960s and 1970s was lost due to the policies of the 1980s.[69]

According to Agostino Paganini, former head of the Bamako Initiative Management Unit of UNICEF, when James Grant arrived at the meeting in Bamako, he walked into a very difficult situation. He had already launched an advocacy effort ("Adjustment with a Human Face") to call attention to the high debt burden in many countries and the need to reschedule the debt.[70] He was in a battle with the World Health Organization, which accused him of not supporting more comprehensive primary health care as called for by the Alma Ata Declaration—a point that was partly true given Grant's unflinching support for *selective* primary health care, a less comprehensive approach that fit well with UNICEF's focus on vaccination and child nutrition. And he walked into a room where there was intense concern that without increased spending on the health sector, it would be impossible to achieve the goals for expansion of primary health care services that had been outlined by those present at the Alma Ata conference a decade earlier.[71] Paganini recalled, "Mr. Grant must have felt that something was to be done urgently if the Child Survival Revolution had to be preserved from the unproductive open-ended process of the WHO approach and the hard-nosed economic vision of the [World Bank]. The surprise launch of the Bamako Initiative during the September 1987 WHO Regional Meeting of the African Ministers of Health was his response to the critics . . . and his attempt to focus the world attention to the African situation."[72]

Grant knew that many health facilities lacked cash for even basic functions, and patients were not getting the care they needed. He recognized that many poor people were already paying for care and medicines (often of dubious quality) at private clinics and private pharmacies. If they could develop a strategy where governments paid salaries and some recurrent costs, and users contributed part of what they were paying in the private market, then perhaps the health system would survive and even be strengthened: "The communities were not expected to contribute *more* resources out of their pocket, but on the contrary to receive better quality services, curative as well as preventive, from a *fraction* of what they were already spending in the informal system."[73] The rest, Paganini explains, was meant to be financed by external bilateral and multilateral donors. In this way, "the availability of a limited, but lifesaving package of health services, both preventive and curative" would be guaranteed. As for the very poor, who could not pay, this would be left to "solidarity mechanisms under community control."[74] Grant presented a model that fit perfectly within the regnant economic orthodoxy.

The responses to Grant's proposal varied. In general, opposition was muted and no real alternatives were proposed. According to Paganini, although the African ministers approved the plan, "the public health community was split along ideological lines on the issue of equity."[75] The staff from the World Health Organization argued that middle- and low-income countries could not all be treated the same.[76] In the end, the World Health Organization went along with the plan but, according to Paganini, "was furious," presumably because the leadership had not been consulted ahead of time and had been one-upped by UNICEF in front of the ministers of health.

And the World Bank? Paganini describes its response as "timid interest." And why not? The plan contained the key principles laid out by neoliberal thinkers. Bamako's solution to the bank's policy of structural adjustment—a policy that restricted public sector health spending—was to turn to financing and organizational mechanisms that promoted user fees to raise revenue and decentralization so that funds would be raised "close to the point of service" and not go into central government coffers.[77] Viewed this way, it was the perfect "common sense" outcome. What was perhaps not obvious to most of those endorsing the proposal was that its principles were born from the mission of the Mont Pèlerin Society, the result of a decade of intense ideological construction. It was as if there was no alternative.

The Bamako Initiative was enthusiastically endorsed at the meeting and in subsequent years was implemented in a number of African and non-African settings. The founding principles of the initiative, which interestingly called for a "national commitment to the development of universally accessible essential health services" and "substantial government financial support for primary healthcare, preserving, and, wherever possible, increasing the proportion of the national budget dedicated to basic health services,"[78] were ignored in most places. Instead, although framed in terms of "cost shifting" from cash-strapped governments to patients seeking care at clinics in often-impoverished locales, the outcome was to relieve governments of the responsibility of looking after their poorest citizens and to put the burden on individuals themselves regardless of their capacity to pay for services. That this exogenous idea had little to do with the desires of the communities in which it was implemented, and in most poor-country settings was entirely unlikely to generate significant funds, also had no dampening effect on the enthusiasm for the Bamako Initiative among those endorsing it.

7 From Bamako to Badakhshan

NEOLIBERALISM'S TRANSPLANTING MECHANISM

Economics are the method; the object is to change the
heart and soul.

Margaret Thatcher

In his 1904 account of the second Danish expedition to the Pamir
Mountains, *Through the Unknown Pamirs,* explorer Ole Olufsen described
Badakhshan's interaction with the outside world as being "slight," "partly
by reason of the secluded situation of the provinces, shut off as they are
from civilization by the most mighty mountains of the world, and partly
on account of the poverty of the people."[1] As mighty as they were, the
mountains of Badakhshan were not high enough to prevent neoliberal
ideas from penetrating into one of the remotest parts of the Soviet empire
in the aftermath of its collapse. That goal was achieved using the very
mechanisms espoused by classical liberalism as a safeguard against tyranny: nongovernmental institutions, distinct from the apparatus of state,
as the vanguard of a vibrant civil society. As part of the struggle between
the capitalist and communist worlds, NGOs, perhaps unwittingly, became
the means by which the ideological shift proposed and planned in Mont
Pèlerin that first week in April 1947 was achieved.

NEOLIBERALISM AS STATECRAFT

In the aftermath of the Second World War and on the eve of the Cold War
with the Soviet Union, the United States launched the Marshall Plan for

the reconstruction of war-ravaged parts of Europe. The plan was designed by General George C. Marshall, the American statesman and military leader credited with the Allied victory in Europe. He believed that economic reconstruction would create the basis for political stability and democracy, and that the plan was a short-term expedient to prevent Europe from descending into abject chaos. In his convocation address at Harvard University on June 5, 1947, Marshall stated that the policy was not directed "against any country or doctrine but against hunger, poverty, desperation, and chaos." "Its purpose," he told the graduates and faculty sitting in Harvard's outdoor Tercentenary Theater, "should be the revival of a working economy in the world so as to permit the emergence of political and social conditions in which free institutions can exist."[2]

The concept of global intervention by providing economic aid made a lot of sense to government policy makers in the United States. In 1953, the Foreign Operations Administration was created to coordinate aid to other countries.[3] By the end of the 1950s, however, there was significant dissatisfaction with the piecemeal and short-term nature of aid from the United States to the developing world, and with its inability to counter the ideological influence of the Soviet Union. Moscow had grasped the strategic benefits of distributing aid to poor countries emerging from colonial rule, and hitherto neglected parts of Africa, Latin America, and Asia seemed poised to become new battlefields of the Cold War. In the 1960 U.S. presidential campaign, John F. Kennedy made creation of a long-range foreign development program a priority. He argued that existing programs did not address the needs of the United States or developing countries, and that helping such countries would benefit the United States politically and the Western world ideologically. After the election, in a special message to the U.S. Congress on March 22, 1961, President Kennedy said:

> In the face of these weaknesses and inadequacies—and with the beginning of a new decade of new problems—it is proper that we draw back and ask with candor a fundamental question: Is a foreign aid program really necessary? Why should we not lay down this burden which our nation has now carried for some fifteen years?
>
> The answer is that there is no escaping our obligations: our moral obligations as a wise leader and good neighbor in the interdependent community

of free nations; our economic obligations as the wealthiest people in a world of largely poor people, as a nation no longer dependent upon the loans from abroad that once helped us develop our own economy; *and our political obligations as the single largest counter to the adversaries of freedom.*

To fail to meet those obligations now would be disastrous; and, in the long run, more expensive. *For widespread poverty and chaos lead to a collapse of existing political and social structures which would inevitably invite the advance of totalitarianism into every weak and unstable area.* Thus our own security would be endangered and our prosperity imperiled. *A program of assistance to the underdeveloped nations must continue because the nation's interest and the cause of political freedom require it.*

We live at a very special moment in history. The whole southern half of the world—Latin America, Africa, the Middle East, and Asia—are *[sic]* caught up in the adventures of asserting their independence and modernizing their old ways of life. These new nations need aid in loans and technical assistance just as we in the northern half of the world drew successively on one another's capital and know-how as we moved into industrialization and regular growth.

But in our time these new nations need help for a special reason. Without exception they are under Communist pressure. In many cases, that pressure is direct and military. In others, it takes the form of intense subversive activity designed to break down and supersede the new—and often frail—modern institutions they have thus far built.

But the fundamental task of our foreign aid program in the 1960's is not negatively to fight Communism: *Its fundamental task is to help make a historical demonstration that in the twentieth century, as in the nineteenth—in the southern half of the globe as in the north—economic growth and political democracy can develop hand in hand.*[4]

On November 3, 1961, President Kennedy established the U.S. Agency for International Development (USAID). USAID's mandate from the Congress was clear: "To further America's foreign policy interests in expanding democracy and free markets while improving the lives of the citizens of the developing world."[5]

In his 2005 book, *A Brief History of Neoliberalism*, David Harvey cites a confidential 1971 memo from Lewis Franklin Powell Jr., a corporate lawyer soon to be appointed to the Supreme Court by President Richard

Nixon, to Eugene Sydnor, a friend of his who headed the U.S. Chamber of Commerce. The memo called on conservative think tanks in the United States to transform the way society conceptualizes the state and its role in the economy, the very task started by Hayek and his colleagues at the Mont Pèlerin Society. Entitled "Attack on American Free Enterprise System," the memo, which is worth reading in its entirety, argues that "strength lies in organization, in careful long-range planning and implementation, in consistency of action over an indefinite period of years, in the scale of financing available only through joint effort, and in the political power available only through united action and national organizations."[6] Powell argued that the Chamber of Commerce should lead an assault upon major institutions—universities, schools, the media, publishing, the courts—to change how individuals think "about the corporation, the law, culture, and the individual."[7] The result was a flurry of activity within think tanks espousing neoliberal principles—the American Enterprise Institute, the Heritage Foundation, the Cato Institute, the Hoover Institution at Stanford University, the Manhattan Institute for Policy Research—and increased grants to support the penetration of neoliberal ideas into mainstream thinking.[8]

The biggest boost for the rise of neoliberalism as a defining paradigm of the late twentieth century, however, came during the period when Margaret Thatcher was prime minister of the United Kingdom (1979–1990) and Ronald Reagan the president of the United States (1981–1988).[9] Thatcher was a self-described disciple of Hayek, saying in her autobiography that "the most powerful critique of socialist planning and the socialist state which I read at this time [the late 1940s], and to which I have returned so often since [is] F. A. Hayek's *The Road to Serfdom*."[10] Speaking of books like Hayek's, Thatcher said that the "clear analytical arguments against socialism . . . gave us the feeling that the other side simply could not win in the end. . . . It left a permanent mark on my own political character, making me a long-term optimist for free enterprise and liberty."[11]

In his chronicle of the Thatcher years, historian John Ranelagh recounts how at a Conservative Party policy meeting in the 1970s, a colleague of Thatcher's had prepared a document suggesting that the party take the middle road on some policy issues. "Before he had finished speaking to his paper, the new Party Leader [Margaret Thatcher] reached into her briefcase and took out a book. It was Friedrich von Hayek's *The Constitution of Liberty*. Interrupting [the speaker], she held the book up for all of us to see. 'This,' she said sternly, 'is what we believe,' and banged Hayek down on the table."[12] According to political scientist Susan George, Thatcher was uncompromising in her implementation of neoliberal economic ideas, justifying her actions with the acronym TINA, "there is no alternative." She later convinced Queen Elizabeth II to appoint Hayek as a member of the Order of Companions of Honour in 1984, for his "services to the study of economics."[13]

Similarly, Reagan cited Mises and Hayek as the philosophical thinkers who most influenced his conduct as a leader.[14] Former White House economist and Reagan associate Martin Anderson, touted as one of the engineers of Reagan's economic policies, described Reagan as having been extremely well informed about the approach his administration had taken, saying he was its principal driver: "For over twenty years he [Reagan] observed the American economy, read and studied the writings of some of the best economists in the world, including the giants of the free market economy—Ludwig von Mises, Friedrich von Hayek and Milton Friedman."[15] When Reagan's successor, George H. W. Bush, presented the Presidential Medal of Freedom to Hayek in 1991, he referred to him as "one of the most influential economic writers of our century," a man "revered by the free people of Central and Eastern Europe as a true visionary, and recognized worldwide as a revolutionary in intellectual and political thought. How magnificent it must be for him to witness his ideas validated before the eyes of the world. We salute him."[16]

THE "TRANSPLANT MECHANISM"

In 1982, President Ronald Reagan traveled to London as part of a multi-country trip through Western Europe. On June 8, he addressed the British Parliament at the Palace of Westminster, delivering one of his most significant foreign policy speeches. He described the West as "approaching the end of a bloody century plagued by a terrible political invention—totalitarianism" and the Soviet Union as on the verge of economic collapse. He then went on: "The hard evidence of totalitarian rule has caused in mankind an uprising of the intellect and will. Whether it is the growth of the new schools of economics in America or England or the appearance of the so-called new philosophers in France, there is one unifying thread running through the intellectual work of these groups—rejection of the arbitrary power of the state, the refusal to subordinate the rights of the individual to the super-state, the realization that collectivism stifles all the best human impulses." Describing democracy as a "fragile flower," Reagan argued that it needed "cultivating," and if freedom and democratic ideals were to grow during the remainder of the twentieth century, "we must take actions to assist the campaign for democracy." He pointed out that "since 1917 the Soviet Union has given covert political training and assistance to Marxist-Leninists in many countries." Praising the German Federal Republic's political foundations—known as *Stiftungen*, these government-funded foundations had assisted their ideological counterparts abroad, most notably in the Iberian Peninsula—he announced, "We in America now intend to take additional steps" to bring about "peaceful and democratic progress."[17] With this, the Reagan administration funded the American Political Foundation, created to promote communication between the two major U.S. political parties and other political parties around the world, to "determine how the U.S. can best contribute—as a nation—to the global campaign for democracy now gathering force."[18] The American Political Foundation's study, funded by a $300,000 grant from USAID, became known as the Democracy Program.[19]

The Democracy Program Report, presented to President Reagan on July 27, 1983, highlighted ideas that had been expressed since the 1950s on how best to "assist democratic institutional development abroad openly and through the private sector."[20] The report drew extensively on the theories of William A. Douglas, a professor of political science at Johns Hopkins University and senior consultant to the Democracy Program, who, in his 1972 book, *Developing Democracy*, argued that the best approach for creating democratic institutions in the Third World was to develop a "transplanting mechanism" capable of operating in different cultural contexts.[21] The Democracy Program ultimately recommended establishing a nonprofit corporation to distribute funds to private organizations linked to each of the major political parties in the United States, the business community, and an existing institute representing U.S. labor unions, for the express purpose of promoting democracy abroad and acting as a counterweight to state power.[22] In 1983, the U.S. government created the National Endowment for Democracy (NED). Closely mirroring the neoliberal belief in the interrelation between economic and political systems, the NED argued that "an open market economy is a prerequisite of a democratic political system. *A dynamic private sector with an active small business community can supply a counter-weight that effectively limits state power and enables democracy to thrive.*"[23]

The creation of the NED set in motion an important ideological shift in the nature of NGOs as institutions of civil society. The term *civil society* had long been used to envision some sort of society distinct from the body politic, "and with moral claims independent of, and sometimes opposed to, the state's authority."[24] Instead of conceiving of civil society (and NGOs) as the *product* of a democratic society, the NED saw components of civil society—both NGOs and other forms of private enterprise, including businesses, foundations, and private educational institutions—as a force against communist and authoritative regimes and a way of *creating* democratic societies by diluting state power.[25] NGOs, in this view, become Douglas's "transplanting mechanism," conveying new ideas to a variety of strategic settings and helping to synchronize foreign policy with political aid.[26]

The rise of NGOs as recipients of aid dollars closely followed the ascendancy of neoliberal thinking in Washington and London. In their studies of the NGO sector, David Hulme and Michael Edwards describe the 1980s and 1990s as a period dominated by a "new policy agenda," which placed a premium on the untested belief that the private sector was a better mechanism for delivering services and that NGOs are more efficient than the government, especially in providing services to poor people.[27] Growing in numbers and budgets—funded by government-sponsored agencies (like the NED), private donations, and intergovernmental organizations—in the 1980s and 1990s, NGOs became a powerful global political force explicitly identified as a meeting place for economic and political aid.[28]

In development circles, NGOs were popularly perceived as desirable for local communities because of their local knowledge. They were seen as a way of holding governments accountable and protecting human rights.[29]

For the architects of the "new policy agenda," however, NGOs were regarded as a necessary remedy for nonperforming state agencies, able to deliver services to the poor cheaply and efficiently and without the participation of the state.[30] As an alternative to state agencies, NGOs became closely aligned with the neoliberal mission, with funds allocated to expand their size and number.[31] Between 1980 and 1993, the number of international NGOs registered in OECD countries grew from 1,600 to 2,970; funding rose from US $2.8 billion (in 1994 dollars) to US $5.7 billion during the same period.[32]

At the same time, the World Bank and the IMF supported the imposition of "structural adjustment" on poor country economies.[33] Cutting government expenditures on health and education opened the door to a decentralized approach to social service delivery and to forms of governance more suited to market-driven economies, creating space for the operation of both international and local NGOs.[34] The lack of funding from the state and the loss of its redistributive powers of taxation created the perfect environment for a misplaced justification of user fees for social services in poor locales.[35]

Though Badakhshan did not participate in an official World Bank or IMF structural adjustment program, the collapse of the government and its inability to deliver social services created a similar scenario. There was no alternative other than to channel emergency funding through NGOs. Thus NGOs, acting as institutions of civil society, became the de facto vehicles through which the market could permeate areas of the social world that previously were under the writ of a social contract and the purview of the state.[36]

Aligning foreign policy and development aid was a critical part of William Douglas's recommendations. Although it is difficult to draw a straight line connecting ideology to praxis, even large, independently financed NGOs would become Douglas's transplanting mechanisms by accepting donor money earmarked for the implementation of specific policies. They would be accountable less to the local communities where they provided services and more to their transnational funding sources: wealthy governments, private foundations, and multilateral organizations.[37] According to the World Bank, in the early 1970s about 1.5 percent of the income of international NGOs derived from individual donor governments (bilateral funding) or large international institutions (multilateral funding); by the mid-1990s, it was around 30 percent. By then, international NGOs based in the United Kingdom and working in other countries were receiving from 20 to 55 percent of their funding from their government; those based in Sweden, 85 percent; in Canada, 70 percent; in the United States, 66 percent; and in Australia, 34 percent.[38]

When I met with USAID officials in Almaty in October 1996 to talk about the revolving drug fund, they told me with unabashed clarity that the reason they were financing the initiative in Badakhshan was to "open new markets" and "foster democracy." As they pointed out, their official documentation clearly states that they work with organizations who share their commitment to the "importance of a flourishing private sector, both as an engine of economic growth and as a repository of the principles of democratic pluralism."[39] Like the World Bank, they saw the privatization of health services as a priority for developing countries because they believed outsourcing health services to the nongovernmental sector would be more efficient.[40] They were in the midst of the ZdravReform project, and although Tajikistan was not one of the target countries, they were grateful for the opportunity to "reform" the health system there.

As the largest donors in global health in the 1980s and 1990s, the World Bank and USAID set the terms for the activities of NGOs that received funding from them.[41] USAID acknowledges in its policy guidance to the private voluntary organization sector with which it works that even though their interests might overlap, it recognizes that "motivations, interests, and responsibilities are not and should not be identical." Furthermore, "it is to be expected that USAID and PVOs [private voluntary organizations] each will pursue goals related to their particular concerns and objectives and, at the same time, will work together on common priorities."[42]

Nevertheless, the structure of their granting process ensured that only approaches that overlapped well with USAID interests would get funded. As Michel Foucault has argued, mechanisms of control and power are often exercised through systems of knowledge and organization, which codify techniques and practices in a certain way.[43] It is through the definition of goals and procedures, using examples of how certain activities should be organized, that what is "normal" or "good" is defined.[44] As Foucault described in his lecture at the Collège de France in February 1978, this approach—employing tactics rather than laws—requires "arranging things so that this or that end may be achieved through a certain number of means."[45] Foucault refers to this exercise of power through *forming* the way citizens and institutions behave and the way their activities are organized as "governmentality."[46] Thus ideology is transmitted through the requirements for funding grant applications, allowable approaches to program implementation, and the metrics used for program evaluation.[47] NGOs and other applicants must in turn reflect this language to qualify for donor funds.[48]

The use of specific language and the promotion of specific programmatic solutions—like the revolving drug fund—shape the way recipients approach potential approaches to a given problem. The grant submitted to USAID by AKF's offices in Geneva and Washington closely mirrored the language used by USAID in their description of the goals of their Central Asian Region ZdravReform project (chapter 5). While there is no doubt in my mind that the individuals involved—from the staff I was working with at AKF to the program officers I interviewed at USAID's office in Almaty—wanted to help the local population, it is interesting to note the ideological focus of the language. In the midst of describing a "reform" that would introduce "specific policy and financing mechanisms that reduce waste and decrease the government's role as the sole financier of health services," achieving expected results, such as "a monetized system for purchasing and supplying pharmaceuticals," there was little mention of preventing premature deaths or preserving the level and quality of health and health care that had been achieved during the Soviet period.

AKF's Geneva staff framed the foundation's program to address the local pharmaceutical crisis in what would appear to be the ideological language and policy imperatives of its donor—something that many NGOs do to survive and provide services to the populations in which they work. In doing so, some element of the ultimate goal—ensuring that the poor of Badakhshan had ready access to life-saving medicines—was diminished.[49] More significantly, it marked a watershed moment for health care delivery in Badakhshan.

PART IV The Aftermath

NEOLIBERAL SUCCESS,
GLOBAL HEALTH FAILURE

8 Privatizing Health Services

REFORMING THE OLD WORLD

> It is no exaggeration to say that, once the more active part
> of the intellectuals has been converted to a set of beliefs,
> the process by which these become generally accepted is
> almost automatic and irresistible.
>
> Friedrich August von Hayek, 1949

British prime minister Margaret Thatcher famously noted that "freedom is not synonymous with an easy life. . . . There are many difficult things about freedom: It does not give you safety, it creates moral dilemmas for you; it requires self-discipline; it imposes great responsibilities."[1] This could not have been truer than for the inhabitants of Badakhshan, the older generation of whom likened the post-Soviet period to the famine and hardship following the Second World War.

And in the midst of that struggle, it was clear by the summer of 1996 that the revolving drug fund proposal was moving forward regardless of whether it would work or whether the people of Badakhshan wanted it, because it was seen as a way to transition from "humanitarian assistance" to some form of "sustainable development." The revolving drug fund carried with it a lot of unexamined assumptions about the fitness of "the market" as the optimal mechanism for distributing social goods to a poor population living at the margins of a collapsed empire in the midst of a profound health crisis. But it seemed there was no alternative. To quote Margaret Thatcher, "TINA."

As Ahmed and I were to see, these assumptions did not stop with the revolving drug fund. Instead, it appeared to us that the idea that privatization was the only logical path forward—an assumption made without critical assessment of potential consequences—was manifesting itself in other ways. It was as if the aspirations of Hayek and his colleagues at the Mont Pèlerin Society were being realized in real time: ideology was operating as common sense. As to other important outcomes—reduced mortality or morbidity, or ensuring justice and dignity—they fell into what I refer to as realms of neoliberal programmatic blindness: areas of programs that are eclipsed by ideological aims.

PRIVATIZING HEALTH

The Central Dental Clinic, located along Khorog's tree-lined central avenue, Lenin Street, was generally a busy place. In normal circumstances it would be full of patients of all ages waiting to be seen for toothaches, bleeding gums, abscesses, and cavities.[2] But that June day in 1996 when we went to start our dental clinic survey was not normal. That day, there were very few people waiting.

Misha, the head dentist, came out to greet us. We had been there before, and he knew we noticed the difference. As he ushered us into his office, he noted that fewer patients were coming to the clinic now that they had to pay out of pocket for care. I asked about the rest of the patients who used to be waiting. There were a lot of poor people who needed treatment, he told us, but they had no money to pay for the services. I asked him if they would be okay without treatment. His face became serious, and he nodded ruefully. He said nothing for a moment. He wanted to help people, he responded, but he could accept only a few people who could not pay. It had to be this way, he said, or else he and his colleagues would not be able to repay the loan they had received to keep the clinic going:

> Now it costs 287 rubles to remove a tooth for somebody, whereas before it was free. Treatment for periodontal conditions or to prevent an infection from going beyond the tooth now costs 405 rubles, whereas before it cost nothing. I don't set the prices; they are set by the Republic Dental Society. . . . We've had a meeting and decided that for people who cannot afford our services, we'll make an allowance and treat them for free. But, since our people are proud, there are few who come forward and say that they don't have money. Recently, we decided to let some people give what they have.

By this point in our relationship—over the previous three months we had met a number of times at both his office and his home to talk about the health transition in the post-Soviet period—Misha knew that I felt strongly about sick people getting the care they needed, and I sensed that he felt the same way. He came from a modest background and knew well the realities of life in a family without much income.

Ahmed and I had become friends with Misha quite by accident in April of that year. In a moment of desperation, when the Central Dental Clinic was on the verge of shutting down because of lack of supplies, Misha had walked into Khorog's central Lenin Park, to the building located slightly off the center of the tree-lined gardens, in the middle of the park. It was in this smart-looking building that the Aga Khan had resided when he visited Badakhshan the year before, and which, after his departure, had become the local headquarters of AKF.

When Misha came to the AKF building and asked to speak to somebody about financial problems at the city's Central Dental Clinic, it was because he saw no other way of saving the facility. Since Dr. Pierre Claquin was in Geneva and no local health officer had yet been appointed, Misha was directed to the office I shared with Ahmed when we were in Khorog. We welcomed him, not sure how we might help. He proceeded to tell us about the crisis at the dental clinic, describing how it had run out of money for supplies and he would soon have to refuse services to people who were facing serious dental emergencies and desperately required care. He had come to ask for an emergency grant and reminded us that if his clinic shut down it would affect a lot of people; it was one of only two facilities in the city (the other was at the main hospital). If AKF gave him a grant, he told us, he would be able to continue providing dental care for free. I nervously asked him what amount he needed, expecting it to be in the thousands of dollars. I was worried that if it was a big amount, he would not get the help that he needed. I was surprised when Misha asked for US $500.

Aside from being relatively modest, Misha's request was compelling. I immediately spoke to Hakim Feerasta, AKF Tajikistan's chief executive officer, who agreed that it would be terrible if the clinic closed and that it made sense to give Misha the money. I informed Misha about the decision, saying that the grant had been approved because of the importance of dental care in people's lives. He would receive the money the following week, when Mr. Feerasta was to be in Badakhshan. I then left Khorog for two weeks.

When I came back, I was surprised to find that the plan had changed. In my absence, it had been decided that rather than providing Misha with a grant, it would be better to *lend* him money from the Enterprise Support Fund, a mechanism to boost local business activities sponsored by AKF and the Aga Khan Fund for Economic Development. And with that, the funds he received became a small-business loan and the dental clinic the first for-profit health provider in Badakhshan.

I was saddened when Misha later told me that if the plans for a grant had not changed, the clinic would still be providing free services to poor people:

> I know your personal feelings about this, Salmaan. You want to help the health situation here. On the other side is ESF [Enterprise Support Fund], which is about business. You said you would help me. Since the help ended up coming in the form of credit, I have had to sweat in order to return it. . . . I told the clinic doctors that this money is from AKF. . . . I told them to think carefully about how to treat the patients so that they do not need to come back twice. If the patient is not happy with the treatment, he can have his money back.

Clearly privatization was meant to foster this outcome: direct accountability to patients, who, in what has proved to be a significant moral transformation in global health, were now viewed as customers. But when he suggested that functioning within the realm of business was different from helping people—perhaps, one could imagine, a difference in moral orientation—it was evident that with the loan something had changed, and we all knew it.

It would be a lie if I said I was indifferent to the transformation of the grant into a loan. I was not against the clinic operating as a business— *someday in the future*. I came from a place where such dental facilities are the norm. I just did not think it should be one of the first "businesses" to be privatized, especially since it was part of what had been a comprehensive health system that was faltering, and at that moment, there was no system of insurance to pool risk and no safety net for those too destitute to pay. Moreover, the clinic was a public entity, and neither the clinic's beneficiaries—now "consumers"—nor the public at large had decided that it should be private.

Of course, I understood that the local government did not have money and was under pressure from the central government in Dushanbe to cut expenses. I also understood that if people paid for services, they might hold their providers accountable for a higher quality of care. But in a population this poor and without any real mechanism (state-run or otherwise) for ensuring that the indigent received care, I was worried. I knew from my time in the villages that although people said that they were willing to pay for services, many simply could not do it, and they would suffer. And in presenting his case to us, Misha had told us that there were many dental emergencies which simply could not wait. I contacted Dr. Claquin in Geneva, who told me that while he could not change the arrangement that had been made with ESF, this would be an opportunity to find out what charging for services meant for people. He gave us the green light to do an official survey of the patients visiting the Central Dental Clinic in June and July 1996.[3]

The survey results provided few surprises. More than 70 percent of patients came to the clinic with a toothache, the rest with gum issues and other conditions. More than 40 percent had waited longer than fourteen days before coming to the clinic. When we asked one patient if waiting this long had been an issue, he looked at us incredulously: "I cannot sleep for nights due to toothaches and other diseases. And I can't be healed. What else can the effect be but adverse?"[4]

The survey was not limited to questions about dental care: we asked many questions about user fees, privatization, and the future of health care in the region. When asked about the privatization of health care—services provided for a fee—there was skepticism about whether such a system would work given the current condition of Badakhshan:

> The major problem [with private health services] will be inaccessibility for the bulk of the population due to their inability to pay for services.[5]

> Then only people with money will have the right to have health. Others won't be able to pay for the treatment.[6]

> Private services can be used by well-off people, but the majority of Badakhshan's population will be deprived from using the health care services, at least for today. We are not ready for that yet.[7]

Interestingly, it was not only the access issues that worried people. The moral transformation in the doctor-patient relationship—from healer and patient to service provider and paying client—also worried respondents. This critical component of neoliberal philosophy had not escaped the local eye. As one respondent described it, "Medicine will turn from a humane profession into an ordinary one: a business."[8]

I found Misha to be an interesting person. He had grown up poor; he was only eighteen when his father died of cancer, leaving him and his three sisters and four brothers to care for their mother. "Of course, we had shoes and we could study for free," he told Ahmed and me, "but we didn't receive food [assistance] then, and we didn't have enough food." When I asked Misha how he had become a dentist, he reminded me that during the Soviet period it was possible even for the poorest person to enter university if he or she was clever and worked hard. "I got admission to the finest medical school but had no money," he recalled. "The ticket to travel there cost sixty-four rubles"—more than half a month's wages at that time—"and my mother did not have enough money for it. I will remember that for the rest of my life."

Misha had come a long way since then. His new Pamiri-style house in Khorog was very different from those in villages like Kuhdeh. This house was not smoky because it had radiators for heating and multiple rooms. In the room where we sat, Misha had a television and a VCR to complement the special woodwork and new bookcases that he had had built. I asked him if it was a mistake to charge for care at this time, when people were poor and sick and the government was too weak to use the distributive power of taxation to create even a rudimentary safety net. Misha thought a bit and told me that while he and the dentists working for him at the clinic felt that it was okay to charge adults, they would never do that for children. To him, to charge for the care of children was unconscionable. I asked about the distinction.

MISHA: I don't want to exaggerate, but we are only 200,000 people, and if we become money oriented, we will simply lose our people. I know we have to help others, just as the imam now helps us. We cannot [completely] transform medicine into a fee-for-service system, because people will not use our services. Ninety percent of people [here] do not have work. If we charge for the children, we will lose a lot. Now that we charge adults, there is already a difference in the number of patients that come to the clinic. There used to be twenty-eight patients for each of the doctors per day. And we had six to eight doctors. Today, we have only five to eight people per doctor per day, and only four doctors. We have had to work very hard because we wanted to pay back our loan quickly because the money came from the imam's organization. We would have worked until our noses bled to pay the money. Also, it was a private debt and we had our reputations at stake.

SALMAAN: But do you believe that privatization was the best thing to do?

MISHA: I believe that privatization is the right path and I will try and privatize the big clinic [at the main hospital] also. There is no other way. We have no choice because the government will not help us. . . . The government in Badakhshan thinks that the Soviet Union will return [one day]; they do not want things to be privatized because they will be ignored after that. Even the Dushanbe government told them they should privatize things.

Salmaan, just imagine, I come to my clinic and I do not have the [necessary] materials. Patients come with the hope of being treated and we cannot treat them. Now that we have become privatized, we can help people. People are selling things on the street; it means that some people can afford the services. With subsidies from those who are able to pay, I can make allowances for large families with ten kids or more, or veterans of the Second World War. For them, it's free. My guidelines are: ten kids or more, veterans of the Second World War, doctors working at this clinic, and the children of staff of the polyclinic and gynecology clinic. From these categories, we allow a maximum of three patients per day, except for Second World War veterans, who can come as much as they need.

I respected the fact that Misha had recognized that there were those who needed care regardless of their financial situation, following the standards set during the Soviet period. I feared, of course, for the more than 80 percent of people in Khorog who were unemployed and the many thousands in the rural areas for whom dental care was sometimes an urgent necessity and for whom no alternative plan existed.

I knew the day would eventually come when Misha would privatize the only other public dental clinic in town, located at the main hospital, an aspiration that he had not hidden from us. Misha was willing to do this because he did not feel it was as consequential as charging for general medical care. But "when the hospital starts to charge," he told me, the government will surely draw the line and not allow it.

Thinking of the health insurance systems in Germany, the United Kingdom, and Canada and other systems of risk pooling that buffered my life and that of most people I knew, I once asked Misha if charging individuals for services, especially when they were sick and vulnerable, was the only way forward, the only way to get quality care to people. His answer was simple and reminiscent of Mrs. Thatcher: "It has to be this way, Salmaan. . . . We do not have another way out. Or else we have to wait for Lenin to come back." TINA.

Given the rapidity of the changes I had observed in Tajikistan in the short period I lived there, it was evident that Lenin, in any form, was not coming back. Instead, the old world created by the Soviet order—which, flawed though it may have been, had been built on an ethical foundation of equity—had dissolved. In its place, a new order based on a different set of social and ethical principles appeared.

This was not just my assessment. People felt it. While many people admitted that they were happy to be free from the negative aspects of the Soviet era, to be able to practice their faith freely and connect with the outside world, they recognized and verbalized the fact that their freedom had come at a price. They had gone from a world where there was a sense of collective struggle and shared commitment to one where the social fabric was changing in a way that people did not recognize. The Rais of Kuhdeh had once told me that in villages where people had in the past given their neighbors milk, they now wanted to sell it; it was the only way to survive. When I asked him why he worried about that, he responded, "It is our tradition to share—that's how we've survived through the ages."

The privatization of the dental system was not earth shattering in and of itself. Like the other "reforms" that had taken place in Tajikistan— including privatization of agricultural plots and the state bus service—it was one more step on the path to a much broader transformation: as the relationship between neighbors, between doctors and patients, between teachers and students became more transactional, a new logic of practice was emerging.[9] One twenty-eight-year-old man spoke eloquently of the changes: "Even sharing with each other, which existed here before the Russians, now, following the collapse, has begun to gradually vanish. People have somehow become estranged from each other. Everyone thinks [only] about his own prosperity. We lost the sincerity and mutual aid that distinguished us from other people."

REDEFINING THE SOCIAL WORLD

Processes of globalization—many of which "are changing the nature of human interaction across a wide range of spheres including the socio-cultural, political, economic, technological and ecological"—are not new.[10] They have occurred in different forms for millennia. What is new at this historical juncture is the coupling of neoliberal ideology as a global force with modern institutions like transnational NGOs, in a manner that allows for the redefinition of geographical space—"reterritorialization"—in innovative ways.[11] With NGOs as the transplanting mechanism, no place is too remote to fall under neoliberalism's ideological reach or to feel its practical impact.

In many ways, the discourse of international development—closely linked to the ideology of neoliberalism in the latter part of the twentieth century—is at the vanguard of globalization. And with it comes a significant cognitive exchange that "is being shaped foremost by a broader context of certain value systems, beliefs, aspirations ... that seek to maintain a particular world order."[12] It is in the transformation of value systems—the shaping of the moral world and the ethical frameworks that govern it, as patients become consumers and markets the distributors of social goods—that the subtleties of neoliberal discourse have the greatest bearing for Badakhshan.

The privatization of the dental clinic is a window into some of the transformations brought to Badakhshan and the region. At the local level, we saw a movement toward what the French sociologist and philosopher Georges Bataille has called the "unrestricted growth of impersonal productive forces."[13] One could argue that privatizing health services set in motion a process that left the distribution of health services—in this case, dental care—in the hands of a small group of people—"the market." Privatization became an end in itself, and "choice" within this system was a choice among products, services, and opportunities provided by the market, *if one could afford it*. Without any mechanism to help those unable to pay, the decision of "the market" becomes final, as if it were a law of nature: you get what you pay for.

In neoliberal terms, individual choices about purchasing goods and services in the private market without so-called government interference constitute "freedom." And this particular type of freedom displaces important considerations such as "freedom for the poor, for those who cannot or who choose not to participate in the marketplace."[14] Karl Polyani, the Hungarian-born historian and philosopher, argues in his 1944 classic *The Great Transformation*—one of the clearest repudiations of neoliberal ideology—that "bad" freedoms can result from a market that operates unlinked to social context and unfettered by any broader societal oversight. These types of freedom have a polarizing effect on society.[15] Among these are "the freedom to exploit one's fellows," "the freedom to make inordinate gains without commensurable service to the community," and "the freedom to keep technological inventions from being used for public benefit."[16] It was the last of these, where the fruits of modern medicine were denied to those who could not pay, that frightened me the most.

The decision to privatize the dental clinic was not part of a strategy to build a pluralistic health sector. In fact, it was largely removed from the local social, economic, and ethical context; it was, given the preceding seventy years of Soviet-provided care, somewhat ahistorical and more ideological than strategic. Economist Amartya Sen points out that when the liberal moral philosopher Adam Smith wrote *The Wealth of Nations* in the eighteenth century, he presented a sound ethical framework as critical to the proper functioning of capitalism *within* society. "While prudence was of all virtues that which is most helpful to the individual," Smith wrote, "humanity, justice, generosity, and public spirit are the qualities most useful to others."[17] In fact, Smith defended public services like free education and poverty relief. He was concerned about the inequality and poverty that might remain in an otherwise successful market economy and even supported regulation and oversight to prevent this: "When the regulation, therefore, is in favour of the workmen, it is always just and equitable; but it is sometimes otherwise when in favour of the masters."[18]

Thus, looking at Misha's story, it is the push toward individualism amid profound societal disruption that causes the greatest disquiet.[19] In this particular form of individualism, where each person is left to look after him or herself, the bonds of community dissolve, resulting in fragmentation and isolation. This is what the French sociologist Emile Durkheim has referred to as the *anomie* of industrialized economies.[20] Even as Misha dives head-on into the new world order, his remark that "if we become money oriented, we'll simply lose our people," indicates where this path will lead.

Although likely done with the best of intentions, the decision to change the dental clinic grant into a loan is telling. The loan was given at a moment when Badakhshan's government was not strong enough to develop its own comprehensive strategy, and input from users of the clinic was neither sought nor heard. Neither equity nor justice nor patient needs were part of the calculus. It seems rather that it was simply a business decision. And Misha, who, when he first came to the AKF offices in Lenin Park could not even envision a world where his dental clinic could be transformed into a business, now saw no other alternative.

The story of the dental clinic demonstrates the power of the globalizing discourse of neoliberalism and its ability to reterritorialize, penetrating everyday life in even the farthest of places so as to become "common sense" and to go unquestioned, even in the face of strong values or clear alternatives.

Of course, it would be simplistic to place the weight of this social transformation in Badakhshan solely on the shoulders of an international NGO. The new ethical framework that had begun to permeate Badakhshani society was undoubtedly linked to the ravages of the civil war, to hunger and starvation, and to the fragmentation of society that occurs amid ethnic, sectarian, and ideological conflicts. It was also linked to global processes associated with the penetration of neoliberalism into the region through other vehicles and mechanisms, and the revaluation of all areas of the social world, including the care-giving professions, in terms of their economic value in "the market." And yet, in the local world of Badakhshan, the small act of changing a grant to a loan, of charging a vulnerable population for a social good, left an indelible mark. This vignette—which exposes how quality was pitted against access, and how caring for those in need was displaced by the requirement to make a profit and repay a loan—illustrates how a social order of a certain kind is created.[21]

9 Revealing the Blind Spot

OUTCOMES THAT MATTER

The ideas of economists and political philosophers, both
when they are right and when they are wrong, are more
powerful than is commonly understood. Indeed the world
is ruled by little else. . . . I am sure that the power of vested
interests is vastly exaggerated compared with the gradual
encroachment of ideas. . . . But, soon or late, it is ideas, not
vested interests, which are dangerous for good or evil.

John Maynard Keynes, 1936

It took almost a year after deciding in 1996 to proceed with the revolving
drug fund before it was implemented. By the time the program began in
Khorog in 1997, I had left Badakhshan. Under a new name—Rationalizing
Pharmaceutical Policy and Management (RPPM)—the revolving drug
fund program expanded one district at a time over the next four years,
until by December 2000 all of Badakhshan's seven districts were included.
In its final project evaluation, AKF reported that by January 2004, only
50 percent of the cost of the medicines purchased for the program were
being recovered from patients; the rest were paid for by Aga Khan Health
Services, part of the Aga Khan Development Network.[1] The reason for the
low cost recovery: 71.6 percent of the population reported difficulty paying for medicines, even with a generous subsidy.

The "rational" use of drugs, which depends on diagnosis, is difficult
to assess. Under the revolving drug fund program, the "appropriateness"
of disease treatment increased from 85 to 95 percent, meaning that
more physicians were using dosages and drugs from the World Health
Organization's essential drugs list. The average number of drugs received

by sick patients when they went to see a doctor decreased from 4.6 to 1.4 between 1997 and 2004. Antibiotics as a proportion of all drugs prescribed decreased from 52 percent to 27 percent during the same period.[2]

During the period of the revolving drug fund, the state-run pharmacy system and distribution network, which had brought medicines to health posts in some of the remotest parts of Badakhshan during the Soviet era, was completely dismantled. In USAID's final evaluation of the revolving drug fund, completed in 2004, the author noted that the Department of Health pharmacy system (TajikFarmatsia) had also been privatized: "The DoH [Department of Health] no longer has the pharmacists or infrastructure for supply and distribution of pharmaceuticals since the privatization of the oblast central pharmacy (TajikFarmatsia) and district pharmacies several years ago. The only provision of essential drugs for PHC [primary health care] is provided by the RPPM project for the entire oblast."[3] The report interestingly alludes to the fact that the government wanted to be involved in providing low-cost medicines to the population but not through for-profit private pharmacies: "Given the current position of the DoH [Department of Health] regarding a state-supported non-profit pharmaceutical system, there is no opportunity at this time or in the near future for integration of RPPM into the DoH [Department of Health]."[4] Government participation in providing medicines was ruled out.

Following the health and nutrition surveys that AKF had conducted in 1994 and 1996, three more were conducted in 1998, 2001, and 2004. The findings told a disturbing story.[5] As far as household economics, the survey showed that only 26 percent of the population were employed; the annual per capita income was US $70.[6] By 2004, an estimated 76 percent of the population lived below the poverty line (down from 91 percent in 1999), with six of Badakhshan's seven districts facing food insecurity at a "high" or "very high" level. Almost 92 percent of respondents reported that their household had sold possessions to pay for food; of those, 63 percent had sold livestock, an important marker of vulnerability.

Acute malnutrition had increased from 3 percent of children surveyed in 1994 to 13.5 percent in 2001; in 2004, it was 8.8 percent, almost triple the first survey results. Similarly, chronic malnutrition increased from 40.3 percent in 1994 to a peak of 53.8 percent in 1998; in 2004 it remained high at 32.3 percent. Weight deficit went from 19.2 percent in 1994 to 23.1

percent in 2004.[7] A nationwide survey cited in the AKF report showed that inhabitants in Tajikistan ate an average of 1.6 meals per day, with 46 percent reporting only one meal per day. Because Badakhshan was the poorest oblast in Tajikistan, the survey's authors concluded that the majority of households in Badakhshan likely consumed less than this average.

Overall, the health status and health needs of Badakhshan's population remained worrisome. Of the 2,370 households visited by AKF in 2004, 29 percent reported a family member hospitalized in the past year, 22 percent reported a household member suffering from chronic illness in the past six months, and 12 percent reported a household member experiencing acute illness in the two weeks prior to the survey. Illness was highest among those younger than five years (28 percent); and a higher number of females (58 percent) appeared to be affected by illness then males. Of those who reported having had an illness, 32 percent cared for themselves, 31 percent went to health posts, and 26 percent went to hospitals. Seven percent went to a religious healer.

For the households reporting at least one illness, a full 72 percent said that they spent roughly 20 percent of their yearly income on care.[8] Patients reported that 59 percent of their total expenses were for medicines. For households reporting chronic illnesses, the mean amount spent per household was roughly 65 percent of yearly income.[9] Medicines constituted 61 percent of these expenses. It is no surprise that the AKF survey showed that 82 percent of households found it difficult to cover health care costs and that 72 percent of respondents reported being unable to acquire prescription medications because they could not pay for them.

The majority of childhood illnesses were found to involve diarrhea and upper respiratory infections—the biggest killers of children globally and diseases that are readily treated with medicines. The survey estimated the crude infant mortality rate (per 1,000 live births) in 2004 to be 38.3 and the crude child mortality rate (per 1,000 live births) to be 52.2.[10] These numbers were very close to the level of infant and child mortality observed in Tajikistan in 1995 and 1996, at the height of the civil war.[11] The percentage of children immunized for childhood diseases decreased from 72 percent in 2001 to 36 percent in 2004, well below that reported in the rest of Central Asia.[12] In the data collected by AKF in their series of health and nutrition surveys, statistics were worse for those living in the poorer regions of Badakhshan.

COST SHIFTING TO NO CARE: THE TRUTH ABOUT USER FEES

While disturbing, the outcomes of the revolving drug fund program and the statistics about the level of ill health in Badakhshan were not particularly surprising. Many questionable assumptions had been made in Bamako about user fees and their potential positive effects on health and quality of care, evidenced by data in the scientific literature years before the intervention in Badakhshan began.

The untested notion that user fees for health services would "rationalize" demand or improve supply turned out to be, by and large, not true. At first blush one could imagine that if user fees were collected and reinvested into the system, they would not only allow users to demand better services but would provide additional resources to fund service provision at health clinics. After all, around the world, many people spend money on health services of dubious quality and effectiveness. If these funds could be directed toward better care, perhaps patients would benefit.

Although a few studies from West Africa conducted in the early 1990s—in Niger, Cameroon, Benin, and Guinea—suggested that user fees might work as billed, subsequent analyses showed that in settings of poverty their effect was detrimental.[13] A number of convincing studies have demonstrated that user fees actually decreased clinic utilization rates, for the same reasons that AKF and USAID outlined in their final reports: people could not afford the cost of the goods and services or the transaction costs (such as transportation and time away from work). For example, in Zambia, health service utilization dropped 33 percent over two years after fees were introduced.[14] Similarly, in Dar es Salaam, Tanzania, government hospitals saw a drop in utilization of 50 percent after user fees were implemented.[15] As might be expected, the effects of fees are not equally distributed: a study in Niger showed that when new fees were introduced, although there was an overall decrease in medical consultations of only 6.3 percent, among the poor it was 32.4 percent.[16] Similar findings were observed in Kenya and Nigeria.[17]

Overall, when user fees were initiated in poor communities, health service utilization went down.[18] Where fees have been removed—in particular for the cost of medicines—there have been significant increases in utilization.[19] Although high utilization does not necessarily translate into better outcomes, when economist Christopher James and colleagues at the London School of Hygiene and Tropical Medicine analyzed twenty-seven studies of programs in a variety of countries that had implemented user fees, they found that in sixteen of the programs there were clear negative effects on both utilization of services and treatment outcomes.[20]

Even creating a community-managed waiver system was not effective in places ranging from West Africa to East Africa to China.[21] According to Najmi Kanji, writing before he was hired to run AKF's revolving drug fund program, although programs like the Bamako Initiative accept that a proportion of the community will not be able to pay for services and should be exempted, "mechanisms and criteria for exemption are . . . simplistic and fail to reflect the complex power relationships that exist at the local levels of health care."[22] For Badakhshan, this is extremely important given the strong networks of patronage and the under-the-table payments from the Soviet era.[23]

While user fees decreased utilization among the destitute sick, the money garnered from charging for care has turned out to be a pittance. In general, fees cover a small proportion of the operating costs of a clinic. For example, in a 2004 report for the Department for International Development in the United Kingdom using data from eighteen African countries, the author found that average revenue from fees accounted for 6.9 percent of the budget, and this was similar to findings elsewhere.[24] As a result, the presence or absence of fees does not have a significant impact on the availability of medicines and supplies.[25] Ironically, administering user fees proves to be expensive; according to one study from Zambia, implementation ended up costing as much as the revenue raised from the fees.[26]

In areas where user fees have been removed for impoverished populations, utilization of health services has increased and health outcomes have improved. In one example from the Bamako Initiative, where access to HIV medicines had decreased and patients had been forced to turn to traditional practices after user fees were introduced, once payments for medicines were removed, there was significant improvement in utilization of and adherence to HIV treatment.[27] Similarly, in Uganda the government removed user fees from the country's health units in 2001. The result was a 155 percent increase in outpatient clinic visits. Even utilization of the most basic preventive health care—services that had not been subject to user fees—increased. In the Ugandan case, immunization rates for diphtheria, pertussis, and tetanus increased from 48 percent to 89 percent, to cite one example.[28] Interestingly, increased utilization remained constant over a two-year period, with the poorest quartile using health services twice as much as the least poor quartile (which was not the case prior to the abolition of these fees). Similar findings have been noted elsewhere.[29] In the *British Medical Journal* in 2005, James and colleagues estimated that more than three million child deaths could have been averted over the past twenty years if user fees had not been charged in impoverished areas, equal to over 150,000 lives saved per year.[30]

At its simplest, charging user fees to very poor people fails for obvious reasons: a system of exchange requires the solvency of the exchange partners as a basic precondition.[31] Certainly, people will make sacrifices for their health, but sometimes they are already too vulnerable. Their position in the social structure limits individual agency. The evidence is now abundant that user fees contribute to the financial burden faced by people who are poor, dissuading them from seeking care. Since most people in the world are not trained to accurately judge the severity of an illness—to distinguish an upper respiratory infection from pneumonia, diarrhea that will resolve from the type that leads to an infant's death, or cardiac pain from musculoskeletal pain—user fees may dissuade people from seeking necessary care rather than diminishing "frivolous" care.[32]

UNPACKING THE REFORM

The task of providing financing for the care of a very vulnerable population in the immediate post-Soviet period in Badakhshan was itself daunting. Planning for the future was an even bigger challenge. Key donors, like USAID and the World Bank, encouraged "reform" of the health system, largely moving away from government-centered universal coverage toward a consumer-based private system.

Yet, as Seedhouse (1995) points out, any reform "must aim to reconstruct an existing structure or system in order to enable it to achieve its original end(s) in an improved way."[33] If improving delivery of pharmaceuticals to a vulnerable population was the aim of the reform, we scarcely have to ask whether adopting the approach of the Bamako Initiative was a sound decision. The revolving drug fund did not make sense for Badakhshan, for reasons that are worth considering.

The mandate of the revolving drug fund was to create a "sustainable" structure that could ultimately survive in the absence of donor support. According to development specialist Anne LaFond, most donor ideas about sustainability involve being able to hand over the program to government at some point:

> They are predicated on the assumption that once initial "start-up" costs are met, donors will "hand over" all project responsibilities to government. Ordinarily these responsibilities consist of operational costs and support activities such as supervision and management. According to the traditional definition sustainability occurs when government absorbs these responsibilities and is able to maintain project benefits. . . . The majority of donor perceptions of sustainability are reflected in the following definition employed by the United States Agency for International Development: Sustainability is the ability of a health project or programme to deliver health services or sustain benefits after major technical, managerial and financial support has ceased.[34]

As the AKF and USAID reports on the revolving drug fund project indicated, the intervention led to the *breakdown* of the state system for pharmaceutical procurement and delivery, making a handover virtually impossible. The main entity of what was formerly the public system (TajikFarmatsia) was privatized, leaving no party with an interest or obligation to ensure that all parts of the population, rich or poor, receive appropriate care. The Department of Health's apparent desire to recreate a not-for-profit system was immediately ruled out as a possibility. Without state involvement—or the creation of some form of public or private pooled-risk insurance mechanisms—the onus for sustainability shifted to the patients, precisely the goal of neoliberalism's advocates.

In general, health care is difficult to distribute as a commodity because there is often a limited competitive market—given their capital costs, such facilities as hospitals can almost be considered public utilities—and most consumers have insufficient information to make informed medical decisions. Unlike many other goods, the users of health care generally do not know exactly what they need (they do not have the requisite technical training), are generally unable to judge quality and price according to a reliable standard, and are often too ill to deliberate or shop around.[35] Other exigencies, such as poverty and lack of transportation, make participation in "the market" more difficult. This is very different from neoliberal assumptions about competition and *Homo economicus*'s perfect knowledge of and access to the commodity being purchased.[36] Therefore, in practice, most people do not "participate in their own health" by making decisions about pharmaceuticals.[37] Instead, they rely on trained health providers.[38]

Even in the United States, "cost sharing"—a buzzword for charging user fees—has been found to entrench inequality of access to medical care. In the past, questions have arisen about whether the high costs of Medicaid (the U.S. government program for the indigent sick) could be cut by "cost shifting" in which patients pay for services, thus discouraging patients from "overusing" the health system and seeking "unnecessary" medical care. In this context, the debate has been framed as one between inefficiency or moral hazard (overconsumption) and risk protection.[39] However, the RAND Health Insurance Experiment conducted in the 1970s and 1980s found that user fees reduced all types of interactions with the health system—physician visits, dental visits, prescriptions, and hospital admissions—adversely affecting health outcomes among the sick poor.[40] For the poor, "cost shifting" often means no care at all.

NEOLIBERAL SUCCESS

Despite the failure of the Bamako Initiative in Badakhshan, the AKDN continued to intervene to ensure access to care. Perhaps reflective of the nature of a multifaceted network like the AKDN, one of its member institutions, Aga Khan Health Services, stepped in to cover the cost of drugs for the many patients who could not pay. As political scientist William DeMars has pointed out, NGOs are not simply monoliths carrying out the latent agendas of their partners, but a "bundle of contradictions," a site of "dynamic cooperation and conflict among its partners" and, arguably, within themselves.[41] Unfortunately, neither this organizational tension nor findings that the revolving drug fund had not worked as billed appeared to greatly affect the overall strategy. In fact, as I discovered during a visit to Badakhshan shortly after USAID's report came out in 2005, the plan was for the program to continue.

Was there any scenario in which persisting with the program would be reasonable? Is there something that can be done to fix the approach? For places like Badakhshan, the answer seems to be no. Data from a USAID-sponsored project in the Kyrgyz Republic has shown that the high costs charged to patients result from fixed costs associated with starting and maintaining private pharmacies in rural areas as well as real costs associated with getting medicines to distant places. This raises serious questions about whether any amount of tinkering would make this a viable approach for a region as poor and isolated as Badakhshan.[42]

Why, then, was an alternative to the revolving drug fund, such as building private or public pooled risk schemes like the health insurance programs found in other settings, not actively sought? The reason, I think, is to be found in the congruence of a number of factors—all linked to the penetration of neoliberalism into political thought and social praxis—which ensured that Margaret Thatcher's maxim, "There is no alternative," would become a reality. The first is placing the idea of the revolving drug fund within the lexicon of global health. To borrow from Milton Friedman, having the idea lying around—and, in this case, endorsed by global health's major donors—keeps the idea alive and adds to its practicability. It becomes "common sense."

The second factor is the state itself becoming a party to the policy. As we saw at the first meeting in Bamako, ministers of health supported the initiative. Charitably, one could argue that this was because of pressure from the World Bank and the International Monetary Fund, who insisted that countries conform to the "structural adjustment" of their economies and cut social sector expenditures. Cynically, it could be posited that governments did not mind being relieved of the burden of looking after their poorest citizens. Since the late 1990s, Tajikistan has been under pressure from multilateral donor agencies like the World Bank and the International Monetary Fund to curtail central government expenditures and commitments, including social services.[43] By 2007, private out-of-pocket payments accounted for 76.2 percent of all health expenditures in the country (an amount that was formally zero during the Soviet period), ranking Tajikistan among those countries with the lowest share of public sector health expenditure as a percentage of total health expenditure in the World Health Organization's European Region.[44] This drive to limit state involvement in the social sector—which Michel Foucault has argued transforms the role of the state by allowing it to control citizens without being responsible for their well-being[45]—led to the government's acceptance of policies like the revolving drug fund. Thus the revolving drug fund was undertaken with the acquiescence of both the Tajik federal government in Dushanbe and Badakhshan's provincial government in Khorog.

The third factor is that a major donor supported continuation of the policy.

This last factor provides considerable insight into the way the program has been evaluated. As we have discussed, USAID is quite open about its objective of building markets, and AKF's application was written in language congruent with and reflective of USAID's ZdravReform regional efforts. Although the funds requested were for medicines, continuation of funding in the face of the relative failure to make medicines accessible to the sick and poor exposes the disconnect between the purpose of health reform and health outcomes.

In this setting it becomes clear that the "reform" aimed far beyond the delivery of health care. For advocates of neoliberalism, success means the creation of markets and the reduction of government involvement in the lives of citizens. One only has to reread the language mirrored in AKF's application to USAID to sense this:

> The strategic use of essential drugs *to catalyse the start of these reforms* is an opportunity that perhaps should not be missed. In many ways, the timing for such an initiative seems right, and if the RDF project can serve *to change the old ways of thinking* at the many levels of this society, then the project will have made a significant contribution. . . .
>
> Though not without risk, staff believe that the RDF project is timely and has the potential of *catalysing the process of reforming* the health system. Although it is unlikely that the project will ever recover more than 50–60%

of the actual drug costs, it is imperative that both government and communities *make the mental switch that the old system is not coming back,* and that any new, viable system will require more community involvement in management as well as in contribution.[46]

When viewed in light of the ideological project laid out in 1947 by Hayek and the thirty-five others at Mont Pèlerin, it is clear that the very act of implementing the revolving drug fund was a success for the advocates of neoliberalism: it catalyzed a change that would be irreversible, regardless of its outcome.

REALMS OF NEOLIBERAL PROGRAMMATIC BLINDNESS

In his analysis of a failed development program in Lesotho, anthropologist James Ferguson (1994) suggests that the most important thing about a development project may rest not in what it fails to do but in what it achieves in failure: its side effects.[47] Quoting Michel Foucault's analysis of the prison system, where Foucault asks, "What is the use of these different phenomena that are continually being criticized?" Ferguson argues that repeated failure allows us to speak about a logic that transcends the program being implemented. In Foucault's language, this is the space of discourse, or what he calls power/knowledge.[48]

Though NGOs were the vehicle William Douglas proposed as the transplanting mechanism, in truth what matters is the policy itself—its exposure to the light of day in places where it had hitherto been unimaginable and alien. The policy itself is the vehicle of change; it is the ideological underpinnings of the policy and not the specific health project (nor the organization) that is being funded. In this case, a policy cloaked in an ostensibly neutral technical activity to which nobody could object—mechanisms for ensuring a steady supply of medicines at a moment of profound vulnerability—had been used to introduce a set of ideas targeted at transforming expectations between citizen and state in Badakhshan, Tajikistan, Central Asia, and beyond.

On a broader level, this very local example explains why the Bamako Initiative, though it had failed to meet its health goals in a number of settings, was funded and replicated again and again in many parts of the world. And though, as Ferguson and Foucault suggest, repeated failure reveals the discursive forces behind the intervention, the programs themselves—as global health interventions likely based on the best of intentions but steeped in the ideological rather than the phenomenological—fall into the trap of neoliberal programmatic blindness. That is to say, because of the ideological underpinnings, which frame the behavior of the donor as well as the recipient in everything from the application for money to the evaluation of the project, the service delivery objectives of the project get lost.

For health projects, the best outcome is to stem the spread of disease and prevent morbidity and mortality. Optimal outcomes may involve the state delivering care, or private markets, or both. However, when policies are driven by a neoliberal agenda—when a medical intervention is used as the means for enacting a broader ideological goal of changing the nature of the state and its relationship with citizens—then the purported outcome of delivering care and improving health, even if measured, becomes less relevant. This may be one reason why it took many years for policy makers in the West to realize that levying user fees on the sick poor has resulted, in many cases, in excess morbidity and death. Instead, the empirically unsupported neoliberal belief that participation in the market is an economic form of political democracy takes precedence.

Badakhshan is one of many examples in global health where ideology, or dogma, overrides both qualitative and quantitative data. In this case, the need to ensure that patients can access medical care and to protect health gains from the Soviet period fell into realms of neoliberal programmatic blindness. To describe and enumerate those losses on both programmatic and moral levels is essential to comprehending the full effects of neoliberalism and its penetration into communities, families, and bodies—the phenomenology of neoliberalism in the most intimate local spaces. More importantly, however, it is a critical step in the moral and programmatic reorientation of global health.

10 Epilogue

REFRAMING THE MORAL DIMENSIONS OF ENGAGEMENT

The reach of markets, and market-oriented thinking, into
aspects of life traditionally governed by nonmarket norms
is one of the most significant developments of our time.

Michael J. Sandel, *What Money Can't Buy*, 2012

Against a tide of utilitarian opinion and worse, we are
offered the chance to insist, *This is not how it should be done.*

Paul Farmer, *Pathologies of Power*, 2003

Neoliberalism has been the defining paradigm in global health since at
least the late 1970s. Because of the untested and unproven belief that the
creation of unfettered markets constitutes an economic form of political
democracy, neoliberalism—particularly neoliberal economics—was conceived as a bulwark against totalitarianism and the rise of a strong, centralized state.[1] The ideology reached its political and policy zenith in the
late 1980s, overlapping the collapse of the Soviet Union. For many, this
was no coincidence and represented the victory of capitalism over communism, of the individual over the communal, and of liberalism over
totalitarianism.[2]

For the poor in the high mountains of Badakhshan, people subject to
large-scale social forces beyond their control—the disintegration of essential state services, a tragic and violent civil war, and a history of persecution, marginalization, and poverty—the collapse of the Soviet Union
spelled disaster. Rising to the occasion, NGOs entered a difficult situation
and, through myriad donor-funded interventions across a number of vital

sectors, saved many lives. That is without doubt.[3] They also, perhaps inadvertently, brought into this physically isolated region at the margin of the Soviet empire an ideological force that would have profound effects in the short term on the organization of the health system, and would forever change the relationship between the citizens of the region and their state.

But Badakhshan is a small place, and this case study is one of many playing out across the globe, from Asia and Africa to South America and Europe.[4] While it is safe to say that the effects of neoliberalism's entry into the world of global health have been felt by many, the suddenness of the shift into a neoliberal world order in the countries of the former Soviet Union—which, at the time it was happening, was referred to as the ascendance of "the new world order" or "late twentieth century capitalism"—has become emblematic of the spread of neoliberal ideology. Even in Russia, which maintained a strong state in the face of the collapse of its empire, neoliberal economic theories contributed to the deaths of millions. In their recent book, *The Body Economic: Why Austerity Kills*, Oxford University sociologist David Stuckler and Stanford University physician-epidemiologist Sanjay Basu point out that the post-Soviet transition resulted in more than ten million deaths.[5] "What became known as 'the post-communist mortality crisis' turned out to be the worst drop in life expectancy in the past half-century in any country that wasn't an active war zone or experiencing famine."[6] The reason for this, they argue, had little to do with the fall of communism and more to do with the rapid transition to a particular type of unfettered capitalism—an economic "shock therapy" to which millions of Russians were exposed.[7] In contrast, health improvements were seen in places like Poland, where economic reforms were introduced slowly and, importantly, where the government maintained systems of social protection.[8]

OUR PREDICAMENT

Every situation where programs are dissonant with the lived experience of local populations—where what matters most to communities falls into realms of (neoliberal) programmatic blindness—should raise important questions about health delivery and about social, economic, and political development. For me, the first question is: why are programs executed in the face of clear and abundant evidence suggesting that they will not achieve good health outcomes? Part of the answer, I have argued, depends on understanding two important factors that have defined global health since the late 1970s.

The first factor is the strength and success of neoliberalism as an intellectual and political movement that defined the late twentieth century, and its hegemonic reach—its penetration—into almost every part of our politics (writ large) and the policies that have emerged from them.[9] Antonio Gramsci argues that hegemony refers to the permeation throughout society of an entire system of values, attitudes, beliefs, morality—an organizing principle—that is diffused by social institutions into almost every area of daily life, so as to become "common sense."[10] This becomes "the natural order" and goes unquestioned. In a very narrow sense, in the world of global health and international development, neoliberalism's hegemonic reach has allowed dogma to supersede data, as the example of the revolving drug fund illustrates.

On a broader level, neoliberal values create, as Harvard University political philosopher Michael Sandel has suggested, a much bigger problem: "Sometimes markets crowd out other nonmarket values worth caring about."[11] Instead of open markets and civic engagement emanating from a liberal polity, neoliberal ideology posits that the opposite will happen: a liberal polity will emanate from participation in an unfettered market. While the empirical basis of this position is highly questionable, it is clear that by making the social world subject to economic considerations— rather than the economic being one part of the social realm—something significant happens: the market becomes the arbiter of all things social and moral. The effects are stark in health and education. Writing about neoliberal health reform in New Zealand in the second half of the 1980s, University of Auckland health economist Toni Ashton concludes that "the ideology underpinning these policies includes a general belief in the superiority of markets over governments, of competition over co-operation, and of self-reliance over community responsibility." As a result, "important values such as human dignity, distributive justice, and social cohesion, have been given second place to the pursuit of efficiency, self-reliance, a fiscal balance, and a more limited state."[12]

Likewise, in his extensive work on understanding the rise and effects of neoliberalism, historian Daniel Stedman Jones argues:

> Neoliberal political success brought with it a number of consequences. There was a newfound acceptance of inequality as a necessary and unavoidable evil. There was a cumulative squeeze of the public sphere—of the space for generously funded, comprehensive, and universal public services, and for collective industrial action and communal activity, of shared public spaces and institutions. A general assumption took hold among policymakers and publics, encouraged by the neoliberal interpretation of Adam Smith's concept of the invisible hand, that self-interest could mean selfishness. Greed, and less pejoratively profit, were to be celebrated. The provision of assistance to the poorest suffered as the public listened to arguments about the "escalating" costs of welfare. That this came during a period when middle- and upper-tier earners benefited more through the tax system from state subsidy than those deprived groups had ever done was rarely mentioned. There was in fact a redistribution from the poorest to the wealthy over the course of the 1980s, and this continued in the 1990s under Bill Clinton and Tony Blair. Whether these were intended effects (they probably weren't, in most cases) is less important than the fact that neoliberal policies tended to affect the most vulnerable members of society in the harshest ways.[13]

Neoliberalism as a system of political and economic thought has had its most profound effects in changing values and expectations about the role government can play in creating a just society—as an entity capable of taking a long view rather than being driven by short-term profit or the vagaries of external funding—and our responsibilities to each other as members of that society.[14]

The second defining factor in global health has been the rise of NGOs in international development. David Lewis, a reader in Social Policy at the London School of Economics, points out in his work on management of NGOs that while the dominant view is that they are "heroic organizations seeking to 'do good' for others in difficult circumstances," they are also a critical part of the global movement "away from donor support to state institutions towards a more privatized—and potentially less accountable—

form of development intervention."[15] Because of the neoliberal belief that markets and private initiative are the only efficient means of providing services to people—with governments simply playing an enabling role— NGOs have become the preferred avenue for service provision, what development experts Edwards and Hulme refer to as a "deliberate substitution for the state."[16] There is no empirical basis for translating this belief into public policy, nor are there data to suggest that improvements in efficiency cannot be achieved through strengthening the public sector.[17] This approach was specifically designed to weaken the state—part of the neoliberal strategy for containing totalitarianism—rather than to protect the vulnerable, increase political participation, build social stability and cohesion, or promote social, economic, and political development.

While it is true that international NGOs may be catalysts for the development of local civil society, most are not accountable to the local communities in which they are working. In the absence of civic engagement by the local population—many of whom are poor and who live in countries where the institutional and social foundations of democratic participation are weak— the semblance of community involvement, a proxy for "democracy," has to be created.[18] As people who have spent a lot of time working in global health programs will recognize, this is often achieved through the conflation of "democracy" with participation in "the market." It is here that neoliberalism's key precept—that an unfettered economic sphere will give rise to political democracy—finds its salience in global development. The very fact that people appear willing or are obliged to pay user fees for medicines or services is seen as a form of community participation—and hence, of participatory democracy.[19] It is by promoting this type of conflation that NGOs not only ignore the lived realities of the local world but become vehicles through which neoliberal ideology enters the most minute level of development.

The collapse of the Soviet Union presented a unique opportunity for NGOs to become Douglas's transplantation mechanism.[20] The ideological and political vacuum left in the aftermath of the collapse—exacerbated in the case of Tajikistan by the civil war and near complete shutdown of state services—provided a fertile historical moment for the ideas of neoliberalism. As the neoliberal economist Milton Friedman so clearly put it, "Only a crisis . . . produces a real change. When a crisis occurs, the actions that are taken depend on the ideas that are lying around."[21] In the case of the Bamako Initiative, the fact that the World Health Organization and others had expressed concerns about the equity of the approach did not diminish the idea.[22] In fact, the system for propagating neoliberal ideology at the expense of health outcomes was well defended by global institutional structures, which had achieved a policy consensus by the late 1980s for the defense of the neoliberal vision, effected through the control of resources and key nodes in the global policy network.[23] This, as Pulitzer-winning science writer Laurie Garrett has so aptly pointed out, is because the idea behind this discourse is not so much to help at a time of crisis but to initiate an ideological shift.[24]

The extent of the crisis and the amount of money required for intervention created the perfect storm: NGOs had little choice but to turn to large donors, often wealthy governments or large international organizations. Together, by the late 1980s the institutions born of Bretton Woods and the Cold War constituted the largest funders in global health. By defining the problem in certain ways—for instance, establishing the state and the public sector as inefficient, the market as a superior means for distributing scarce resources, and user fees as a form of community participation—and reifying these representations through processes of grant applications and program evaluation, these institutions define the way health programs are conceived and implemented.[25] It is through the structuring of grants—a form of what Michel Foucault refers to as governmentality, in which the application criteria and the definition of performance shape the behavior of the recipients—that many NGOs become both the subject of neoliberal ideology (they are formed by it) and its transplantation mechanism.[26] Because funding streams are controlled by organizations closely linked to the propagation of the neoliberal vision, it is difficult for alternative ideas to emerge and easy for programs to mirror the foreign and economic policies of donor nations and institutions.[27]

This is not to suggest that NGOs are monolithic and naïve. In fact, as we have seen, many NGOs are, as political scientist William DeMars says, "a bundle of contradictions." DeMars argues, "To view partner latent agendas solely as a threat to the purity of NGO missions is to misunderstand the contradictory nature of the relationship. An NGO that carries no latent agenda is one that makes a negligible impact, because it has little

money, few projects and difficulty recruiting staff. Smart NGO professionals develop complex scripts for playing off one partner against another,
and using partner latent agendas to fuel the NGO salient mission."[28]

IS THERE A WAY OUT?

Almost twenty-five years after the African ministers of health met in
Bamako and more than twenty years after I started learning about neoliberalism and the Bamako Initiative, I remain astonished at the enthusiasm
with which this policy has been adopted by so many well-meaning people
around the world. I imagine that some adopted the approach out of necessity or a misplaced sense of pragmatism, others out of belief in its correct-
ness and apparent common sense, and a few, perhaps, because they sought
an ideological transformation. For the poor and sick in Badakhshan and
many other settings, the outcome was the same. Yet sadly, the unexamined
ideas of neoliberalism discussed in this book continue to be propagated
through discourse, policy, and practice.

I have come to the conclusion that the way out of the amber is both
complex and simple. At its most complex, it will require careful recalibration of our goals as a society and the type of world we wish to create.
Philosopher Michael Sandel has argued that we have drifted from *having*
a market economy, which is a valuable and effective tool for organizing
productive activity, to *being* a market society—a way of life in which social
relations are made in the image of the market. Observing that our "reluc-
tance to engage in moral and spiritual argument, together with our
embrace of markets, has exacted a heavy price" that "has drained public
discourse of moral and civic energy, and contributed to the technocratic
and managerial policies that afflict many societies today," Sandel argues
that it is time for us to think through the moral limits of markets.[29]

At its most simple, this will require recalibrating our focus in global
health and development from "sustainability" and "local ownership"—
buzzwords that run the risk of serving as doublespeak for a neoliberal
agenda—to an approach that puts equity and patient outcomes first.[30] In
health and education, equity of access often means equity of outcome.
While *equity* has different meanings, I am inclined to call any policy that

is biased toward serving those with the greatest need, which improves outcomes for the poor and marginalized, a move toward equity.[31] By promoting the market as the sole distributor of health care, neoliberal economics has failed to prove itself an instrument of equity and is therefore not good for the health of poor populations. Competitive markets may have an important role to play, but they should not be the sole mechanism through which health care and health goods are distributed to vulnerable populations. A recalibration of focus toward equity of access and equity of outcome will allow NGOs to again take up the mantle as the vanguard of a moral order that finds poverty and structural violence unacceptable.[32]

In the last decade, activists' and patients' demands for HIV treatment for people living in the world's poorest communities have resulted in a sea change in global health: a transformation from an "international health" preoccupied with cost and false calculations of utility to a "global health" concerned with equity. Today, large global health initiatives, such as the President's Emergency Plan for AIDS Relief in the United States and the Global Fund to Fight AIDS, Tuberculosis and Malaria, are providing diagnostic tests and medicines to the poor without charge. These examples are an important first step in realizing a global health equity agenda, but much more needs to be done.

For practitioners and academics working in global health, the road ahead can be both simple and complex. By acquiescing to the dominant discourse in fear that we will be cut off from funding streams and projects, we as practitioners and researchers do a disservice to the communities where we work. In the case of global health, a commitment to health delivery—not to mention a commitment to equity and justice—requires that we examine what has fallen into the realms of neoliberal programmatic blindness and attempt to fix it. Paramount in this process is accepting that we must not continue to privilege the fiscal over the moral.[33]

The French sociologist Pierre Bourdieu has argued that part of the intellectual challenge we face is not to take the neoliberal view for granted, as self-evident. We need to analyze the production of this discourse, its circulation, and its effects.[34] As he so eloquently puts it:

> The ideal of the collective intellectual, to which I have tried to conform whenever I could make common cause with others on some particular point, is not always easy to put into effect. And if, to be effective, I have

sometimes had to commit myself in my own person and in my own name, I have always done it in the hope—if not of triggering a mobilization, or even one of those debates without object or subject which arise periodically in the world of the media—at least of breaking the appearance of unanimity which is the greatest part of the symbolic force of the dominant discourse.[35]

Health and health care delivery are not neutral; they are intimately tied to political economy. Our voices for the promotion of an intellectual and policy framework for equity in care delivery and outcomes are the logical counterforce. TINA.

Notes

FOREWORD

1. Thomas Piketty, *Capital in the Twenty-First Century* (Cambridge, MA: Belknap Press, 2014), 186.

2. "The Bamako Initiative," *Lancet* 332, no. 8621 (1988): 1177–78.

3. J. Y. Kim, J. V. Millen, A. Irwin, and J. Gershman, *Dying for Growth: Global Inequality and the Health of the Poor* (Monroe, ME: Common Courage Press, 2000), 147.

4. Ibid., 146.

5. Ibid., 145–46.

6. M. B. Steger, *Globalization: A Very Short Introduction* (Oxford: Oxford University Press, 2013), 104–6.

7. Pope Francis, *Apostolic Exhortation Evangelii Gaudium of the Holy Father Francis to the Bishops, Clergy, Consecrated Persons and the Lay Faithful on the Proclamation of the Gospel in Today's World* (Vatican City: Vatican Press, 2013), 47.

8. Steger, *Globalization*, 107.

9. A. Krishna, *One Illness Away: Why People Become Poor and How They Escape Poverty* (Oxford: Oxford University Press, 2010).

10. Piketty, *Capital in the Twenty-First Century*, 264.

11. Jean Drèze and Amartya Sen, *An Uncertain Glory: India and Its Contradictions* (Princeton, NJ: Princeton University Press, 2013).

12. Kim et al., *Dying for Growth*.

13. Drèze and Sen, *An Uncertain Glory*, 155.

PREFACE

1. In a recent article in the *International Herald Tribune* on the effects of post-2008 austerity in Portugal, journalist Raphael Minder (2013), referring to the International Monetary Fund/European Commission/European Central Bank (the "troika") bailout of the Portuguese economy, points out that austerity raises some important philosophical questions: "Can governments afford the social welfare states their citizens cherish? If not, how far can they go in cutting state benefits without further stifling economic recovery, intensifying social imbalances and forfeiting the welfare of future generations?" Minder quotes a teacher at one of Lisbon's public schools, a system that has faced drastic cuts under the troika's regime: "The austerity reforms mean that education has become soulless and only about financial numbers rather than people." See also Stuckler and Basu 2013; Sandel 2012; Stuckler, King, and Basu 2008.

2. Stein 2008; Rowden 2009.

3. Smith 1982b; Dhanagare 2001; O'Connell 1999; Stewart 1997.

4. Douglas 1972.

5. Edwards and Hulme 1996b.

6. Stuckler and Basu 2013; Rowden 2009; Stein 2008; Harvey 2005; Harvey 1990.

1. INTRODUCTION

1. The name of this village has been changed to disguise its identity and protect the anonymity of its residents.

2. Village clinics were referred to as feldsher-accoucheur points, or FAP points. The facility is usually staffed by a *feldsher*, a medical doctor's assistant, or an accoucheur, an individual who assists during childbirth.

3. See Schoeberlein-Engel 1994; Tadjbakhsh 1993a; Keshavjee 1998.

4. See Slim and Hodizoda 2001. For a description of the war, see Schoeberlein-Engel 1994; Keshavjee 1998; and Matveeva 2009.

5. Matveeva 2009.

6. According to the World Bank (1998), Tajikistan had a per capita GNP of US $330 in 1996. The economy is primarily based on agriculture, which accounts for 25 percent of output and 50 percent of employment. The country's main agricultural products are cotton, silk, fruits, and vegetables. Industry accounts for 35 percent of output and 12 percent of employment. The per capita GDP of the

Soviet Union was estimated at $2,870 in 1990 (World Bank 1992). By some estimates, Tajikistan's per capita GDP likely ranged between 36 percent and 53 percent of that number, giving it a per capita income in 1990 between $1,033 and $1,521. See also Falkingham 2000: 10; UNDP 1998.

7. See UNDP 1998; International Monetary Fund 1998.

8. The rate of inflation reached 635 percent in 1995; in 1996 it was 42 percent (World Bank 1998). See World Bank 1998; OCHA 1998; UNICEF/WHO Mission 1992.

9. Falkingham 2000.

10. EOHCS 2000: 4.

11. EOHCS (2000) reported that the infant mortality rate in Tajikistan is likely an underestimate because prevailing Soviet-era definitions do not count premature and low birth weight newborns who did not survive the first week. It is also in the interest of hospitals not to record neonatal mortality (4).

12. EOHCS 2000.

13. In 1997, 3,540 cases of measles were reported in Tajikistan (WHO 1999). Rates of diphtheria were much higher in Tajikistan than in other republics, with 1,464 cases reported in 1996 (Vitek and Wharton 1998). See Hampton et al. 1998; UNDP 1998; Keshavjee and Becerra 2000.

14. With a land surface of 64,100 square kilometers (about half the country), Badakhshan has only approximately 216,000 inhabitants.

15. See Robinson 1993; Moore 1993; Edwards and Hulme 1996a.

16. Jones 2012: 123.

17. Colclough and Manor 1991; World Bank 1993; World Bank 1987; Abel-Smith 1986; Brugha and Zwi 2002; Skaar 1998; Mills 1997. See also Isin 2000: 154; Ilcan and Lacey 2011.

18. Salamon 1993: 1.

19. Shah and Shah 1996: 217.

20. UNICEF 1988a.

21. See Gilson et al. 2001; Abel-Smith and Dua 1998.

22. Gilson et al. 2001; WHO 1988; UNICEF 1990b; Keshavjee 1998.

23. McPake 2002: 124; De Ferranti 1985; Birdsall 1986.

24. Amin 1996.

25. Brugha and Zwi 2002: 64. See also World Bank 1987; World Bank 1993; Abel-Smith 1986; Pfeiffer 2004; USAID 1995; World Bank 1997; Buse and Walt 1996; Green and Matthias 1997; De Beyer et al. 2000.

26. Carrin and Vereecke (1992) point out that the constraint on international aid and on public health budgets forces governments to produce as much health as possible within predetermined budgets (23).

27. Shore and Wright 1997: 11; Burchell 1991: 279.

28. Edwards and Hulme 1996a; Green and Matthias 1997; Zaidi 1999; Turshen 1999.

29. Edwards and Hulme 1996a; Powell and Seddon 1997; Turshen 1999; Stewart 1997; Hanlon 1996; Drabek 1987.

30. Ferguson 1994: v.

31. For a broader discussion of this, see Marcus and Fischer (1986).

32. Hall 1992.

33. For a broader discussion of this, see Marcus and Fischer (1986).

34. This, of course, is situated within the ongoing debate in anthropology between individual agency and social structure (Bourgois, 1995; Bourdieu 1977, 1984, 1990; Sahlins 1985; Moore 1987, 1994; Leach 1977; Yalman 1967).

35. In *Culture and Practical Reason* (1976), Sahlins criticizes Marx for taking for granted that goods are produced to answer needs. He argues that for Marx, exchange is the cultural part and the consumption code does not enter the argument (consumption is subordinate to use-value). For Sahlins, consumption is important. He argues that the cultural scheme is "variously inflected by a dominant site of symbolic production, which supplies the major idiom of other relations and activities. One can thus speak of a privileged institutional locus of the symbolic process, whence emanates a classificatory grid imposed upon the total culture" (211). In capitalist societies, this institutional locus is the economy. Because medicines meet an urgent need, demand is unlimited. Since people must always maintain or re-establish their health—a need is always created—medicines are extremely profitable and their consumption necessary (Van der Geest and Whyte 1989: 350). See also Kim 1993: 156.

36. Kim (1993) points out that as valuable commodities, pharmaceuticals are subject to "paths and diversions": legal and nonlegal mechanisms of exchange (Appadurai 1986). In both the Soviet and post-Soviet systems, pharmaceuticals were subject to theft, bribery, and so on. According to James Ferguson (1988), focusing on paths and diversions means addressing the cultural issues surrounding objects, as well as the political dimensions. "Paths," then, "are not simply inert, neutral cultural principles, but political instruments, while the inevitable diversions are the subversive and sometimes transformative challenge to the commodity status quo" (493). In beginning to study the movement of pharmaceuticals in Tajikistan, one is immediately confronted with the question of how pharmaceuticals, provided free by Western NGOs and allegedly kept under constant lock and key and inventory control in hospital pharmacies, end up being sold in the informal economy.

37. Under Soviet rule, medicines were provided for free to some groups of people and all hospitalized patients. Soviet citizens came to regard the provision of prescription drugs as a routine function of the state. Despite medicines and medical products being subject to the pitfalls of Soviet industrial distribution—a system plagued by periodic interruptions in supply—there were still enough medicines available for emergency needs. In this sense, they were "fetishized" in the Marxian sense: a certain meaning is considered as an inherent part of an

object's physical existence, when in fact it is due to their integration in a larger system of meaning. "The mind does not create the fetishism (as in other forms of it) but registers it in a mistaken fashion . . . [so as to] naturalize a social [object]" (Jhally 1987: 29). In Sahlins's words, "it is culture which constitutes utility" (1976: viii).

One could add to this the possibility that since, as Baudrillard (1975) has argued, in "late capitalism" everything can be understood in terms of its exchange-value (including human emotions, knowledge, concern, and even consciousness), control over the economy is in the hands of those who can manipulate both demand and consumption through mastery of the symbolic code (Kim 1993). Therefore, what may have started as a benign system of overdrugging a population to alleviate general suffering in the Soviet period has, because if its associations with modernity, resulted in a commodity fetish where pharmaceuticals are intimately linked with development and modernity, making their manipulation a sensitive marker for changes in social relations. See Van der Geest and Whyte (1988), who argue that medicines are consumed as "signs and symbols" and that people "attribute meaning and value to differences in products and to different ways of utilizing them" (6). They go on to say that to suggest that people take Western medicines simply because of their innate capacity to cure obfuscates the question of why people are so inclined to believe in the efficacy of drugs (347-48).

38. Nichter 1989.

39. In Tajikistan this occurred through the distribution of Western pharmaceuticals by international NGOs, thereby exposing the population to products for which there was no advertising and, presumably, for which no market previously existed (the former Soviet Union procured most of its drugs from Eastern European producers). Furthermore, the profit that could be made from pharmaceuticals undoubtedly encouraged their importation and sale by local entrepreneurs, and their dispensation by physicians.

40. In order to ascertain that pharmaceuticals being provided by Western NGOs were being dispensed "correctly" and in "sustainable" doses—in the same way they were dispensed in North America and Europe—Médecins Sans Frontières produced a medical guide in Russian to instruct local physicians. The practices in this manual sometimes differed from local practices and were a way of bringing local doctors in line with "international" practices. See Médecins Sans Frontières 1993, 1995. Thus, the practice of local physicians—and expectations of patients—was changed at the level of the prescriber.

41. Samuel P. Huntington (1993) refers to this encounter from a political perspective by stating that the collapse of the former Soviet Union marks a "new pattern of conflict," the clash of civilizations in world politics. I am referring to this encounter, in a more positive sense, as a meeting of cultural systems.

42. Cf. Harvey 1990.

43. Harvey 2005; Stein 2008; Rowden 2009.

44. Gordon (1991) points out that in his 1982 essay, "The Subject of Power," Foucault argues that "power is only power (rather than mere physical force or violence) when addressed to individuals who are free to act in one way or another. Power is defined as 'actions on others' actions': that it, it presupposes rather than annuls their capacity as agents; it acts upon, and through, an open set of practical and ethical possibilities" (5). See also Brown 2003. Governmentality is the process by which choices are actively shaped.

45. Harvey (1989) points out that "close scrutiny of the micro-politics of power relations in different localities, contexts, and social situations leads [Foucault] to conclude that there is an intimate relation between the systems of knowledge ('discourses') which codify techniques and practices for the exercise of social control and domination within particular localized contexts" (45). Power and knowledge act in such a way as to 'normalize society'. They operate, "by establishing a common definition of goals and procedures . . . [and] agreed-upon examples of how a well-ordered domain of human activity should be organized. These exemplars . . . immediately define what is normal; at the same time, they define practices which fall outside their system as deviant behavior in need of normalization" (Dreyfus and Rabinow 1983: 198). See also Escobar 1995: 5, 9; Crewe and Harrison 1988; Sachs 1992; Dahl and Rabo 1992; Pigg 1992.

46. Cf. Bellah et al. 1985.

47. Ferguson 1994: 254.

2. HEALTH IN THE TIME OF THE USSR

Epigraph: Chekhov 1899: 16.

1. Slonimskaia 1965.

2. The word zemstvo comes from the Russian word zemlya, which means "soil" or "earth." It has more of a sense of district/rural medicine, and was used to describe a system of bringing medical care closer to the people.

3. The government stimulated the economy through attractive fiscal and monetary policies and the development of railway and other infrastructure. As a result, industrial output grew at an annual rate of 5.72 percent from 1861 to 1913. Despite this growth, by 1913, Russia's per capita industrial production was still only 4.8 percent that of the United States (Navarro 1977: 2). See also Lane 1970: 25.

4. Frieden 1977: 544.

5. Frieden 1981: 78.

6. Field 1967: 20–21.

7. Frieden 1977: 542.

8. Frieden 1981: 90.

9. Karpov, *Zemskaia sanitarnaia organizatsiia v Rossii,* 49–50, quoted in Frieden 1981: 90.

10. Navarro 1977: 10.

11. Navarro 1977.

12. Frieden 1981: 78.

13. Frieden 1981: 91.

14. Frieden 1981: 338.

15. Bulgakov 1975.

16. It must be remembered that this was in the preantibiotic and prevaccination era, so the *zemstvo* physicians had limited tools to help them.

17. Frieden 1981: 64; Field 1967: 22, 89.

18. Frieden 1977: 542.

19. Frieden 1977: 75.

20. Navarro 1977: 12; Frieden 1981: 75.

21. Frieden 1981: 104; Hyde 1974; Knaus 1981; Ryan 1978.

22. The Julian calendar was used in Russia at that time. The revolution occurred in November 1917 according to the Gregorian calendar.

23. Frieden 1981: 91.

24. For more on the impact of the Industrial Revolution, see Marx 1990: vol. 1, chs. 27–28; Engels 1958. See also Hobsbawm 1964; Thompson 1968.

25. Banerji 1979; Doyal 1979; Igun 1992; Field 1967.

26. For a broader overview of the Soviet welfare state, see Madison 1968; Yonowitch 1977.

27. Ravitch 1937: 165–68.

28. Veressayev 1916: 191.

29. Hyde 1974: 19–20.

30. Mark Field (1967), a sociologist who studied health care in the Soviet Union extensively, suggests that some of the Bolshevik ideas about medical services in a new society, including the expectation that physicians must serve the proletariat, the new ruling class in Communist society, were contrary to the ethical universalism of medicine, and as such, clashed with the basic medical ethics of most physicians. The Bolsheviks, Field says, countered that this position of ethical universalism did not seem to have existed before the revolution. They accused the doctors of "medical sabotage," which, Field says, was difficult to believe of this group with "its traditions and a strong sense of social duty and professional ethics" (57). See also Navarro 1977.

31. Although doctors were implicated in supporting White Guardists and sometimes withholding assistance from Bolsheviks, Field says that this was an excuse used by the Bolsheviks to justify "the gradual elimination of the medical profession as a corporate body" (1967: 57). Navarro counters by saying that it would be absurd to assume that the medical profession would not fight curtailment of their prerogatives. Citing the support by the Chilean Medical Association

for forces opposed to President Salvador Allende, he says that "when having to choose between the defense of its privileges and the Hippocratic oath, the choice is quite clear" (1977: 20).

32. See Lenin 1926: 346, 420.

33. Navarro 1977: 28.

34. For a more detailed discussion of this subject, see Pipes 1990.

35. *Sobranie ukazanii I rasporiashenii rabochego I krest'ianskogo pravitel'stva,* no. 5, otdel pervyi, 16 dekabria, st. 81 1917: 72–73, quoted in Hutchinson 1990: 178.

36. Hutchinson 1990: 178.

37. Navarro 1977: 17.

38. Schecter 1992: 34; Field 1967: 57, 89; Navarro 1977: 19.

39. See Ryan 1978: 160. The Soviet view of medicine—as a service to man and society—is captured by the compulsory oath of Soviet doctors, which differs from the Hippocratic Oath professed by physicians in other countries:

- Having received the lofty title of doctor and having taken up a doctor's occupation I solemnly swear:
- to devote all my knowledge and powers to the protection and improvement of man's health and the cure and prevention of illness; to work conscientiously in the place demanded by the interests of society;
- to be prepared always to provide medical care, to treat patients with attention and solicitude; to keep medical secrets;
- to improve continuously my medical knowledge and skills as a doctor; to assist through my work the development of the science and practice of medicine;
- to turn for advice, if the interests of the patient demand this, to professional colleagues and never to refuse advice and assistance to them;
- to preserve and develop the noble traditions of our country's medicine; in all my actions to guide myself by the principles of communist morality; to remember always a Soviet doctor's lofty calling and responsibility to the people and the Soviet government.
- I swear to remain faithful to this oath throughout the whole of my life.

40. Collective workers councils.

41. Navarro 1977: 26.

42. Ryan 1978: 7.

43. Navarro 1977: 16.

44. This was aimed at stimulating the economy, with a focus on consumer goods rather than capital goods. Certain sectors of industry were preferentially encouraged. "It was during this period the Lenin coined the frequently-quoted aphorism that communism was Soviet power plus electricity" (Navarro 1977:32).

45. Hyde 1974: 88.

46. Field 1967.

47. Though many physicians died in the civil war and the numerous epidemics in that period, the early reforms resulted in an increase in the number of physicians from 22,000 in 1917 to 63,162 in 1928. See Navarro 1977: 25.

48. Soloviev 1940, quoted in Field 1967: 63. Originally presented by Dr. Z. P. Soloviev at the Fifth All-Russian Congress of Health Departments, held in Moscow in the summer of 1924.

49. Navarro says that collectivization was necessary to allow the extraction of surplus value from agricultural labor for the support of industrialization (1977:42).

50. Stalin quoted in Navarro 1977: 35.

51. Following Trotsky, who had said, "The strength and stability of regimes is defined in the last analysis by the relative productivity of labor" (quoted in Bettelheim 1976: 27).

52. See Field 1967: 65; Navarro 1977: 43. Field argues that while this placed a lot of political pressure on the health system, it was not accompanied with sufficient resources to ensure that everybody had access to such care.

53. Hyde 1974: 100.

54. Quoted in Navarro 1977: 42. Navarro cites Gaston Rimlinger's 1971 book, *Welfare Policy and Industrialization in Europe, America and Russia.*

55. Segregated subsystems existed for workers of specialty occupational groups. For example, during the expansion of the railways and the construction of the trans-Siberian railroad, an extensive network of medical units designated specifically for treating personnel connected to the railroad industry grew across the country. By 1975, this network was estimated to include some 6,000 separate facilities and 126,000 staff, including 34,000 doctors. These facilities were "considered to provide such high-quality care that workers from other sectors of the economy occasionally [sought] admission by back-door methods" (Ryan 1978: 112). This further fragmentation and duplication of the health care system caused problems on several levels, including administrative, budgetary, and quality of care.

56. Lenin saw the struggle against illness as part of the communist struggle. Ideologically Marxism defines illness as a product of the biosocial: physiological threat and destructive social conditions (such as the exploitation of the worker under capitalism). So as not to cede ideological ground after the push for rapid industrialization starting in 1928, the Soviet health services redefined the therapeutic process as a "socialist productive process," emphasizing its meaning as a scientific and rational battle against pathogenesis, and held that as communist society was perfected toward true socialism, illness would diminish and disappear. See Field 1967: 160.

57. Field 1967: 163.

58. Field 1967: 6.

59. Field 1967: 70.

60. Harvard Medical School and Open Society Institute 1999.

61. Navarro 1977: 64–65.

62. For example, in the system there were few generalist doctors, and medical points and ambulatoria had to send patients to either the *rayon* (district) or

oblast (provincial) hospitals for further care. Thus there was little continuity of care between the hospital or ambulatory systems, and the lack of coordination led to unnecessary hospitalization. For example, in the town of Uryupwisk, it was found that 28 percent of inpatients could have been treated in domiciliary care under the supervision of a primary care physician (Ryan 1972). See also Hyde 1974: 127; Navarro 1977.

63. Shimkin 1958: 1384.

64. Field 1967: 98.

65. Field 1967: 114.

66. Field 1967: 112.

67. Field 1967: 115.

68. See Field 1967: 170. Field cites an original publication: T. F. Fox, "Russia Revisited," *Lancet,* Oct. 9 and 16, 1954, pp. 748-53, 803-7. Field says that "in actual practice the physicians are so overburdened with the task of providing clinical services that they have little time and energy (except in the most formal manner) to give to prevention, and they feel that this task belongs exclusively to those working in the SES stations" (169).

69. Eberstadt 2006: 1384.

70. Schecter 1992: 78; Mezentseva and Rimachevskaya 1990; Field 1995.

71. Field 1995; Ryan 1978.

72. Field 1995. Another offshoot of the limited funding in the no-fee health system was that health care became highly stratified, with hospitals for elites *(nachalstvo)*—usually Politburo and Central Committee members, leading academicians, and athletes—stocked with medicines and functioning equipment. A disproportionate share of limited health resources went to this group free of charge, while common people had to settle for less (Field 1995; Ryan 1978). This system was institutionalized as a subsystem of the health system, run by a group within the Ministry of Health known as the "Fourth Division." See also Knaus 1981: 135.

73. Communist Party of the Soviet Union 1961: 87-88.

74. Health care was underwritten as a public service paid for through general state revenues and taxation, and therefore paid for indirectly by the population.

75. According to Hyde (1974), "Health resorts and sanatoria have played a significant role in reducing morbidity, strengthening health and prolonging human life, and have helped to compensate people for many deficiencies suffered as a result of priorities for rapid industrialization and defense expenditure" (80). In fact, some industrial enterprises had private sanatoria for their workers; those that did not shared in the cost of the visit.

76. Field points out that people were never made aware of the nature of the financing for services: payments made by industrial and agricultural organizations from their profits, income tax, and the hidden turnover tax charged on consumer goods (1967: 191)

77. Ryan 1978: 29.

78. Ryan 1978: 28.

79. Ryan 1978: 131; Knaus 1981: 157.

80. Ryan 1978: 132.

81. Knaus 1981:114.

82. Knaus 1981: 129.

83. Schecter 1992; Helmstadter 1990.

84. Knaus 1981: 129.

85. Davis and Feshbach 1980. As Cockerham (1999) points out, "This situation is without precedent in modern history. Nowhere else has health worsened so seriously in peacetime among industrialized nations. . . . The likelihood that an entire group of industrialized societies under a stable administrative system would experience such a prolonged deterioration in public health was completely unexpected" (1). The original report of age-specific mortality rates as compiled by Davis showed that only the mortality rates of groups of ages five to twenty stayed level between 1964 and 1976; all other age-group specific mortality rates increased distinctly, some by almost 40 percent (zero to one year and forty to fifty years). Overall mortality increased by 32 percent (Davis 2006, table 1, p. 1403). Infant mortality increased by more than a third between 1970 and 1975, and reached 40 per 1,000 (compared with <13 per 1,000 in Europe) by 1980 (Eberstadt 2006: 1384). As Eberstadt (2006) points out, "The only country in modern times to have suffered a more serious setback in life expectancy was . . . Pol Pot's Cambodia. Clearly, something in Russia is going very, very wrong" (1384–85). See also Cockerham 1999: 9.

86. Cockerham 1999: 9–10.

87. Eberstadt 2006: 1385.

88. A *samizdat*—a self-published work circulated informally through underground channels—by a "Boris Komarov" claimed to cite suppressed official data showing that birth defects in the USSR were rising by 6 percent each year because of the effects of pollution (and probably alcohol consumption) on pregnancies (Boris Komarov (pseud.), *The Destruction of Nature: The Intensification of the Ecological Crisis in the USSR*, Frankfurt/Main: Posev Verlag, 1978, later published in English by M. E. Sharpe, quoted in Eberstadt 2006).

89. Eberstadt 2006: 1385; Goldman 1972.

90. Eberstadt 2006: 1386.

91. Eberstadt, 2006: 1386. According to a Soviet official quoted in the Davis-Feshbach report, health expenditures as a share of the national budget were 6.6 percent in 1965, and decreased to 5.2 percent in 1978 (1386). See also Field 1995.

92. Mezentseva and Rimachevskaya 1990; Field 1995.

93. Helmstadter 1990: 12.

94. Schecter 1992: 96.

95. Herxheimer 1991: 1135.

96. Helmstadter 1990: 12.

97. Herxheimer 1991: 1135; Schecter 1992: 98; Nichols 1991: 38.

98. Internal production of medicines had dropped markedly, such that during the first six months of 1990, medicine imports were up 50 percent compared to 1989 (Helmstadter 1990: 12).

99. World Health Organization 1996.

100. According to Chandani (1998) in 1996 emergency aid covered 80 percent of the total drug volume, with Médecins Sans Frontières providing $200,000 in essential drugs and AKF providing $180,000 in specialty medicines.

101. In addition, the lack of laboratory reagents and other consumable supplies has meant that the local hospital laboratories have been forced to discontinue all but the simplest of tests, including screening blood for infectious agents (e.g., HIV, Hepatitis A, Hepatitis B, Hepatitis C, and VDRL).

102. Sigerist 1947.

103. Stuckler and Basu 2013.

3. SEEKING HELP AT THE END OF EMPIRE

1. Unlike their western Tajik neighbors who speak Tajik, a dialect of Persian (Farsi), the inhabitants of Badakhshan speak languages classified in the Eastern Iranian language family, thought to be linked to the language spoken by the Eastern Iranian Sogdians. The Sogdians are an ancient Iranian civilization (529-323 B.C.). Sogdia was a province of the Achaemenid Persian Empire. Sogdian is a Middle Iranian language.

2. In fact, as Bliss (2006) points out, to this day in parts of Badakhshan local rulers cite Alexander in matters of ideology and claim descent from him (55). After Alexander, the region fell under the control of the Persians, the Indians, the Bactrians, and ultimately the Chinese (eastern Pamir region). By the third century A.D., the region had fallen under the Persian Sassanid empire, at which point the Sogdians, an eastern Iranian people practicing Zoroastrianism, occupied Badakhshan (ancient Sogdia). They fell under the influence of the Hephthalites, also known as the White Huns, in the fifth century A.D. Also see Wilhelm Tomasheck, *Centralasiatische Studien I. Sogdiana. Wien,* quoted in Bliss 2006.

3. Bliss 2006: 56-58.

4. The Emirate of Bukhara was a Central Asian state that existed from 1785 to 1920 and was based in the Persian (Tajik) city of Bukhara, now in Uzbekistan. Also see Bliss 2006: 60-63.

5. Bliss 2006: 72-74.

6. Within Shi'ism there are many branches, the largest being the Twelve-Imam Shi'a, *Ithna Ashari,* and the Isma'ilis. See Esmail and Nanji 1977: 232; Makarem

1967: 47; Nasr 1966: 147–58. Shi'a Islam, like Sunni Islam, stems from an orthodox interpretation about religious authority that existed from the very inception of the religion. The split between the two interpretations is linked to an event said to have taken place in 632 A.D., five days before the month of pilgrimage (*hajj*). According to Shi'a Muslims, during a stopover at the pond (*ghadir*) of Khumm, the Prophet Muhammad was said to have received a revelation from God, after which the Prophet declared his cousin (and son-in-law) Ali Ibn Abu Talib as his vice-regent, or imam. See the Qur'an, V:67. According to tradition, the Prophet is then said to have prayed to God: "Oh God, help whomever helps him, opposes whomever opposes him, support whomever supports him, forsake whomever forsakes him, and turn the right to whatever direction he turns" (Makarem 1967: 29). Those who believed in *Imamat* as a divine mechanism for the continuing guidance of the human race—a means of interpreting the Qur'anic law, *shari'ah*, after the death of the Prophet in 632 A.D.—became known as "followers of Ali," the *shī'atul 'Alī* (Shi'a). Those who believed that the Prophet had left no instructions furthering the passage of divine authority were known as "the people of tradition and the consensus of opinion," *ahl al-sunna wa'l-jama'ah* (Sunni). See Makarem 1967; Dabashi 1993: 98; Esmail and Nanji 1977: 230; Nasr 1966: 148.

7. Thobani 1993.

8. Aga Khan IV, who was designated as the next imam on the death of his grandfather, while he was a student at Harvard, lives in his chateau, Aiglemont, near Paris, France. His followers believe the imam is imbued with the religious legitimacy to interpret the Message of Islam in a dynamic and temporal way, allowing Isma'ili Muslims to refer to the Qur'an, the Hadith (the teachings of the Prophet Muhammed), and to their living imam for guidance. See Bocock 1971: 366; cf. Aga Khan III 1954. Also see Daftary 1994: 2.

9. Bliss 2006: 60.

10. By the tenth century, the Isma'ilis had risen to power in North Africa. This empire, named *al-Fatimiyyun* (Fatimid) after the Prophet Muhammed's daughter, Fatima, lasted for over two hundred years. In 969 A.D., the Fatimids, under the direction of their imam, al-Mu'izz, founded the city of Cairo (al-Qahira), which was to serve as both their capital and the seat of intellectual and political development (Esmail and Nanji 1977: 234). The Fatimid Empire encompassed large parts of North Africa and the Middle East—including Mecca, Jerusalem, and Sicily—with a political and religious network that went as far as India (Steinberg 2011: 34). This center, driven by Fatimid patronage of scientific research and cultural activity, attracted mathematicians, physicians, astronomers, and thinkers from all over the Muslim world, particularly to its two great universities, al-Azhar and Dar al-Hikmah (Nanji 1987: 180). It was during this period that the major Isma'ili works emerged, including those of the Persian poet and philosopher, Nasir Khusrow, who was the missionary (*da'i*) that was ultimately sent to Badakhshan (Nasr 1966: 159).

11. See Daftary 1994: 44. Following the reign of the eighth Fatimid caliph (and 18th Isma'ili Imam), Imam al-Mustansir, in 1095 A.D., a schism occurred in the Fatimid court and the Isma'ili movement branched into two parts (Daftary 1994: 3). Some of the followers accepted Nizar ibn al-Mustansir, al-Mustansir's oldest son, as the Imam, while others followed his younger brother, al-Musta'li bi'llah. After a short military campaign, Nizar was captured and imprisoned. His young son, Hadi bin al-Nizar, was forced to flee with his father's followers—believed by some historians to be the forebears of the present-day Isma'ilis of Badakhshan—to Isma'ili-controlled mountain fortresses in the South Caspian Rudbar region of present-day Iran. This series of forts—the most famous of which was called Alamut ("eagle's nest")—had been established during the time of the Fatimids under the guidance of Hasan-i Sabbah, the representative (*hujja*, "proof") of the imam. The imams assumed control of the different Iranian communities from Hasan and consolidated an empire involving a number of mountaintop strongholds that was to last for over 150 years from 1090 to 1256 A.D. (Esmail and Nanji 1977: 248).

Based at Alamut, the Isma'ili communities of the region faced the threat of destruction from a number of different dynasties. Initially the biggest threat came from the Sunni Seljuq dynasty in Turkey. At the beginning of the twelfth century, the Seljuq army, "conquered and destroyed Tabas [in southern Khurasan of present-day Iran] and other Isma'ili castles, pillaged the Isma'ili settlements and enslaved some of their inhabitants" (Lewis 1980: 52). In Isfahan, western Persia, the sultan encouraged the massacre of Isma'ilis, which spread as far west as Baghdad, where Isma'ili books were burned. In 1126, the Seljuq sultan, Sanjar, again launched an offensive against the Isma'ilis in the eastern part of the kingdom (present-day Quhistan, Nishapur, and Khurasan), where the vizier gave orders to "make war against the Isma'ilis," to "kill them wherever they were," and "to pillage their property and enslave their women" (Lewis 1980: 64).

A later threat came from Jenghiz Khan, who by 1220 had captured the Persian cities of Balkh, Marv, and Nishapur, and made himself master of eastern Iran (Lewis 1980: 89). In 1256, the Isma'ili Empire around Alamut was destroyed by the Mongol invasion, which resulted in the massacre of various Isma'ili communities. Those Nizari Isma'ilis who survived the Mongol massacres sought refuge in Afghanistan, India, and other regions of Central Asia, including Badakhshan (Daftary 1994: 44). Following the Mongol invasion and waning of Isma'ili influence in Persia, the movement went underground, and as a result, knowledge of its history was lost. The faith continued to survive despite considerable religious and political persecution. The imams later resettled in southeast Iran among a preexisting Isma'ili community. In 1817, the Isma'ili imam Khalil Allah, who had settled in the town of Yezd, was assassinated by elements within the Persian Qajar court. Fearing a massive political crisis, the ruling shah of Iran granted Qum and Mahallat to his son, Hasan Ali Shah, and conferred upon him the title of Aga Khan (great leader) (Esmail and Nanji 1977: 253). In 1848, Hasan Ali Shah Aga Khan migrated from Iran to India, to eventually settle among his followers in Bombay (Gellner 1981: 105–6). From there, under the leadership of his grandson, Muhammad Shah Aga Khan III, the Imamat shifted its focus to education, health, economic, and cultural life (Nanji 1987: 183; Esmail and Nanji 1977: 255).

12. According to Bliss (2006) Isma'ilis in Badakhshan were described by Sunnis as "shameful" and as *kafir* (infidels), and even Shi'a groups sometimes viewed them with resentment. See Bliss 2006: 222; Biddulph 1880: 121.

13. According to Bliss (2006) during this period the population was treated harshly, with the aim of "exterminating and subjugating the shameful Shiites and false Ismaelites, who live in those regions of Badakhshan and Chitral" (Kreutzmann 1996: 79, quoted in Bliss 2006: 63).

14. Bliss 2006: 222; Becker 1968: 215.

15. See Poladi 1989. Accounts of these pogroms not only filtered back to remote areas of the Isma'ili dominated Pamiri mountains, but in certain low-lying areas such as Yazgulam, the entire Isma'ili population was forced to convert. Stein 1933: 283, quoted in Bliss 2006.

16. Although welcomed by the residents of Badakhshan, like many other European colonial powers, the Russians were on a "civilizing mission" that was at times brutal. Russian colonialism was predicated on the grounds that through the "Russification" and concurrent modernization of Central Asia, people could be freed from the burdensome "traditions" that were perceived to keep them mired in the past. Islamic beliefs and practices were often considered antimodern, oppressive, antiprogressive, and of course, an "opiate of the people," and were thus seen as a legitimate object for destruction (Shahrani 1995: 277). Shahrani (1995) notes that this continued from tsarist times into the Soviet colonial project in Central Asia, which, though operating under the aegis of Marxism-Leninism—and unlike most Western colonial ventures was not aimed at economic exploitation and territorial control alone—still used ruthless tactics of superior arms and military technology to realize their goals (thus being both revolutionary and colonial) (277). While many people, mostly peasants, benefited from Soviet rule in Central Asia—by lifting the yoke of direct feudalism, allowing them to benefit directly from the output of the lands they worked, and providing literacy, higher education, housing and health care—many suffered (Pipes 1990; Fitzpatrick 1992; Allworth 1994; Hobsbawm 1994). The Russians, and later the Bolsheviks, had a complex relationship with the practice of Islam. In 1917, following the Bolshevik Revolution, the Soviet government declared to the Muslims: "Henceforth your beliefs and customs, your national and cultural institutions are declared free and inviolable. Arrange your national life freely and unimpeded. You are entitled to this" (Vakhabov 1980:12). This feeling, however, was not to last for long. While Lenin may have believed that the Central Asians

had the right to self-rule along their own cultural lines, Stalin's ascendance changed that (Vakhabov 1980; Lenin 1926; Suny 1992: 28–29). Under Stalin, Islam was anathema to the Soviets because it represented backwardness to a state desirous of rapid industrialization and Europeanization (cf. Bataille 1988; Shahrani 1995; Allworth 1994). During the collectivization of the 1930s, there was a period when "traditionalism" and "anti-Sovietism" were considered synonymous (Poliakov 1992).

17. For example, it is said that the Soviet state used this to "divide and rule" in Tajikistan (Atkin 1989). According to Lewis (1980), Russian scholars, who had already received some Isma'ili manuscripts from Syria, discovered that they had Isma'ilis within the frontiers of their empire, and in 1902 Count Alexis Bobrinskoy published an account of the organization and distribution of the Isma'ilis in Russian Central Asia (Bobrinskoy 1902). At about the same time, a colonial official, A. Polovtsev, acquired a copy of an Isma'ili religious book written in Persian; it was deposited in the Asiatic Museum of the Imperial Russian Academy of the Sciences. Another copy followed, and between 1914 and 1918 the museum acquired a collection of Isma'ili manuscripts, brought from Shugnan by the orientalists I. I. Zarubin and A. A. Semyonov. With these and other subsequently acquired manuscripts, Russian scholars were able to examine the religious literature and beliefs of the Isma'ilis of the Pamir and of the adjoining Afghan districts of Badakhshan. See Ivanov 1932: 418; Minorsky 1960; Bobrinskoy 1902; Bertel 1962: 11–16.

18. In his memoirs, Aga Khan III wrote that he was aware that he had many followers in Russia and Central Asia (Aga Khan III 1954: 20–22). There is some indication that the Soviet government was aware of occasional communications between the Aga Khan and his followers (Sergeyev 1965).

19. According to anthropologist Jonah Steinberg, the arrival of these men was seen as a momentous event, and became fabled (2011: 89).

20. According to Felmy (1996) Aga Khan III opened schools in Hunza, Pakistan, using the funds he had received from his followers: his weight in diamonds. The same funds, expanded by his own contribution, were used to create the Diamond Jubilee Investment Trust (Felmy 1996: 74).

21. The family of the Aga Khan has participated actively in nation-state politics and the institutions associated with them. As Williams (1988) writes: "The Aga Khan's family exhibits exemplary involvement in international affairs. The current Imam's grandfather, Sultan Muhammad Shah, Aga Khan III, was President of the League of Nations, and his father, Prince Aly, was Pakistan's Ambassador to the United Nations. His uncle, Prince Sadruddin Aga Khan, was United Nations High Commissioner for Refugees from 1965 to 1977 . . . and his brother, Prince Amyn, served from 1965 to 1968 with the United Nations Secretariat" (206–7).

22. Steinberg 2011: 11. See also Kaiser 1994 and Kaiser 1996 for a discussion of the Aga Khan Development Network.

23. Although nondenominational by charter, the AKF looks to the Isma'ili community for financial contributions and voluntary service. Also see Steinberg 2011: 11; cf. Kaiser 1994.

24. Aga Khan Foundation 1997: 3.

25. See Slim and Hodizoda 2001: 517. For a description of the war, see Keshavjee 1998 and Matveeva 2009.

26. Matveeva 2009.

27. The Aga Khan spoke about Tajikistan at the Massachusetts Institute of Technology graduation ceremony in Cambridge, Massachusetts, in May 1994. After telling the graduates and their families that the country had become the focus of one of the "most interesting encounters of the day," he went on at length:

> It is here [in Tajikistan], and in the other Central Asian republics, that three great cultures encounter one another: the ex-Communist world, the Muslim world, and the Western world. It is here that those three cultures could forge a success that would contrast starkly with the brutal failure in Bosnia. The result of the encounter in Tajikistan may determine much about the way history unfolds over the coming decades, so it is worth thinking a bit about the stance that each of these cultures might take in preparing for this encounter. That thought might lead one to ask what it would take for this, or any, encounter to be constructive. *I suggest that there are four pre-requisites for success. For each of the cultures, the result should, first, draw on its strengths and, second, be consistent with its goals. Third, the result should be a sustainable improvement in the current situation. And fourth, the transition should be humane.*
>
> Each of these three cultures has something to bring to the solution of the problems of Tajikistan. The West has many strengths, but prominent among them are science and democracy (with their public mechanisms for self-correction) and also private institutions, liberal economics, and a recognition of fundamental human rights. The Muslim world offers deep roots in a system of values, emphasizing service, charity and a sense of common responsibility, and denying what it sees to be the false dichotomy between religious and secular lives. The ex-Communist world, although it failed economically, made important investments in social welfare, with particular emphasis on the status of women, and was able to achieve in Tajikistan impressive social cohesion. These are a powerful array of strengths and goals. Just how to combine them to solve Tajikistan's problems is not clear. But if the outcome is to be sustainable, it seems necessary to concentrate resources on the development of private institutions, of accountable public institutions and of human potential.
>
> But how to get from here to there without inflicting cruel damage on a people already buffeted by shortages and change? Again, the way is not entirely clear, but one should strive to retain the powerful ties of mutual support that—in different ways—bind individuals together in Muslim and Communist societies. *And one should see that the impressive gains in health and education are not lost in the transition, for it would be unconscionable to allow, for example, the equality of men and women that has been achieved in Tajikistan over the last 60 years to be erased in the transition to a market economy.*
>
> These are the prerequisites that I hope the representatives of these three important cultures will keep in mind as they have their encounter over Tajikistan. If the encounter of the Muslim world, the West and the ex-Communist world takes

account of the need for each to draw on its own strengths, to be consistent with its goals, to strive for a sustainable, improved outcome and to ensure a humane transition, then the encounter will have been as successful as it is important. Indeed, the importance of Tajikistan has, if anything, increased in recent years, as events in neighboring countries continue to remind us. (Aga Khan IV 1994; italics added)

28. Aga Khan Development Network 2012; Steinberg 2011: 11.

29. Cf. Kaiser 1994; Kaiser 1996; Steinberg 2011.

30. Aga Khan IV 1967.

31. Kaiser 1994: 26. According to Kaiser, institutions in the Aga Khan's network operate in a manner similar to subsidiaries of a large multinational corporation, the profits of which remain within the network for reinvestment in social development projects. Also see Becker and Sklar 1987: 2.

32. Kaiser 1994: 219.

33. Aga Khan IV 1976: 7.

34. Aga Khan IV 1982; Kaiser 1996: 1.

35. Aga Khan IV 1982.

36. Although the Aga Khan has argued that strengthening institutions of civil society is one way to strengthen democratic competence and accountability, he has been careful to uphold ideas of popular sovereignty, justice, and dignity (Aga Khan IV 2008: 104, 110, 116). In a speech at the annual meeting of the European Bank for Reconstruction and Development in Tashkent, Uzbekistan, in May 2003, the Aga Khan suggested it would be a mistake to simply support the growth of the private sector in lieu of the state; more important was better understanding how institutions of civil society should relate to government (Aga Khan IV 2008: 18–21). Even participation in the free market, which the Aga Khan has stated is essential to his community's future in the global economy, has been placed in a particular context. "Economic development—increasing the production and consumption of goods and services in the economy and expanding and improving the quality of employment opportunities for a country's population and its disposable income—is certainly critical," he has argued. But while "growth plays a central role in increasing human welfare and dignity," he said, "other dimensions and challenges to development play at least an equally important role." "Unfortunately," he continued, "many of them are not easily measured in conventional economic terms or addressed through usual economic programs and policies" (Aga Khan IV 2008: 18–21). Also see *Daily News*, September 20, 1982, quoted in Kaiser 1994: 80.

37. Steinberg 2011.

38. Lewis 2007: 19. See also Edwards 1996; Fowler 1997; Leat 1995.

39. Lewis 2007: 19. See also Pollit 1993.

40. Edwards and Hulme 1996a: 12.

41. Kaiser 1994: 219.

42. Kaiser 1994: 216–17. See also Becker and Sklar 1987.

4. THE HEALTH CRISIS IN BADAKHSHAN

Epigraphs: Keshavjee 1998.

1. *Moom* is the word for "grandmother" in Shugni, a local language from one of Badakhshan's districts that is used as a lingua franca in the region. The conversation that follows did not occur in one sitting but over one and a half months in and around the same setting, often with exactly the same people present, and with the children hiding behind various beams and structural supports. The text has been presented in a single sequence for stylistic purposes only.

2. Poliakov 1992: 88–90.

3. Poliakov 1992: 59. Cf. Farmer 1992 and Ryan 1971 for a discussion of how blaming the victim obscures structural violence.

4. One U.S. dollar was the equivalent of three hundred Tajik rubles, the currency being used at the time.

5. See UNDP 1995.

6. According to a water and sanitation study contracted by the Aga Khan Foundation, the problem in Khorog is not just emptying the toilets but the day-to-day cleaning of the facilities. Furthermore, no public toilets have functioning sinks. From an unpublished internal report written by Eric Dudle, September 1995.

7. Keshavjee 1998; Jain 1985; Meegama 1980.

8. Keshavjee 1998: 130.

9. Local physicians attribute the prevalence of rickets to the swaddling of young infants by their mothers and the resulting lack of exposure to direct sunlight, as well as to improper diet. See Keshavjee 1998.

10. According to a report conducted by Epicentre for the Aga Khan Foundation in 1994, 9.4 percent of pregnant women exhibited signs of severe anemia and an additional 10.9 percent of moderate anemia ("Demographic, Mortality, Nutrition and Immunization survey in Gorno Badakhshan," by Philippe Cavailler and Serge Doussantousse, March 1995). Anemia may actually be more common than indicated by these figures: normal hemoglobin values at lower altitudes might indicate anemia at a higher altitude, such as Badakhshan's.

11. Chen et al. 1981; Martorell and Ho 1984; Scrimshaw 1978.

12. Birkenes 1996.

13. Because the Pharmaceutical Use Survey relied on individual honesty and self-reporting, the values may be an underestimate of true household income. One U.S. dollar was the equivalent of three hundred Tajik rubles at that time.

14. Material is taken from "Health and Nutrition Survey, Autonomous Oblast of Gorno Badakhshan (Tajikistan)," July–August 1996, revised February 1997.

15. This corresponded to 2,877 Tajik rubles at the time. See also Médecins Sans Frontières 1993: 47. Values given in the text are the average price of generic drugs in 1988 in French francs. The values have been increased by 5 percent per annum, compounded, and divided by 5.5 to convert to 1997 U.S. dollars.

16. Keshavjee 1998.

17. As the health system disintegrated, many poor people turned to traditional medicine—Badakhshan has a long tradition of using high-mountain herbs for healing—and religious healers for help. Traditional medicine had been used also during Soviet times, but in the crisis of the post-Soviet period—which some people I spoke to cited as the cause of the "revival of folk medicine"—people began to turn to traditional healers to treat serious illnesses, for which they would have gone to the hospital during the Soviet era. As we went through villages surveying households, we found many people using amulets and blessed water to cure their ailments. They told us that they would have preferred to use medicines but either could not find any or could not afford them. In the thousand-household pharmaceutical use study that Ahmed and I carried out for AKF, 62 percent of respondents reported taking nonallopathic medicines for their illness, while 67 percent reported having consulted a *khalifa*, or religious leader, for medical help.

18. Aga Khan Foundation 1997: 20, emphasis added.

19. Farmer 1999.

20. For a full text of the letters, see Keshavjee 1998, appendix D.

21. Because the social structures that allow structural violence seem so ordinary in our ways of understanding the world, they are almost invisible. Differential access to resources, political power, education, health care, and legal standing are just a few examples. The idea of *structural violence* is closely linked to *social injustice* and the social machinery of oppression. See Galtung 1969: 167–91; Farmer 2005: 191; Galtung 1993: 106; Gilligan 1997: 306. See also Farmer 1992 and Ryan 1971 for further discussion of how blaming the victim obscures structural violence.

22. Keshavjee 2006: 72–93.

23. Keshavjee 1998, emphasis added.

24. Equally worrisome are changes that affect the status of women and, in turn, infant mortality. See Caldwell 1986; Chen et al. 1981; Farah and Preston 1982; Caldwell and McDonald 1982; Black 1984. See also Wise et al. 1985; Carstairs and Morris 1989; Brennan and Lancashire 1978; Gortmaker 1979; Flegg 1982; Frenzen and Hogan 1982; Bor et al. 1993; Lundberg 1993.

25. Blackburn 1991: 41–42.

26. Desjarlais et al. 1995; Blackburn 1991.

27. For example, even in the Soviet period, household income directly affected variables such as diet, use of health care, and housing quality, as well as access to care (it was customary to give doctors a bribe) (Ryan 1989). There was certainly a large gap between services provided in urban and rural areas. For example, Sovietwide data indicates that in 1986, only 35 percent of rural district hospitals had hot water, 27 percent had no indoor toilet facilities, and 17 percent had no running water (Velkoff 1992: 7).

5. MINDING THE GAP?

Epigraph: Dostoyevsky 1955.

1. ZdravReform 1994: 1.

2. USAID 1997: 1.

3. USAID 1997: 12.

4. This included the following countries: Armenia, Georgia, Kyrgyzstan, Azerbaijan, Moldova, Tajikistan, Russia, Belarus, Ukraine, Kazakhstan, Turkmenistan, and Uzbekistan. See Aksartova 2005: 116.

5. Aksartova 2005: 91.

6. USAID had to work through nongovernmental contractors, Aksartova suggests, because they faced the "very non-trivial task of finding ways to commit billions of dollars," without working through governments (2005: 125).

7. ZdravReform 1996.

8. ZdravReform 1999: 7.

9. ZdravReform 1999: 6; italics added.

10. ZdravReform 1999: 6.

11. Jones 2012.

12. ZdravReform 1999: 7.

13. Borowitz et al. 1999: 33.

14. Borowitz et al. 1999: 33.

15. Tajikistan was not part of USAID's ZdravReform project at that time, mostly because of security issues. Tajikistan later became part of ZdravPlus, USAID's successor program to ZdravReform.

16. I discuss the reasons for why the doctors were doing this in Keshavjee 1998.

17. Cueto 2004: 1864–74.

18. Hardon and Kanji 1992: 114. See also UNICEF 1988b.

19. McPake 2002: 120–39.

20. Gilson et al. 2001: 37–67; WHO 1988; UNICEF 1990a, 1990b; Litvack and Bodart 1993: 369–83; McPake et al. 1993: 1383–95.

21. Lee and Goodman 2002: 97–119.

22. "The Bamako Initiative" 1988.

23. Kanji (1992) points out that the involvement of donors in the drug field is linked to the strength of their own drug industry: "On the whole, US, Swiss, German and Japanese aid agencies have been negative about the essential drugs concept and, where they have supported drugs programmes, the support has tended to reinforce their vested interest. The US, Switzerland, Germany and Japan all have large and powerful drugs industries and their lobbying power and influence over government policy is significant" (76). See also Akin et al. 1987.

24. Chabot 1988; "The Bamako Initiative" 1988; and Kanji 1989.

25. Kanji 1989: 113. Kanji has written extensively on pharmaceuticals in poor countries, including the dangers of the Bamako Initiative. See Kanji 1989, 1992; Kanji and Hardon 1992; and Hardon and Kanji 1992.

26. Kanji 1989: 113.

27. Kanji 1989: 115.

28. Dahlgren 1991; Foltz 1994.

29. Waddington and Enyimayew 1989; Yoder 1989; Moses et al. 1992; Awofeso 1998.

30. Kanji 1989: 115.

31. "The Bamako Initiative" 1988, italics added.

32. Hecht et al. 1993: 213–42.

33. Creese 1990.

34. Dumoulin and Kaddar 1993, quoted in Desclaux 2004.

35. The World Health Organization argued that middle- and low-income countries were not uniform and could not all be treated the same. See WHO 1991. See also Dahlgren 1991; Abel-Smith and Rawall 1992; Cross et al. 1986; Gilson 1988; Foster 1989; Waddington and Enyimayew 1989.

36. Lee and Goodman 2002; McPake et al. 1993.

37. Keshavjee 1998: 146.

38. Keshavjee 1998: 517.

39. In their proposal to USAID, the foundation set several explicit goals:

1. Improved availability and accessibility of essential drugs in project areas.

2. Greater efficiency and effectiveness of clinical case management and prescribing practices directly at the primary level of health care, and indirectly at all levels of care.

3. The establishment of a monetised system for purchasing and supplying pharmaceuticals which supports national plans for health sector reform and improved self-sufficiency in financing and resource management.

4. Increased involvement of communities in decision making for essential drugs management. (AKF, cited in Keshavjee 1998)

40. Given its role in Badakhshan as an institution of the imamat, AKF was worried that if they took on the role of providing pharmaceuticals in addition to supplying food and fuel, it would appear that they were taking over from the government. They also feared that once they entered into providing pharmaceuticals, "it would be difficult to withdraw from this activity" (Keshavjee 1998: 517).

41. The term "international guidelines" in some ways sanitizes the real story about how neoliberalism gets into the bodies of the poor through norms and guidelines that shape practice. The guidelines were, after all, not truly "international" since they did not include Soviet practices and guidelines. In fact, the Soviet Union had an extensive scientific community that conducted research on clinical medicine and published them in peer-reviewed journals. Years of Soviet scientific discourse, practice and guidelines were overlooked to bring in Western

"essential drugs" guidelines, which were based on providing poor people with the minimal type and dosages of drugs that deemed necessary for basic survival. The Soviet health system provided care that went well beyond this. Instead, the "international guidelines" were the only norms accepted and funded by donors.

42. According to Kanji and Hardon (1992: 94), programs that are implemented in the absence of a national policy or consensus tend to become vertical, resulting in parallel systems of procurement, distribution, and training.

43. AKF, cited in Keshavjee 1998: 517, emphasis added.

44. When I informed Médecins Sans Frontières of this, they came to Kuhdeh to assess the situation and make sure the community was receiving its allotment of free humanitarian assistance medicines.

45. AKF, cited in Keshavjee 1998.

6. BRETTON WOODS TO BAMAKO

Epigraph: Friedman 2002: xiv.

1. Markwell 2006.

2. U.S. Department of State, Office of the Historian 2012.

3. Keynes is associated with the post–World War II social reform that was part of the ideological waning of liberalism, and a recognition that capitalism (postindustrialization) brought in its wake social problems. The basis of this was that the state had to be involved. In some ways, like the New Deal in the United States, it provided a foundation for more state involvement in the market.

4. Palley 2005.

5. Harvey 2005; Rowden 2009.

6. In fact, in its pure form, neoclassical economic theory saw no role for the state except to guarantee property rights, print money, and have a central bank to control credit creation. See also Rowden 2009: 63; Pfeiffer 2004. For an extended discussion on Keynes and monetarism, see Jones 2012: 180–214. Jones argues that post–Second World War neoliberal economics was framed in direct opposition to three of Keynes's ideas: (1) "the use of government and the power of the public purse to alleviate the worst effects of economic downturns;" (2) his invention of macroeconomic analysis; and (3) "the uses to which his ideas were put in British and U.S. economic policy in the postwar years" (184, 187).

7. Milton Friedman trained at the University of Chicago and taught in the department of economics starting in the late 1940s. Von Hayek came to the university in the 1950s and taught in the Committee on Social Thought. According to Jones (2012), Hayek had tried build a society of scholars as early as 1938. The term *neoliberalism* was used to describe a group of like-minded scholars who first gathered in August 1938 at the Colloque Walter Lippmann in Paris, convened by the French philosopher Louis Rougier. It is believed that at this meeting

the term *neoliberalism* was coined by Alexander Rüstow (Mirowski and Plehwe 2009). "The label was chosen for strategic reasons: to be 'neoliberal' implied one recognized that laissez-faire economics was not enough and that, in the name of liberalism, a modern economic policy was needed" (Jones 2012: 31).

8. See Steil 2013; Jones 2012. Interestingly, Dennis Robertson represented Britain in the discussions on the stabilization fund that was created at Bretton Woods. Both Robertson and Keynes are said to have not participated in the final formulation of the Articles of Agreement, which were drafted by Harry White (Jones 2012: 251).

9. According to Jones (2012), "Classical and neoclassical economics had always assumed that supply and demand would tend toward full employment equilibrium in the long run. Keynes, however, believed both that this was untrue and that it defined a laissez-faire approach that brought with it unacceptable social and economic costs. For him, the economy ought to be managed according to the large-scale relationships that were in operation, which in turn influenced the many economic decisions of individual actors in the marketplace. The relationships he had in mind were among money, tax, credit, debt and expenditure" (186).

10. Bird 1992: 288, 290–91.

11. Stein 2008: 9. According to Stein, the idea to create an agency that could support less developed countries was raised in 1951 by a U.S. presidential commission led by Nelson Rockefeller. The United States formally submitted the IDA proposal in July 1959.

12. Stein 2008: 9.

13. Prior to his role at the U.S. State Department, Dillon was undersecretary of state for economic affairs from 1958 to 1959.He was secretary of the treasury of the United States from 1961 to 1965.

14. Stein 2008: 9. See also Kapur et al. 1997 for more examples, including from Latin America.

15. Stein 2008; Kapur et al. 1997: 1150; Wade 2002.

16. See Mises 1949: chapter 15; Mises 1951. Mises, the leader of the Austrian school of economics, was best known for his argument that socialism would fail economically because of the "economic calculation problem," an inability to set prices and make the complex economic calculations required to put capital goods to their most productive use. In one of his better known works, *Human Action*, Mises laid the foundation for the idea of the "sovereignty of the consumer" in a free-market economy: "Merciless egoistic bosses, full of whims and fancies, changeable and unpredictable. For them nothing counts other than their own satisfaction" (270). For the capitalist economy to succeed, he argued, "in the conduct of their business affairs they must be unfeeling and stony-hearted because the consumers, their bosses, are themselves unfeeling and stony-hearted" (271).

17. This is ironic, of course, since neoliberalism came to be associated with oppressive regimes, such as Pinochet in Chile. Numerous examples make clear that free markets and democracy do not necessarily go hand in hand.

18. Jones 2012: 123.

19. Keynes's ideas were quite popular in the 1920s and 1930s, especially in Roosevelt's New Deal policies. According to Keynes, government intervention in the economy was critical to raise consumer demand in a depressed economy and boost production. This approach was in contrast to the Austrian economists Hayek and Mises, who argued that government intervention was inflationary (Jones 2012: 184).

20. Rowden 2009: 63.

21. According to Jones (2012), Hayek's efforts to bring thinkers together had started in the 1930s. He refers to the Colloque Walter Lippmann in Paris, organized by philosopher Louis Rougier.

22. Haegeman 2004; Mirowski and Plehwe 2009.

23. The complete text was:

> The central values of civilization are in danger. Over large stretches of the Earth's surface the essential conditions of human dignity and freedom have already disappeared. In others they are under constant menace from the development of current tendencies of policy. The position of the individual and the voluntary group are progressively undermined by extensions of arbitrary power. Even that most precious possession of Western Man, freedom of thought and expression, is threatened by the spread of creeds which, claiming the privilege of tolerance when in the position of a minority, seek only to establish a position of power in which they can suppress and obliterate all views but their own.
>
> The group holds that these developments have been fostered by the growth of a view of history which denies all absolute moral standards and by the growth of theories which question the desirability of the rule of law. It holds further that they have been fostered by a decline of belief in private property and the competitive market; for without the diffused power and initiative associated with these institutions it is difficult to imagine a society in which freedom may be effectively preserved.
>
> Believing that what is essentially an ideological movement must be met by intellectual argument and the reassertion of valid ideals, the group, having made a preliminary exploration of the ground, is of the opinion that further study is desirable inter alia in regard to the following matters:
>
> 1. The analysis and exploration of the nature of the present crisis so as to bring home to others its essential moral and economic origins.
> 2. The redefinition of the functions of the state so as to distinguish more clearly between the totalitarian and the liberal order.
> 3. Methods of re-establishing the rule of law and of assuring its development in such manner that individuals and groups are not in a position to encroach upon the freedom of others and private rights are not allowed to become a basis of predatory power.
> 4. The possibility of establishing minimum standards by means not inimical to initiative and functioning of the market.

5. Methods of combating the misuse of history for the furtherance of creeds hostile to liberty.

6. The problem of the creation of an international order conducive to the safeguarding of peace and liberty and permitting the establishment of harmonious international economic relations.

The group does not aspire to conduct propaganda. It seeks to establish no meticulous and hampering orthodoxy. It aligns itself with no particular party. Its object is solely, by facilitating the exchange of views among minds inspired by certain ideals and broad conceptions held in common, to contribute to the preservation and improvement of the free society. (Mont Pèlerin Society 1947)

24. Think Tank Watch 2007.

25. Hartwell 1995.

26. Jones (2012) argues that the "neo" in neoliberal itself implies that laissez-faire economics is not enough and a modern form of liberalism is required (31).

27. Rowden 2009: 62. This idea is drawn from Leon Walras's *Elements of Pure Economics*, where he laid out the ideas of general equilibrium theory.

28. Rowden 2009: 62; Stein 2008: 61.

29. Clarke 2005: 50-59.

30. Brown 2003.

31. Brown 2003: 7, 37.

32. Brown 2003: 37. According to Brown, "Governmentality is a rich term which Foucault defines as the 'conduct of conduct.' The term is also intended to signify the modern importance of *governing* over ruling, and the critical role of *mentality* in governing as opposed to the notion that power and ideas are separate phenomena. Governmentality moves away from sovereign and state-centered notions of political power (though it does not eschew the state as a site of governmentality), from the division between violence and law, and from a distinction between ideological and material power. Finally governmentality features state formation of subjects rather than state control of subjects; put slightly differently, it features control achieved through formation rather than repression or punishment" (Brown 2003: 48).

33. Brown 2003: 40.

34. Brown 2003: 41.

35. Brown 2003: 41.

36. Lemke 2001: 201.

37. Harvey 2005: 21.

38. Ong 2006.

39. Jones 2012: 344.

40. Goldman 2005: 60-65.

41. McNamara also became quite interested in alleviating poverty. He gave a famous speech to the bank's Board of Governors in Nairobi, Kenya, on September 24, 1973, where he called for a reorientation of development policies (World Bank

1973). In the speech, McNamara defined relative poverty and absolute poverty for the bank:

> Relative poverty means simply that some countries are less affluent than other countries, or that some citizens of a given country have less personal abundance than their neighbors. . . . But absolute poverty is a condition of life so degraded by disease, illiteracy, malnutrition, and squalor as to deny its victims basic human necessities. It is a condition of life suffered by relatively few in the developed nations but by hundreds of millions of the citizens of the developing countries represented in this room.

He said this, of course, speaking to the board members, many from poor countries. He continued:

> This is absolute poverty: a condition of life so limited as to prevent realization of the potential of the genes with which one is born; a condition of life so degrading as to insult human dignity—and yet a condition of life so common as to be the lot of some 40% of the peoples of the developing countries. And are not we who tolerate such poverty, when it is within our power to reduce the number afflicted by it, failing to fulfill the fundamental obligations accepted by civilized men since the beginning of time?

Because his remarks were presumably so surprising, McNamara felt obliged to qualify his statements by saying, "I do not wish you to interpret my remarks as those of a zealot. But you have hired me to examine the problems of the developing world and to report to you the facts. These are the facts."

He then called for a reorientation of the bank's policies, saying that countries should make serious moves toward more equitable distribution of the benefits of economic growth. He told the board, "And I should stress that unless national governments redirect their policies toward better distribution, there is very little that international agencies such as the World Bank can do to accomplish this objective."

42. Stein 2008.

43. Stein 2008: 210.

44. Stein 2008: 212.

45. Golladay and Liese 1980: 47; quoted in Stein 2008: 212.

46. Stein 2008: 213.

47. Stein 2008.

48. Rowden 2009: 65.

49. Stein 2008; Beder 2006.

50. Rowden (2009) argues that to make sure this would happen, the largest creditor countries created what became known as the Baker Plan, which ensured that all multilateral donors and bilateral donors would check with the IMF for a green light before they lent more money or changed the terms of any loans. Thus the IMF became the leader of the "aid cartel" (66). For an alternate view on these arrangements, see Bogdanowicz-Bindert 1986. See also Stein 2008: 25–26.

51. Lapeyre 2004.
52. Rowden 2009: 146
53. Prescott and de Ferranti 1985.
54. Prescott and de Ferranti 1985; Lee and Goodman 2002.
55. In a recent blog in the British newspaper *The Guardian*, health editor Sarah Boseley (2012) wrote about how de Ferranti had undergone a Damascene conversion, moving from his 1985 argument that "there appears to be considerable scope for having users bear a larger share of healthcare costs" to now saying that paying a fee to a provider is "a practice that effectively burdens sick and needy people, a small and vulnerable segment of the population, with most of the healthcare costs." Whereas in the past he had argued for fees for services or fees for coverage, in *The Lancet* he argued that fees have "meant choosing between going without needed services or facing financial ruin" (Rodin and de Ferranti 2012).

Boseley asked de Ferranti about his support for universal health coverage, despite his rejection of the idea in the 1980s. With thirty years of hindsight, he replied:

> If you go back to that time, the actual point that I was making was different than just saying user fees are good. I recognise that other voices in the bank and other voices talking about the bank put it that way. But the point I was making was if there is no money to get healthcare to remote areas, to poor areas or to rural areas, then the cry for free healthcare for all means no healthcare for many. And so it wasn't a sense that user fees are good in their own right but with so few resources available, one needs to look to—that was the argument being made then—those who can pay, so that those who cannot pay would be more able to get services. That's the argument that was being made.
>
> Since then—I guess it is now 30 years—economic growth rates, higher incomes, all the forces that have led to this florescence of interest and action by countries towards universal healthcare [have] shown that more resources were available and more that could be applied to health—so that older argument no longer applies. The world has completely changed. Thirty years. Three decades. That's a long time. Things change and arguments should change. And in the presence of more resources and the ability not just financially but administratively of countries to manage these programmes, which was again not there 30 years ago, it just now makes eminent sense and I have been outspoken in this—to move towards universal health coverage systems.

Boseley goes on to quote Rick Rowden, author of *The Deadly Ideas of Neoliberalism* and a harsh critic of the user fees policy of the past, who argues that de Ferranti and others who took a similar line were simply part of their era—"riding the political wave of the time—Reagan, Thatcher and the free market."

At the end of the blog, Robert Yates, who wrote extensively about the corrosive effects of user fees (see Yates 2006, 2009) comments:

> It is indeed to his credit, that Dr de Ferranti acknowledges that the argument for user fees "no longer applies." Many other people and agencies have also changed

their minds over the last thirty years. I must admit that I was at best agnostic on this issue, until 2001 when I witnessed people queuing into the desert for free health care, following the removal of user fees in Uganda.

But now the evidence is clear. If countries replace user fees with higher levels of public spending and allocate and manage these resources properly, utilization of key health services will increase, particularly by the poor and vulnerable. More importantly this will lead to improvements in population health indicators as the recent Lancet UHC series and this case study from Niger demonstrates. . . . The Lancet UHC series (involving authors with previously divergent views) shows that we are now well beyond a tipping point in the user fees debate. Now the issue isn't whether to introduce or retain fees at the point of delivery, it is how to replace them with more efficient and equitable public financing mechanisms. All the collaborators on the Lancet series should be congratulated for highlighting the need to do this in order to achieve Universal Health Coverage.

56. Stein 2008: 213.

57. De Ferranti 1985.

58. Stein 2008: 218.

59. Stein 2008: 219.

60. Stein 2008: 217.

61. Nobel Prize 1974.

62. Stein 2008: 215.

63. Sahn 1992.

64. Kapur et al. 1997: 520.

65. Stein 2008: 39. See also Stein and Nafziger 1991.

66. For example, in Liberia spending went down from US $7 per capita to US $1.50; in Nigeria spending dropped from US $3 to US $1.81 (the WHO recommends US $32 per capita) (World Bank 1980, 2004).

67. Paganini 2004.

68. In fact, between 1973 and 1986, the share of health services in twenty developing countries fell from 5.5 percent of government expenditure to 4.2 percent, while the share of defense spending went from 12.7 percent to 15.2 percent.

69. Rowden 2009.

70. Jolly et al. 1992.

71. Cueto 2004.

72. Paganini 2004.

73. Paganini 2004: 12..

74. Paganini 2004: 12..

75. Paganini 2004: 11..

76. See WHO 1991.

77. Cassels 1995; Zwi and Mills 1995; Abel-Smith 1986; Ebrahim and Ranken 1988.

78. Ridde 2011: 176.

7. FROM BAMAKO TO BADAKHSHAN

Epigraph: Butt 1981.

1. Olufsen 1904: 146.

2. Marshall 1947.

3. With the Mutual Security Act of 1954, this agency was merged with the International Cooperation Administration, and strengthened through the creation of a Development Loan Fund.

4. Kennedy 1961, emphasis added.

5. USAID 2013. This occurred after the U.S. Congress passed the Foreign Assistance Act in September 1961, which separated military and nonmilitary aid. For an example of the theories driving foreign policy, see also Rostow 1960.

6. Powell 1971.

7. Harvey 2005: 43.

8. George 1997; Jones 2012.

9. Historian Daniel Stedman Jones (2012) argues that the move toward neoliberalism actually preceded Thatcher and Reagan, starting during the previous administrations.

10. Thatcher 1995: 50.

11. Thatcher 1993: 12–13.

12. Ranelagh 1991.

13. Ebenstein 2003.

14. Evans and Novak 1981: 229.

15. Anderson 1988: 164.

16. Bush 1991.

17. Reagan 1982; see also Lowe 2012; Democracy Program 1983.

18. Lowe 2012; see also Center for Media and Democracy 2013; Democracy Program 1983.

19. Center for Media and Democracy 2013.

20. Democracy Program 1983.

21. Douglas 1972: 28.

22. Hulme and Edwards 1997.

23. National Endowment for Democracy 2012, emphasis added.

24. Wood 2012: 211. Although there is no agreed-upon definition of civil society, in the post-Enlightenment period it has become associated with the idea of the social contract. The seventeenth-century English philosopher Thomas Hobbes outlined two distinct social relationships: that between citizens and the state (Leviathan) and that among citizens (civil society). The modern liberal understanding of civil society, outlined by the late eighteenth-century German philosopher G. W. F. Hegel, inserted ideas of individual rights and property into the equation (Dhanagare 2001). Thereafter, civil society came to represent a sphere of human relations

and activity differentiated from the state and embodying social interactions apart from the private sphere of the household and the public sphere of the state, including the marketplace (Wood 1990: 245). Hegel differentiated sharply between civil society and political society, which, although it didn't refer solely to the economic institutions of capitalism, required a modern economy, a sphere of existence separate from the state, as a precondition (Wood 1990: 239–40).

25. Alagappa 2004: 29.

26. Douglas 1972: 28; Robinson 1995.

27. Robinson 1993; Meyer 1992; Colclough and Manor 1991; Sollis 1992; Vivian 1994.

28. Wiktorowicz 2001; Douglas 1972: xiii.

29. Hulme and Edwards 1997: 4.

30. Clarke 1998.

31. Hibou 1998.

32. Deakin 2001: 167; Hulme and Edwards 1997.

33. The process of structural adjustment is now referred to as "Poverty Reduction Strategy Papers," a new comprehensive approach being used by the World Bank.

34. Fisher 1991; Jessop 2002.

35. PAHO 1991.

36. In this setting, the idea of NGOs as an extension of "global civil society" is called into question. Even in its loosest interpretation, civil society exists in a space where community, voluntary action, government, business, and individual intersect to "protect and nurture the individual and where the individual operates to provide those same protections and liberating opportunities for others" (O'Connell 1999: 10). See also Mohan and Stokke 2000.

37. Fisher 1991; Harvey 1989; Nagar and Raju 2003; Townsend et al. 2004.

38. Hulme and Edwards 1997.

39. USAID 1995.

40. World Bank 1997; Buse and Walt 1996; Green and Matthias 1997; De Beyer et al. 2000; Edwards and Hulme 1996a; Zaidi 1999; Turshen 1999.

41. By setting the terms for the activities, USAID was able to define the areas of potential intervention, the modes of intervention, and how these are expected to relate to each other. Escobar (1995) describes this process well: "Development was not merely the result of the combination, study, or gradual elaboration of these elements (some of these topics had existed for some time); nor the product of the introduction of new ideas (some of which were already appearing or perhaps were bound to appear); nor the effect of the new international organizations or financial institutions (which had some predecessors, such as the League of Nations). It was rather the result of the establishment of a set of relations among these elements, institutions, and practices and of the systematization of

these relations to form a whole. The development discourse was constituted not by the array of possible objects under its domain but by the way in which, thanks to this set of relations, it was able to form systematically the objects of which it spoke, to group them and arrange them in certain ways, and to give them a unity of their own. . . . In sum, the system of relations establishes a discursive practice that sets the rules of the game: who can speak, from what points of view, with what authority, and according to what criteria of expertise; it sets the rules that must be followed for this or that problem, theory, or object to emerge and be named, analyzed, and eventually transformed into a policy or plan" (40).

42. USAID 1995.

43. Harvey 1989: 45.

44. Dreyfus and Rabinow 1983: 198.

45. Foucault 2007: 99.

46. In his 1982 essay, "The Subject of Power," Foucault argues that "power is only power (rather than mere physical force or violence) when addressed to individuals who are free to act in one way or another. Power is defined as 'actions on others' actions': that is, it presupposes rather than annuls their capacity as agents; it acts upon, and through, an open set of practical and ethical possibilities" (Gordon 1991, 5). According to Brown (2003), "The term is also intended to signify the modern importance of *governing* over ruling, and the critical role of *mentality* in governing as opposed to the notion that power and ideas are separate phenomena. Governmentality moves away from sovereign and state-centered notions of political power (though it does not eschew the state as a site of governmentality), from the division between violence and law, and from a distinction between ideological and material power. Finally governmentality features state formation of subjects rather than state control of subjects; put slightly differently, it features control achieved through formation rather than repression or punishment".

47. Harvey (1989) points out that "close scrutiny of the micro-politics of power relations in different localities, contexts, and social situations leads [Foucault] to conclude that there is an intimate relation between the systems of knowledge ('discourses') which codify techniques and practices for the exercise of social control and domination within particular localized contexts" (45). Power and knowledge act in such a way as to "normalize society." They operate "by establishing a common definition of goals and procedures . . . [and] agreed-upon examples of how a well-ordered domain of human activity should be organized. These exemplars . . . immediately define what is normal; at the same time, they define practices which fall outside their system as deviant behavior in need of normalization" (Dreyfus and Rabinow 1983: 198). See also Escobar 1995: 5; Crewe and Harrison, 1988: 9; Sachs 1992; Dahl and Rabo 1992; Pigg 1992.

48. Aksartova 2005.

49. While it is true that the Aga Khan has spoken about the importance of private initiatives and private enterprise—the local development of civil society via

the empowerment of nonstate actors in terms of "pluralization of the institutional environment" (Bratton 1989: 570)—it is also clear that AKF's framing of the revolving drug fund in their application to USAID takes a different tone. In fact, in speaking of the goals of development at a speech he gave at Evora University in Portugal in 2006, the Aga Khan said: "What are our ultimate goals? Whose interests do we seek to serve? . . . The search for justice and security, the struggle for equality of opportunity, the quest for tolerance and harmony, the pursuit of human dignity: these are moral imperatives we must work towards and think about daily" (Aga Khan IV 2008: 110).

8. PRIVATIZING HEALTH SERVICES

Epigraph: Hayek 1949: 420.
1. Thatcher 1978.
2. Pashaev et al. 1997.
3. I realized that this was a biased sample of people who actually had made it to the dentist, but I was banking that some people were there because they could afford it while others were there simply out of desperation. From the survey results, it turned out that this was mostly true. Also, the survey gave us a good idea of what people had to give up to get to the dentist and what they felt about the privatization of the clinic.
4. Keshavjee 1998: 116.
5. Keshavjee 1998: 407, respondent 21.
6. Keshavjee 1998: 407–8, respondent 35.
7. Keshavjee 1998: 408, respondent 23.
8. Keshavjee 1998, respondent 11.
9. Bourdieu 1990.
10. Lee 2001.
11. Lee et al. 2002; Scholte 2000; Dicken 1998.
12. Lee et al. 2002: 9.
13. Bataille 1988: 125.
14. Wuthnow 1987: 88.
15. Polyani 1954; Epstein 1998. For a discussion of the fragmentation in American life, see Putnam 1995
16. Polyani 1954: 256–58. Citing Hayek's views, Polyani argues that the path to a truly just and free society is blocked by the drive for liberal utopianism. "Free enterprise and private ownership are declared to be essentials of freedom." Any regulation, he says, is "attacked as a denial of freedom," and the "justice, liberty and welfare it offers are decried as a camouflage of slavery." Harvey 2005: 35. Also see Harvey 2005: 37.
17. Smith 1982a: 190. See also Sen 2009; Smith 1982b.

18. Smith 1982b: 246. In *The Protestant Ethic and the Spirit of Capitalism*, while sociologist Max Weber highlighted Calvinism's emphasis on individual salvation and the attribution of material prosperity to personal merit, even that individualism was framed within the need to share and to care for the community, something that has been seen historically (Weber 1930). For example, John Winthrop (1588–1649), a lawyer and one of the first Puritans to land on American shores, governor of the Massachusetts Bay Colony for twelve of its first twenty years, described, in a sermon delivered on board a ship in Salem harbor just before landing on American shores in 1630, his vision of what life in America was to be: "We must delight in each other, make others' conditions our own, rejoyce together, mourn together, labor and suffer together, always having before our eyes our community as members of the same body" (quoted in Bellah et al. 1985: 28). He saw success as tied to the creation of a certain kind of ethical community, and freedom as a form of "moral freedom." Also see Sen 2009; Smith 1982b.

19. Alexis de Tocqueville, a classic liberal scholar, wrote in 1835 in his classic *Democracy In America* that "individualism is a calm and considered feeling which disposes each citizen to isolate himself from the mass of his fellows and withdraw into the circle of family and friends; with this little society formed to his taste, he gladly leaves the greater society to look after itself" (Tocqueville 1969: 506).

20. Durkheim 1933, 1951. See also Berman 1988: 111.

21. Escobar 1995: 58.

9. REVEALING THE BLIND SPOT

Epigraph: Keynes 1936: 383–84.

1. Aga Khan Foundation 2004.

2. Data from the American Association of Retired Persons collected in 2004 suggests that the average number of prescription drugs taken daily by people between fifty and sixty-four years of age is 3.31; that number increases to 4.45 for people sixty-five to seventy-four. See AARP 2005. See also Gu et al. (2010), which presents data from the U.S. National Health and Nutrition Examination Survey showing that in 2007–2008, 48.3 percent of Americans used one or more drugs in the month of the survey. Almost one third (31.2 percent) used two or more drugs, and a tenth (10.7 percent) used five or more drugs.

3. Bethune 2004.

4. Bethune 2004.

5. Aga Khan Foundation Tajikistan and Department of Health Badakhshan 2005.

6. This is equivalent to 207 somoni. The Tajik currency was changed from the Tajik ruble to the somoni on October 30, 2000. At its introduction, one somoni was the equivalent of one thousand Tajik rubles.

7. Aga Khan Foundation Tajikistan and Department of Health Badakhshan 2005.

8. A mean amount of 42.0 somoni.

9. A mean amount of 132.9 somoni.

10. AKF notes in the report that these numbers may not be reliable because the study's sample size was small.

11. WHO 1997a. Infant mortality rates were taken from "Updated Statistics April 1997," issued as an addendum to the same report. Also see EOHCS 2000.

12. Brown et al. 2011. Rates of vaccine coverage in other parts of Central Asia are reported to be in excess of 90 percent.

13. Diop et al. 1995; Litvack and Bodart 1993; Knippenberg et al. 1997.

14. Blas and Limbambala 2001.

15. Rowden 2009: 156.

16. Rowden 2009: 156.

17. Moses et al. 1992; Awofeso 1998.

18. Waddington and Enyimayew 1989; Yoder 1989; Lee and Goodman 2002.

19. Desclaux 2004.

20. James et al. 2006.

21. Meng et al. 2002; Kivumbi and Kintu 2002; Paphassarang et al. 2002; Ridde 2003; Dumoulin and Kaddar 1993; Jaffré and de Sardan 2003.

22. Hardon and Kanji 1992: 114.

23. Field 1995; Knaus 1981; Ryan 1978.

24. Pearson 2004. See also Creese 1990; Gilson 1997.

25. Hecht et al. 1993.

26. Masiye et al. 2005.

27. Desclaux 2004.

28. Yates 2006.

29. Yates 2009.

30. James et al. 2005.

31. Rist 2008.

32. Yates 2009, 2006.

33. Seedhouse 1995: 2.

34. LaFond 1995: 27–28.

35. Loewy 1995: 156; Drake 1994: 11.

36. Lee et al. 2002.

37. Ugalde and Jackson 1995; Bhat 1999; Carrin et al. 1992: 92–93.

38. Rosenthal and Newbrander 1996.

39. Arrow 1968; Pauly 1968; Zeckhauser 1970; Feldstein 1973; Newhouse and the Insurance Experiment Group 1993: 138.

40. Newhouse and the Insurance Experiment Group 1993: 338–39.

41. DeMars 2005: 45.

42. Waning et al. 2010; World Health Organization and Health Action International 2008.

43. Tajikistan began receiving loans from the International Monetary Fund in 1998.

44. Khodjamurodov and Rechel 2010; Falkingham 2004.

45. See Lemke 2001 for a discussion of Foucault's reasoning.

46. Keshavjee 1998: 516–17, emphasis added.

47. Ferguson 1994: 254.

48. Foucault 1979.

10. EPILOGUE

Epigraphs: Sandel 2012: 7; Farmer 2003: 177.

1. Jones 2012.

2. Fukuyama 1992.

3. I shudder to think of what would have happened to the people of Badakhshan if AKF had not come to the region when it did, if people had not been given food and fuel. As bad as the infant mortality and infection rates have been since the collapse, without the assistance of the Aga Khan Foundation, Médecins Sans Frontières, and the Red Cross, these rates surely would have been worse.

4. Minder 2013; Stuckler and Basu 2013; Rylko-Bauer and Farmer 2002.

5. Stuckler and Basu 2013: 21.

6. Stuckler and Basu 2013: 23.

7. Stuckler and Basu 2013: 29.

8. Stuckler and Basu (2013) argue that while Poland became healthier in the post-Soviet period, Russia became sicker. Before communism fell, they had the same death rates. In the first three years after communism fell, the death rate in Russia went up by 35 percent while that in Poland fell by 10 percent. The rates in some countries (e.g., Kazakhstan, Latvia, and Estonia) went up, while others (e.g., Belarus, Slovenia, and the Czech Republic) went down. This, they say, had to do with policy choices on how to transition from communism to capitalism. Those countries that pursued a rapid transition faced more death and worse health. These are the "rapid privatizers." Those who reformed more slowly and maintained social protection systems saw health improvements. They go on to argue that IMF-sponsored economic reform programs are associated with worsened tuberculosis incidence, prevalence, and mortality rates in postcommunist former-Soviet countries (independent of other political, economic, or demographic changes). Lending from non-IMF sources of funding was associated with lower tuberculosis mortality because IMF programs were associated with reduced government expenditure on tuberculosis and health (28–29).

9. As historian Daniel Stedman Jones points out, understanding neoliberalism "reveals the manner in which a body of thought was imperfectly translated into policy and, ultimately, into politics. . . . The process by which ideas were mixed with power involved compromise, but it also involved the creation of a vast network that achieved a large measure of political influence" (Jones 2012: 18). Also see Stein 2008; Rowden 2009.

10. While Gramsci's theory of hegemony is associated here with the structuralist position, it must be noted that he does not view ideology as a simple reflection of economic infrastructure. In fact, he has criticized historical materialism for being overdeterministic because it assumes that a change to a new mode of production is built into history (Bocock 1986: 83). Instead, Gramsci views the relationship between superstructure and infrastructure as constantly changing and reciprocal in historical complexities. According to Gramsci, politics, ideas, religion, culture, etc., are not autonomous, and domination does not occur only in the sphere of production. Through his notion of hegemony, Gramsci wanted to describe the subtle, yet pervasive, forms of ideological control that perpetuate repressive societal structures. Additionally, many theorists have attempted to explain the dynamics of social change (Lévi-Strauss 1963; Yalman 1967; Foucault 1973; Leach 1977; Bourdieu 1977; Sahlins 1985), often invoking traditional theories of cultural hegemony (cf. Gramsci 1971; Williams 1977; Femia 1981), and situating their argument within the structure-agency debate. In contrast to discussions of hegemony, resistance literature (cf. Foucault 1973; Scott 1985, 1990; Bourdieu 1977, 1984; de Certeau 1984) argues that the focus on hegemony is merely a focus on the dominant groups in a society and ultimately ignores everyday forms of resistance that lead to change.

Foucault's idea of discourse is that it is a knowledge system, a totalizing field of activity that continually extends its range of prediction and control (Foucault 1973). The idea of discourse is broader than that of text in that it also includes action and speech that occur within its domain of totalization. It is within the field of discourse that knowledge-power is simultaneously produced and practiced. Harvey (1989) points out that "close scrutiny of the micro-politics of power relations in different localities, contexts, and social situations leads [Foucault] to conclude that there is an intimate relation between the systems of knowledge ('discourses') which codify techniques and practices for the exercise of social control and domination within particular localized contexts" (45). Power and knowledge act in such a way as to "normalize society." They operate "by establishing a common definition of goals and procedures . . . [and] agreed-upon examples of how a well-ordered domain of human activity should be organized. These exemplars . . . immediately define what is normal; at the same time, they define practices which fall outside their system as deviant behavior in need of normalization" (Dreyfus and Rabinow, 1983: 198). Also see Bocock 1986: 83.

11. Sandel 2012: 9.

12. Ashton 1995: 87. While the drive to weaken the state may have some appeal in certain political contexts, people should worry about what happens in places like Tajikistan. The implications for letting Tajikistan undergo a "reverse health transition" are significant. Not only are there profound moral and ethical implications for both the local community and the international community, but there are also very significant political considerations. Since Tajikistan is located beside China, Afghanistan, and essentially, Pakistan, the region's geopolitical importance cannot be overestimated. Ignoring poverty and ill health in poor communities can have significant local and global repercussions. The cost of poor health places a heavy burden on national governments and national stability. According to Price-Smith (1999), declining health status correlates over time with a decline in state capacity by depleting human capital and wealth, and this, in turn, leads to political instability. In fact, a 1998 CIA study found infant mortality to be one of the best predictors of state failure (cf. Esty et al., 1998; Kassalow 2001). Other data examining the regions of the former Soviet Union, including Central Asia, have found that poor health correlates strongly with distrust in the local government and levels of crime (Kennedy et al. 1998). Also see Ashton 1995: 88.

13. Jones 2012: 338.

14. See Farmer 2003: 160–78, for an extended critique of market-based medicine and its effects on values and expectations in health care.

15. Lewis 2007: 10. Lewis (2007) argues that some critics have accused NGOs of supporting/facilitating neoliberal policies by "cleaning up the mess" left by destructive policies, such as the World Bank's structural adjustment programs, and crowding out grassroots movements and opposition (10). Also see Tandon 1996; Abdel Ati 1993; De Waal and Omaar 1993; Hanlon 1991; Tvedt 1998.

16. Edwards and Hulme 1996a: 2. See also Colclough and Manor 1991; World Bank 1987; World Bank 1993; Abel-Smith 1986.

17. Brugha and Zwi 2002; Skaar 1998; Mills 1997.

18. To speak of community participation in the absence of an equitable distribution of goods excludes certain options for social action, independent of the consciousness of the actors (Asad 1993: 15; cf. Sen 1992). Those with lower incomes vote less often than those with higher incomes in democratic systems (Filer et al. 1993: 72; Navarro 1993: 46), and political inequality is generated by inequalities in wealth (Greider 1992). Participation and volunteerism are also adversely affected by poverty (Verba et al. 1995). Also see Habermas 1984, 1987. An advocate of modernity, Habermas argues that only with fair and democratic conditions in place will the voices of the weak be heard. Therefore, the effective communication assumed by the hermeneutical tradition can only occur when appropriate and supportive social conditions apply.

19. De Ferranti 1985; Birdsall 1986; UNICEF 1990a, 1990b; McPake 1993a, 1993b; Clarke 1998; Hirschman 1987; Gupte 1993: 25–26.

20. Douglas 1972.

21. Friedman 2002: xiv.

22. As discussed previously, the World Health Organization had concerns about the plan, arguing that middle and low-income countries differed and could not all be treated the same. See WHO 1991; Cross et al. 1986; Gilson 1988; Foster 1989; Waddington and Enyimayew 1989; Dahlgren 1991; Abel-Smith and Rawall 1992.

23. Cox 1987; Lee and Goodman 2002; Amin 1996.

24. Garrett 2000.

25. Edwards and Hulme (1996a) argue that "given the financial and political muscle of official agencies, there is an obvious fear that donor funding may reorient accountability upward, and away from the grassroots, and bias performance measurement towards criteria defined by donors" (12). Also see Escobar 1995: 5; Crewe and Harrison 1988.

26. Bourdieu 1977: 166.

27. Escobar 1995: 9; Sachs 1992; Dahl and Rabo 1992; Pigg 1992.

28. DeMars 2005: 47. Political scientist David Lewis points out that today there is a neoconservative critique of NGOs. Some neoconservative critics see NGOs as harmful to U.S. policy and business interests. He gives the example of the American Enterprise Institute, which has set up a watchdog site for NGOs. "It lists a set of grievances in relation to NGO's that includes their support of 'global governance' agendas, their efforts to restrict US room for maneuver in foreign policy and their attempts to influence the power of corporations and, by extension, the 'free market.'" (Lewis 2007: 10). The result, according to Lewis, is that NGOs, in some circles, are being viewed as a left-wing program, with a move to rely more on the use of private contractors in place of NGOs, and tighter regulations governing the contracting between USAID and NGOs.

29. Sandel 2012: 7, 10, 14.

30. As Adams (2013) points out, "sustainability" is not a health outcome (71).

31. Carrin et al. 1992; Gilson 1988; cf. Mooney 1983, 1987.

32. Edwards et al. 2000.

33. Adams 2013: 71.

34. Bourdieu 1998: 29.

35. Bourdieu 1998: viii.

Bibliography

AARP (American Association of Retired Persons). 2005. "Prescription Drug Use among Midlife and Older Americans." AARP, http://assets.aarp.org/rgcenter/health/rx_midlife_plus.pdf.

Abdel Ati, H. A. 1993. "The Development Impact of NGO Activities in the Red Sea Province of Sudan: A Critique." *Development and Change* 24: 103–30.

Abel-Smith, Brian. 1986. "The World Economic Crisis. Part 1: Repercussions on Health." *Health Policy and Planning* 1 (3): 202–13.

Abel-Smith, B., and A. Dua. 1998. "Community Financing in Developing Countries: The Potential for the Health Sector." *Health Policy and Planning* 3 (2): 95–109.

Abel-Smith, Brian, and Pankaj Rawall. 1992. "Can the Poor Afford 'Free' Health Care? A Case Study of Tanzania." *Health Policy and Planning* 7 (4): 329–41.

Adams, Vincanne. 2013. "Evidence-Based Global Public Health." In *When People Come First: Critical Studies in Global Health*, ed. João Biehl and Adriana Petryna. Princeton, NJ: Princeton University Press.

Aga Khan III. 1954. *The Memoirs of Aga Khan*. New York: Simon and Schuster.

Aga Khan IV. 1967. "In The Muslim World: Yesterday, Today and Tomorrow." Convocation address delivered at Peshawar University, Peshwar, Pakistan, November 30.

———. 1976. "The Role of Private Initiative in Developing Countries." Speech delivered at the Swiss-American Chamber of Commerce, Zurich, January 14, 1976.

———. 1982. "The Enabling Environment." Speech delivered at a dinner hosted by President Daniel T. Arap Moi, Kenya, October.

———. 1994. "Commencement Speech by His Highness the Aga Khan." Address at Massachusetts Institute of Technology, Cambridge, May 27, www.akdn.org/Content/665/Massachusetts-Institute-of-Technology.

———. 2008. *Where Hope Takes Root: Democracy and Pluralism in an Interdependent World*. Vancouver: Douglas and McIntyre.

Aga Khan Foundation. 1997. "Health and Nutrition Survey: Autonomous Oblast of Gorno Badakhshan (Tajikistan), July–August 1996." Geneva: Aga Khan Foundation.

———. 2004. "Rationalizing Pharmaceutical Policy and Management (RPPM): Final Report (August 1997–October 2004)." Tajikistan: Aga Khan Foundation.

Aga Khan Development Network. 2012. "About the Aga Khan Development Network." Aga Khan Development Network, www.akdn.org/about.asp.

Aga Khan Foundation Tajikistan and Department of Health Badakhshan. 2005. "Health and Nutrition Survey 2004, Gorno-Badakhshan Autonomous Oblast, Tajikistan." Tajikistan: Aga Khan Foundation.

Akin, John S., with Charles C. Griffin, David K. Guilkey, and Barry M. Popkin. 1986. "The Demand for Adult Outpatient Services in the Bicol Region of the Philippines." *Social Science and Medicine* 22 (3): 321–28.

Akin, John S., with Nancy Birdsall and David M. De Ferranti. 1987. *Financing Health Services in Developing Countries: An Agenda for Reform*. World Bank Policy Study. Washington, DC: World Bank.

Akiner, Shirin. 1983. *Islamic Peoples of the Soviet Union*. London: Kegan Paul International.

Aksartova, Sada (Saadat). 2005. "Civil Society from Abroad: U.S. Donors in the Former Soviet Union." PhD diss., Princeton University.

Alagappa, Muthiah. 2004. "Civil Society and Political Change in Asia: An Analytical Framework." In *Civil Society and Political Change in Asia: Expanding and Contracting Democratic Space*, 25–60. Stanford, CA: Stanford University Press.

Allworth, Edward, ed. 1994. *Central Asia: 130 Years of Russian Dominance, A Historical Overview*. Durham, NC: Duke University Press.

Amin, Samir. 1996. "The Challenge of Globalization." *Review of International Political Economy* 3 (2): 216–59.

Anderson, Benedict. 1991. *Imagined Communities*. London: Verso Press.

Anderson, John. 1997. "Islam, Ethnicity and Regional Conflict: The Case of Tajikistan." In *The International Politics of Central Asia*. Manchester: Manchester University Press.

Anderson, Martin. 1988. *Revolution*. New York: Harcourt Brace Jovanovich.

Appadurai, Arjun. 1986. "Introduction: Commodities and the Politics of Value." In *The Social Life of Things: Commodities in Cultural Perspective*. Cambridge: Cambridge University Press.

———. 1991. "Global Ethnoscapes, Notes and Queries for a Transnational Anthropology." In *Recapturing Anthropology*, ed. Richard Fox. Sante Fe, NM: School of American Research Press.

Arrow, Kenneth J. 1968. "The Economics of Moral Hazard: Further Comment." *American Economic Review* 58: 537–39.

Asad, Talal. 1972. "Market Model, Class Structure, and Consent: A Reconsideration of Swat Political Organization." *Man* 7 (2): 74–94.

———. 1973. "Two European Images of Non-European Rule." In *Anthropology and the Colonial Encounter*, ed. Talal Asad. Atlantic Highlands, NJ: Humanities Press.

———. 1993. *Genealogies of Religion: Discipline and Reasons of Power in Christianity and Islam*. Baltimore, MD: Johns Hopkins University Press.

———, ed. 1973. *Anthropology and the Colonial Encounter*. Atlantic Highlands, NJ: Humanities Press.

Ashton, Toni. 1995. "From Evolution to Revolution: Restructuring the New Zealand Health System." In *Reforming Health Care: The Philosophy and Practice of International Health Reform*, ed. David Seedhouse. New York: John Wiley & Sons.

Asimov, Mukhamed. 1987. *Tajikistan*. Moscow: Novosti Press Agency Publishing House.

Aslund, Anders. 1997. "The Role of the State in the Transition to Capitalism." In *Legacies of the Collapse of Marxism*, ed. John H. Moore, 181–97. Fairfax, VA: George Mason University Press.

Atkin, Murial. 1980. *Russia and Iran: 1780–1828*. Minneapolis: University of Minnesota Press.

———. 1989. *The Subtlest Battle: Islam in Soviet Tajikistan*. Philadelphia: Foreign Policy Research Institute.

———. 1992. "Religious, National, and Other Identities in Central Asia." In *Muslims in Central Asia: Expressions of Identity and Change*, ed. Jo-Ann Gross, 46–72. Durham, NC: Duke University Press.

———. 1993. "Islam, Nationalism and Democracy in Tajikistan." Public lecture, Russia Research Center, Harvard University, Cambridge, MA, November 17.

———. 1994. "The Politics of Polarization in Tajikistan." In *Central Asia: Its Strategic Influence and Future Prospects*, ed. Hafeez Malik. Houndmills, Basingstoke: Macmillan.

———. 1995. "Islam as Faith, Politics, and Bogeyman in Tajikistan." In *The Politics of Religion in Russia and the New States of Eurasia*, ed. Michael Bourdeaux. London: M. E. Sharpe.

Awofeso, Niyi. 1998. "Implementing Tuberculosis Control Programmes in Kaduna State, Nigeria." *International Journal of Tuberculosis and Lung Disease* 2 (4): 336–37.

Banerji, Debabar. 1979. "The Place of the Indigenous and the Western Systems of Medicine in the Health Services of India." *International Journal of Health Services* 9 (3): 511–19.

Banuazizi, Ali, and Myron Weiner, eds. 1994. *The New Geopolitics of Central Asia and Its Borderlands*. Bloomington: Indiana University Press.

Bataille, Georges. 1988. *The Accursed Share: An Essay on General Economy, vol. 1: Consumption*. New York: Zone Books.

Baudrillard, Jean. 1975. *The Mirror of Production*. Translated by Mark Poster. St. Louis: Telos Press.

Becker, David G., and Richard Sklar. 1987. "Why Postimperialism?" In *Post Imperialism: International Capitalism and Development in the Late Twentieth Century*, ed. David G. Becker, Jeff Frieden, Sayre P. Schatz, and Richard Sklar, 1–19. Boulder, CO: Lynne Reinner Publishers.

Becker, Seymour. 1968. *Russia's Protectorates in Central Asia: Bukhara and Khiva, 1865–1924*. Cambridge: Routledge.

Beder, Sharon. 2006. *Free Market Missionaries: The Corporate Manipulation of Community Values*. New York: Earthscan.

Beissinger, Mark R. 1992. "Elites and Ethnic Identities in Soviet and Post-Soviet Politics." In *The Post-Soviet Nations*, ed. Alexander J. Motyl, 141–69. New York: Columbia University Press.

Bellah, Robert N., with Richard Madsen, William M. Sullivan, Ann Swindler, and Steven M. Tipton. 1985. *Habits of the Heart: Individualism and Commitment in American Life*. New York: Perennial Library.

Benson, John S. 2001. "The Impact of Privatization on Access in Tanzania." *Social Science and Medicine* 52 (12): 1903–15.

Berger, Peter L. 1969a. *Marxism and Sociology: Views from Eastern Europe*. New York: Appleton-Century-Crofts.

———. 1969b. *The Sacred Canopy: Elements of a Sociological Theory of Religion*. Garden City, NY: Doubleday.

Berger, Peter L., and Thomas Luckmann. 1966. *The Social Construction of Reality*. Garden City, NY: Doubleday.

Berman, Marshall. 1988. *All That Is Solid Melts into Air: The Experience of Modernity*. New York: Penguin Books.

Berman, Peter A. 1995. "Health Sector Reform: Making Health Development Sustainable." In *Health Sector Reform in Developing Countries: Making Health Development Sustainable*. Boston: Harvard University Press.

Bertel, A. E. 1962. "Otcet o rabote pamirskoy ekspeditsii . . ." *Izvestya Akad Nauk Tadzhikskoy SSR*, 11–16.

Bethune, B. Lea. 2004. *Final Evaluation: Matching Grants Projects Implemented by the Aga Khan Foundation, Gorno Badakhshan Autonomous Oblast, Tajikistan, October 1998 to September 2004.* Cooperative Agreement FAO-A-00-98-00078-00.

Bettelheim, Charles. 1976. *Class Struggles in the USSR.* Translated by Brian Pearce. New York: Monthly Review Press.

Bhat, Ramesh. 1999. "Characteristics of Private Medical Practice in India: A Provider Perspective." *Health Policy and Planning* 14 (1): 26–37.

Bhatti, N., with M. R. Law, J. K. Morris, R. Halliday, and J. Moore-Gillon. 1995. "Increasing Incidence of Tuberculosis in England and Wales: A Study of Likely Causes." *British Medical Journal* 310 (6985): 967–69.

Biddulph, John. 1880. *Tribes of the Hindoo Koosh.* Calcutta: Adamant Media.

Biehl, João, and Adriana Petryna, eds. 2013. *When People Come First: Critical Studies in Global Health.* Princeton, NJ: Princeton University Press.

Bird, Kai. 1992. *The Chairman: John J. McCloy, the Making of the American Establishment.* New York: Simon and Schuster.

Birdsall, Nancy. 1986. *Cost Recovery in Health and Education: Bank Policy and Operations.* PHN Technical Note 86–24. Washington, DC: World Bank.

———. 1992. "Health and Development: What Can Research Contribute?" In *Advancing Health in Developing Countries: The Role of Social Research,* ed. Lincoln C. Chen, Arthur Kleinman, and Norma C. Ware. New York: Auburn House.

Biritwum, R. 1994. "The Cost of Sustaining Ghana's "Cash and Carry" System of Health Care Financing at a Rural Health Centre." *West African Journal of Medicine* 13 (2): 124–27.

Birkenes, Robert M. 1996. "Tajikistan: Survey of the Household and Bazaar Economies." Dushanbe: Save the Children.

Bitran, Ricardo. 1988. *Health Care Demand Studies in Developing Countries: A Critical Review and Agenda for Research.* Arlington, VA: Reach, Resources for Child Health Project, JSI.

Black, Robert E. 1984. "Diarrheal Diseases and Child Morbidity and Mortality." *Population and Development Review,* 10 (suppl.): 141–61.

Blackburn, Clare. 1991. *Poverty and Health: Working with Families.* Philadelphia: Open University Press.

Blas, E., and Limbambala M. 2001. "User-Payments, Decentralization and Health Service Utilization in Zambia." *Health Policy and Planning* 16 (suppl. 2): 19–28.

Bliss, Frank. 2006. *Social and Economic Change in the Pamirs (Gorno-Badakhshan, Tajikistan).* London: Routledge.

Bobrinskoy, A. 1902. *Secta Isma'iliya v russkikh I bukharshikh predelakh.* Moscow.

Bocock, Robert J. 1971. "The Isma'ilis in Tanzania: A Weberian Analysis." *British Journal of Sociology* 22 (4): 365–81.

————. 1986. *Hegemony*. London: Tavistock.

Bogdanowicz-Bindert, Christine A. 1986. "The Debt Crisis: The Baker Plan Revisited." *Journal of Interamerican Studies and World Affairs* 28 (3): 33–45.

Bor, W., with J. M. Najman, M. Andersen, J. Morrison, and G. Williams. 1993. "Socioeconomic Disadvantage and Child Morbidity: An Australian Longitudinal Study." *Social Science and Medicine* 36 (8): 1053–61.

Borowitz, Michael, with Sheila O'Dougherty, Cheryl Wickham, Grace Hafner, Julian Simidjiyski, Cari Ann VanDevelde, and Mark McEuen. 1999. *Conceptual Foundations for Central Asian Republics Health Reform Model.* Almaty, Kazakhstan: ZdravReform, http://pdf.usaid.gov/pdf_docs/PNACK456.pdf.

Boseley, Sarah. 2012. "From User Fees to Universal Healthcare—a 30-Year Journey." *Guardian*, October 1, www.guardian.co.uk/society/sarah-boseley-global-health/2012/oct/01/worldbank-healthinsurance.

Bourdieu, Pierre. 1977. *Outline of a Theory of Practice*. Cambridge: Cambridge University Press.

————. 1984. *Distinction*. Cambridge, MA: Harvard University Press.

————. 1990. *The Logic of Practice*. Translated by R. Nice. Stanford, CA: Stanford University Press.

————. 1993. *The Field of Cultural Production: Essays on Art and Literature*. New York: Columbia University Press.

————. 1998. *Acts of Resistance: Against the Tyranny of the Market*. New York: New Press.

Bourgois, Philippe I. 1995. *In Search of Respect: Selling Crack in El Barrio*. Cambridge: Cambridge University Press.

Bowen, John R. 1993. *Muslims through Discourse*. Princeton, NJ: Princeton University Press.

Boyce, Mary. 1985. *Zoroastrians: Their Religious Beliefs and Practices*. London: Routledge and Kegan Paul.

Brain, Peter. 1986. *Galen on Bloodletting: A Study of the Origins, Development and Validity of His Opinions, with a Translation of the Three Works*. Cambridge: Cambridge University Press.

Bratton, Michael. 1989. "The Politics of Government-NGO Relations in Africa." *World Development* 17 (4): 569–86.

Breman, A., and C. Shelton. 2006. "Structural Adjustment Programs and Health." In *Globalization and Health*, ed. I. Kawachi and S. Wamala. Oxford: Oxford University Press.

Brennan, M. E., and R. Lancashire. 1978. "Association of Childhood Mortality with Housing Status and Unemployment." *Journal of Epidemiology and Community Health* 32 (1): 28–33.

Breuilly, John. 1982. *Nationalism and the State*. Chicago: University of Chicago Press.

Bronner, Stephen E., and Douglas M. Kellner, eds. 1989. *Critical Theory and Society: A Reader.* London: Routledge.

Brown, David W., with Anthony Burton, Marta Gacic-Dobo, and Rouslan Karimov. 2011. "A Summary of Global Routine Immunization Coverage through 2010." *Open Infectious Disease Journal* 5: 115–17.

Brown, Lawrence D., and Theodore R. Marmor. 1995. "Health Care Reform in the United States: Clinton or Canada?" In *Reforming Health Care: The Philosophy and Practice of International Health Reform,* ed. David Seedhouse. New York: John Wiley & Sons.

Brown, Wendy. 2003. "Neoliberalism and the End of Liberal Democracy." *Theory and Event* 7 (1), brisbin.polisci.wvu.edu/r/download/114178.

Browne, Edward G. 1921. *Arabian Medicine.* Cambridge: Cambridge University Press.

Browning, Genia. 1987. *Women and Politics in the USSR.* London: St. Martin.

Brubaker, Roger. 1993. "Social Theory as Habitus." In *Bourdieu: Critical Perspectives,* ed. Craig Calhoun, Edward LiPuma, and Moishe Postone. Chicago: University of Chicago Press.

Brugha, Ruairi, and Anthony Zwi. 2002. "Global Approaches to Private Sector Provision: Where Is the Evidence?" In *Health Policy in a Globalizing World,* ed. Kelley Lee, Kent Buse, and Suzanne Fustukian, 63–77. Cambridge: Cambridge University Press.

Bulgakov, Mikhail. 1975. *A Country Doctor's Notebook.* Translated by Michael Glenny. London: Collins and Harvill Press.

Burchell, Graham, with Colin Gordon and Peter Miller. 1991. *The Foucault Effect: Studies in Governmentality.* Chicago: University of Chicago Press.

Buse, Kent, and Gill Walt. 1996. "Aid Coordination for Health Sector Reform: A Conceptual Framework for Analysis and Assessment." *Health Policy* 38 (3): 173–87.

Bush, George H. W. 1991. "Remarks on Presenting the Presidential Medal of Freedom Awards." *George Bush Presidential Library and Museum,* http://bushlibrary.tamu.edu/research/public_papers.php?id=3642&year=&month=.

Butt, Ronald. 1981. "Mrs. Thatcher: The First Two Years." *Sunday Times,* May 3, www.margaretthatcher.org/document/104475.

Caldwell, Jane C. 1979. "Education as a Factor in Mortality Decline: An Examination of Nigerian Data." *Population Studies* 33 (3): 395–413.

Caldwell, Jane C., and Peter McDonald. 1982. "Influence of Maternal Education on Infant and Child Mortality: Levels and Causes." *Health Policy and Education* 2 (3–4): 251–56.

Caldwell, John. 1986. "Routes to Low Mortality in Poor Countries." *Population and Development Review* 12 (2): 171–220.

Caldwell, John C., and Pat Caldwell. 1991. "What Have We Learnt about the Cultural, Social and Behavioral Determinants of Health? From Selected Readings to the First Health Transitions Workshop." *Health Transition Review* 1 (1): 3–20.

Caldwell, John C., and Gigi Santow. 1991. "Preface." *Health Transition Review* 1 (1): 3–20.

Calhoun, Craig. 1993. "Habitus, Field, and Capital: The Question of Historical Specificity." In *Bourdieu: Critical Perspectives,* ed. Craig Calhoun, Edward LiPuma, and Moishe Postone. Chicago: University of Chicago Press.

———. 1994. "Nationalism, Civil Society and Democracy." In *Legacies of the Collapse of Marxism,* ed. John H. Moore, 81–105. Fairfax, VA: George Mason University Press.

Campbell, Donald. 1926. *Trubner's Oriental Series: Arabian Medicine and Its Influences on the Middle Ages.* 2 vols. London: Kegan Paul, Trench, Trubner.

Carrin, Guy. 1984. *Economic Evaluation of Health Care in Developing Countries.* Kent: Croom Helm.

———. 1986. "Drug Prescribing: A Discussion of Its Variability and (Ir)rationality." *Health Policy* 7 (1): 73–94.

Carrin, Guy, with Phillip Autier, Barou Djouater, and Marc Vereecke. 1992. "Direct Payment for Drugs at the Public Pharmacy in Fianga (Chad)." In *Strategies for Health Care Finance in Developing Countries: With a Focus on Community Financing in Sub-Saharan Africa,* ed. Guy Carrin and Marc Vereecke, 75–95. London: Macmillan.

Carrin, Guy, and Marc Vereecke. 1992. *Strategies for Health Care Finance in Developing Countries: With a Focus on Community Financing in Sub-Saharan Africa.* London: Macmillan.

Carstairs, Vera, and Russell Morris. 1989. "Deprivation and Mortality: An Alternative to Social Class." *Community Medicine* 11 (3): 210–19.

Cassels, Andrews. 1995. "Health Sector Reform: Key Issues in Less Developed Countries." *Journal of International Development* 7 (3): 329–48.

Center for Media and Democracy. 2013. "American Political Foundation." Sourcewatch, www.sourcewatch.org/index.php/American_Political_Foundation.

Chabot, Jarl. 1988. "The Bamako Initiative: Letter to the Editor." *Lancet* 8624: 1366.

Chandani, Yasmin. 1998. "Utilizing Prescribing Patterns to Determine Rational Drug Use in Khorog, GBAO, Tajikistan." Master's thesis, Yale University.

Charlton, Sue E., with Jana Everett and Kathleen Staudt, eds. 1989. *Women, the State, and Development.* New York: State University of New York Press.

Chatterjee, Partha. 1986. *Nationalist Thought and the Colonial World: A Derivative Discourse?* Minneapolis: University of Minnesota Press.

———. 1993. *The Nation and Its Fragments: Colonial and Postcolonial Histories*. Princeton, NJ: Princeton University Press.

Chekhov, Anton. 1899. "Uncle Vanya: Scenes from Country Life in Four Acts." In *Swan Song: Plays by Anton Chekhov*, trans. Marian Fell. New York: Scribner..

Chen, Lincoln C., with Emdadul Huq and Stan D'Souza. 1981. "Sex Bias in the Family Allocation of Food and Health Care in Rural Bangladesh." *Population and Development Review* 7 (1): 55–70.

Chen, Lincoln C., with Arthur Kleinman and Norma C. Ware. 1994. *Health and Social Change in International Perspective*. Boston: Harvard School of Public Health.

Chishti, Hakim G. M. 1991. *The Traditional Healer's Handbook: A Classic Guide to the Medicine of Avicenna*. Rochester, VT: Healing Arts Press.

Chowdhury, Zafrullah. 1995. *The Politics of Essential Drugs, The Makings of a Successful Health Strategy: Lessons from Bangladesh*. London: Zed Books.

Christiansen, Palle. 1969. *The Melanesian Cargo Cult: Millenarianism as a Factor in Cultural Change*. Copenhagen: Akademisk Forlag (DBK).

Chylinski, Ewa A. 1991. "Ritualism of Family Life in Soviet Central Asia: The Sunnat (Circumcision)." In *Cultural Continuity and Change in Central Asia*, ed. Shirin Akiner. London: Kegan Paul.

Clarke, Gerard. 1998. "Non-Governmental Organizations (NGOs) and Politics in the Developing World." *Political Studies* 46 (1): 36–52.

Clarke, Simon. 2005. "The Neoliberal Theory of Society." In *Neoliberalism: A Critical Reader*, ed. Alfredo Saad-Filho and Deborah Johnston, 50–59. London: Pluto Press.

Clifford, James. 1988. *Predicament of Culture*. Cambridge, MA: Harvard University Press.

Clifford, James, and George E. Marcus. 1986. *Writing Culture: The Poetics and Politics of Ethnography*. Berkeley: University of California Press.

Cockerham, William C. 1999. *Health and Social Change in Russia and Eastern Europe*. New York: Routledge.

Colclough, Christopher, and James Manor, eds. 1991. *States or Markets? Neo-liberalism and the Development Policy Debate*. Oxford: Clarendon Press.

Comaroff, Jean, and John Comaroff. 1991. *Of Revelation and Revolution*. Chicago: University of Chicago Press.

Communist Party of the Soviet Union. 1961. *Programme of the Communist Party of the Soviet Union*. Moscow: Foreign Languages Publishing House.

Connor, Walter D. 1991. "Equality and Opportunity." In *Soviet Social Problems*, ed. Anthony Jones, Walter D. Conner, and David E. Powell, 137–53. Boulder, CO: Westview Press.

Conroy, Mary Schaeffer. 1994. *In Health and in Sickness: Pharmacy, Pharmacists, and the Pharmaceutical Industry in Late Imperial, Early Soviet Russia*. Boulder, CO: East European Monographs.

Costello, Anthony, with Fiona Watson and David Woodward. 1994. *Human Face or Human Façade? Adjustment and the Health of Mothers and Children*. London: Centre for International Child Health, University of London.

Cox, Robert W. 1987. *Production, Power and World Order: Social Forces in the Making of History*. New York: Columbia University Press.

Creese, Andrew L. 1990. *User Charges for Health Care: A Review of Recent Experience*. Geneva: World Health Organization.

Crewe, Emma, and Elizabeth Harrison. 1988. *Whose Development? An Ethnography of Aid*. London: Zed Books.

Cribb, Alan. 1995. "A Turn for the Better? Philosophical Issues in Evaluating Health Care Reforms." In *Reforming Health Care: The Philosophy and Practice of International Health Reform*, ed. David Seedhouse. New York: John Wiley & Sons.

Cross, Peter N., with Maggie A. Huff, Jonathan D. Quick, and James A. Bates. 1986. "Revolving Drug Funds: Conducting Business in the Public Sector." *Social Science and Medicine* 22 (3): 335–43.

Cruikshank, Barbara. 1994. "The Will to Empower: Technologies of Citizenship and the War on Poverty." *Socialist Review* 23 (4): 29–55.

Csordas, Thomas J. 1993. *Embodiment and Experience: The Existential Ground of Culture and Self*. Cambridge: Cambridge University Press.

Cueto, Marcos. 2004. "The Origins of Primary Health Care and Selective Primary Health Care." *American Journal of Public Health* 94 (11): 1864–74.

Culyer, A. 1983. "Effectiveness and Efficiency of Health Services." *Effective Health Care* 1: 7–9.

Dabashi, Hamid. 1993. *Authority in Islam: From the Rise of Muhammad to the Establishment of the Umayyads*. London: Transaction.

Daftary, Farhad. 1990. *The Isma'ilis: Their History and Doctrines*. Cambridge: Cambridge University Press.

———. 1994. *The Assassin Legends: Myths of the Isma'ilis*. London: I. B. Tauris.

———. 1996. "Introduction: Isma'ilis and Isma'ili Studies." In *Mediaeval Isma'ili History and Thought*. Cambridge: Cambridge University Press.

———, ed. 1996. *Mediaeval Isma'ili History and Thought*. Cambridge: Cambridge University Press.

Dahl, Gudrun, and Annika Rabo, eds. 1992. *Kam-Ap or Take-Off: Local Notions of Development*. Stockholm: Stockholm Studies in Social Anthropology.

Dahlgren, Goran. 1991. "Strategies for Health Financing in Kenya—the Difficult Birth of a New Policy." *Scandanavian Journal of Social Medicine Suppl.* 46: 67–81.

Das, Veena. 1995. *Critical Events: An Anthropological Perspective on Contemporary India*. New Delhi: Oxford University Press.

Davis, Christopher. 2006. "Commentary: The Health Crisis in the USSR: Reflections on the Nicholas Eberstadt 1981 Review of *Rising Infant Mortality in the USSR in the 1970s*." *International Journal of Epidemiology* 35: 1400–1405.

Davis, Christopher, and Murray Feshbach. 1980. *Rising Infant Mortality in the USSR in the 1970s*. Washington, DC: US Department of Commerce.

Deakin, Nicholas. 2001. *In Search of Civil Society*. Basingstoke, Hampshire: Palgrave.

Dean, M. 2007. *Governing Societies: Political Perspectives on Domestic and International Law*. Berkshire: Open University Press/McGraw Hill.

De Beyer, Joy A., with Alexander S. Preker and Richard G. A. Feachem. 2000. "The Role of the World Bank in International Health: Renewed Commitment and Partnership." *Social Science and Medicine* 50 (2): 169–76.

De Brun, Suzanne, and Ray H. Elling. 1987. "Cuba and the Philippines: Contrasting Cases in World-System Analysis." *International Journal of Health Services* 17 (4): 681–701.

De Certeau, Michel. 1980. "On the Oppositional Practices of Everyday Life." *Social Text* 3: 3–43.

———. 1984. *The Practice of Everyday Life*. Berkeley: University of California Press.

De Ferranti, David M. 1985. "Paying for Health Services in Developing Countries: An Overview." World Bank Staff Working Papers, no. 721. Washington, DC: World Bank.

DeMars, William E. 2005. *NGOs and Transnational Networks: Wild Cards in World Politics*. London: Pluto Press.

Democracy Program. 1983. "Report to the President." National Endowment for Democracy, www.ned.org/docs/democracyProgram.pdf.

D'Encausse, Helene Carrere. 1966. *Islam and the Russian Empire: Reform and Revolution in Central Asia*. London: I. B. Tauris.

Denig, P., with F. M. Haaijer-Ruskamp, H. Wesseling, and A. Versluis. 1993. "Towards Understanding Treatment Preferences of Hospital Physicians." *Social Science and Medicine* 36 (7): 915–24.

Denig, P., with F. M. Haaijer-Ruskamp and D. H. Zijsling. 1988. "How Physicians Choose Their Drugs." *Social Science and Medicine* 27 (12): 1381–86.

Desclaux, Alice. 2004. "Equity in Access to AIDS Treatment in Africa: Pitfalls among Achievements." In *Unhealthy Health Policy: A Critical Anthropological Examination*, ed. Arachu Castro and Merill Singer, 115–32. New York: Altamira Press.

Desjarlais, Robert, with Leon Eisenberg, Byron Good, and Arthur Kleinman, eds. 1995. *World Mental Health: Problems and Priorities in Low-Income Countries*. New York: Oxford University Press.

De Vogli, Robert, and Gretchen Birbeck. 2005. "Structural Adjustment and HIV/AIDS: Potential Impact of Adjustment Policies on Vulnerabilities of Women and Children to HIV/AIDS in Sub-Saharan Africa." *Journal of Health, Population and Nutrition* 23 (2): 105–20.

De Waal, A., and R. Omaar. 1993. "Doing Harm by Doing Good? The International Relief Effort in Somalia." *Current History* 92 (574): 198–202.

Dhanagare D. N. 2001. "Civil Society, State and Democracy: Contextualizing a Discourse." *Sociological Bulletin* 50 (2): 167–91.

Dicken, Peter. 1998. *Global Shift: Transforming the World Economy.* 3rd ed. London: Sage Publications.

Diop, F., with A. Yazbeck and R. Bitrán. 1995. "The Impact of Alternative Cost Recovery Schemes on Access and Equity in Niger." *Health Policy Planning* 10 (3): 223–40.

Dostoyevsky, Fyodor. 1945. *The Brothers Karamazov.* Translated by Constance Garnett. New York: Random House.

———. 1955. *Best Short Stories, translated with an introduction by Davis Magarshack.* New York: Modern Library.

Douglas, Mary, and Baron Isherwood. 1979. *The World of Goods.* New York: Basic Books.

Douglas, William A. 1972. *Developing Democracy.* Washington, DC: Heldref Publications.

Doyal, Lesley. 1979. *The Political Economy of Health.* London: Pluto Press.

Doyle, Michael. 1986. *Empires.* Ithaca, NY: Cornell University Press.

Drabek, Anne G. 1987. "Development Alternatives: The Challenge for NGOs— An Overview of the Issues." *World Development* 15 (suppl.): ix–xv.

Drake, David F. 1994. *Reforming the Health Care Market: An Interpretive Economic History.* Washington, DC: Georgetown University Press.

Dreyfus, Herbert L., and Paul Rabinow. 1983. *Michel Foucault: Beyond Structuralism and Hermeneutics.* 2nd ed. Chicago: University of Chicago Press.

Dumoulin, J., and M. Kaddar. 1993. "Le paiement des soins par les usagers dans le pays d'Afrique sub-saharienne: Rationalité économique et autres questions subséquentes." *Sciences Sociales et Santé* 11 (2): 81–119.

Durkheim, Emile. 1933. *The Division of Labor in Society.* New York: Free Press.

———. 1951. *Suicide.* New York: Free Press.

Ebenstein, Alan O. 2003. *Friedrich Hayek: A Biography.* Chicago: University of Chicago Press.

Eberstadt, Nicholas. 1981. "The Health Crisis in the USSR." *International Journal of Epidemiology* 35 (6): 1384–94.

———. 2006. "Commentary: Reflections on 'The Health Crisis in the USSR.'" *International Journal of Epidemiology* 35: 1394–97.

Ebrahim, G. J., and J. P. Ranken. 1988. *Primary Health Care.* London: MacMillan.

Edmondson, Linda, ed. 1992. *Women and Society in Russia and the Soviet Union*. Cambridge: Cambridge University Press.

Edwards, M., with D. Hulme and T. Wallace. 2000. "Increasing Leverage for Development: Challenges for NGOs in a Global Future." In *New Roles and Relevance: Development NGOs and the Challenge of Change*, ed. D. Lewis and T. Wallace. Hartford, CT: Kumarian Press.

Edwards, Michael. 1996. "International Development NGOS: Legitimacy, Accountability, Regulation and Roles." London: Commission of the Future of the Voluntary Sector and the British Overseas Aid Group.

Edwards, Michael, and David Hulme. 1996a. "Introduction." In *Beyond the Magic Bullet: NGO Performance and Accountability in the Post-Cold War World*, 1–22. West Harford: Kumarian.

———. 1996b. "Too Close for Comfort? The Impact of Official Aid on Non-Governmental Organizations." *World Development* 24 (6): 961–73.

Eickelman, Dale F., ed. 1993. *Russia's Muslim Frontiers: New Directions in Cross-Cultural Analysis*. Bloomington: Indiana University Press.

Eisenstadt, S. N., and Louis Roninger. 1980. "Patron-Client Relations as a Model of Structuring Social Exchange." *Comparative Studies in Society and History* 22 (1): 42–77.

Eisenstein, Zila. 1989. "Reflections." In *Promissory Notes: Women in the Transition to Socialism*, ed. Rayn Rapp and Marilyn Young. New York: Monthly Review Press.

Elgood, Cyril. 1934. *Medicine in Persia*. New York: Paul B. Hoeber.

Emin, Leon. 1984. *Muslims in the USSR*. Moscow: Novosti Press Agency Publishing House.

Engels, Friedrich. 1958. *Conditions of the Working Class in England*. New York: Macmillan.

———. 1993. *The Condition of the Working Class in England*. Oxford: Oxford University Press.

EOHCS (European Observatory on Health Care Systems). 2000. *Health Care Systems in Transition: Tajikistan*. Copenhagen: WHO Regional Office for Europe.

Epstein, Helen. 1998. "Life and Death on the Social Ladder." *New York Review of Books* 45 (12): 26–30.

Escobar, Arturo. 1995. *Encountering Development: The Making and Unmaking of the Third World*. Princeton, NJ: Princeton University Press.

Esmail, Aziz, and Azim Nanji. 1977. "The Isma'ilis in History." In *Isma'ili Contributions to Islamic Culture*, ed. Seyyed H Nasr, 227–65. Tehran: Imperial Iranian Academy of Philosophy.

Esty, D. C., with J. A. Goldstone, T. R. Gurr, B. Harff, M. Levy, G. D. Dabelko, et al. 1998. *State Failure Task Force Report: Phase II Findings*. Washington, DC: Central Intelligence Agency.

Etkin, Nina L. 1988. "Cultural Constructions of Efficacy." In *The Context of Medicines in Developing Countries: Studies in Pharmaceutical Anthropology*, ed. Sjaak Van Der Geest and Susan Reynolds Whyte, 299–326. Dordrecht: Kluwer Academic Publishers.

Evans, I. 1995. "SAPing Maternal Health." *Lancet* 346 (8982): 1046.

Evans, Rowland, and Robert Novak. 1981. *The Reagan Revolution*. New York: E. P. Dutton.

Evans-Pritchard, E. E. 1937. *Witchcraft, Oracles and Magic among the Azande*. Oxford: Clarendon Press.

Falkingham, Jane. 2000. *Women and Gender Relations in Tajikistan*. London: Department of Social Policy, London School of Economics.

———. 2002. "Poverty, Affordability and Access to Health Care." In *Health Care in Central Asia*, ed. Martin McKee, Judith Healy, Jane Falkingham, 42–56. European Observatory on Health Care Systems Series. Buckingham: Open University Press.

———. 2004. "Poverty, Out-of-pocket Payments and Access to Health Care: Evidence from Tajikistan." *Social Science and Medicine* 58: 247–58.

Fanon, Franz. 1963. *The Wretched of the Earth*. New York: Grove Press.

Farah, Abdul-Aziz, and Samuel H. Preston. 1982. "Child Mortality Differentials in Sudan." *Population and Development Review* 8 (2): 365–83.

Farmer, Paul. 1992. *AIDS and Accusation: Haiti and the Geography of Blame*. Berkeley: University of California Press.

———. 1999. *Infections and Inequalities: The Modern Plagues*. Berkeley: University of California Press.

———. 2003. *Pathologies of Power: Health, Human Rights and the New War on the Poor*. Berkeley: University of California Press.

———. 2004. "An Anthropology of Structural Violence." *Current Anthropology* 45 (3): 305–26.

———. 2005. *Pathologies of Power: Health, Human Rights, and the New War on the Poor*. Berkeley: University of California Press.

Farmer, Paul, and Byron Good. 1991. "Illness Representations in Medical Anthropology: A Critical Review and a Case Study of the Representation of AIDS in Haiti." In *The Mental Representation of Health and Illness*, ed. J. Skelton and R. Croyle, 131–67. New York: Springer-Verlag.

Feldstein, Martin S. 1973. "The Welfare Loss of Excess Health Insurance." *Journal of Political Economy* 81: 251–58.

Felmy, Sabine. 1996. *The Voice of the Nightingale: A Personal Account of the Wakhi Culture in Hunza*. Karachi: Oxford University Press.

Femia, Joseph. 1981. *Gramsci's Political Thought: Hegemony, Consciousness, and the Revolutionary Process*. New York: Clarendon Press.

Ferguson, Anne. 1988. "Commercial Pharmaceutical Medicine and Medicalization: A Case Study from El Salvador." In *The Context of Medicines in*

Developing Countries: Studies in Pharmaceutical Anthropology, ed. Sjaak van der Geest and Susan Reynolds Whyte, 19–46. Boston: Kluwer Academic Publishers.

Ferguson, James. 1988. "Cultural Exchange: New Development in the Anthropology of Commodities." *Cultural Anthropology* 3: 488–513.

———. 1994. *The Anti-politics Machine: "Development," Depoliticization, and Bureaucratic Power in Lesotho.* Minneapolis: University of Minnesota Press.

Field, Mark G. 1967. *Soviet Socialized Medicine: An Introduction.* New York: Free Press.

———. 1976. "The Modern Medical System: The Soviet Variant." In *Asian Medical Systems,* ed. Charles Leslie. Berkeley: University of California Press.

———. 1986. "Soviet Infant Mortality: A Mystery Story." In *Advances in International Maternal and Child Health,* vol. 6, ed. D. B. Jelliffe and E. F. P. Jellife, 25–65. Oxford: Clarendon Press.

———. 1995. "The Health Crisis in the Former Soviet Union: A Report from the 'Post-War' Zone." *Social Science and Medicine* 41 (11): 1469–78.

Fierman, William, ed. 1991. *Soviet Central Asia: The Failed Transformation.* Boulder, CO: Westview Press.

Filer, J., with L. W. Kenny and R. B. Morton. 1993. "Redistribution, Income, and Voting." *American Journal of Political Science* 37 (1): 63–87.

Firth, Raymond. 1983. *We the Tikopia: A Sociological Study of Kinship in Primitive Polynesia.* Stanford, CA: Stanford University Press.

———. 1984. "The Plasticity of Myth: Cases from Tikopia." In *Sacred Narrative: Readings in the Theory of Myth,* ed. Alan Dundes, 207–16. Berkeley: University of California Press.

Fish, M. S. 1994. "Russia's Fourth Transition." *Journal of Democracy* 5 (3): 31–42.

Fisher, W. F. 1991. "Doing Good? The Politics and Antipolitics of NGO Practices." *Annual Review of Anthropology* 26 (1): 439–64.

Fitzpatrick, Sheila. 1992. *The Cultural Front: Power and Culture in Revolutionary Russia.* Ithaca, NY: Cornell University Press.

Flegg, A. T. 1982. "Inequality of Income, Illiteracy and Medical Care as Determinants of Infant Mortality in Underdeveloped Countries." *Population Studies* 36 (3): 441–58.

Foltz, A. 1994. "Donor Funding for Health Reform in Africa: Is Non-Project Assistance the Right Prescription?" *Health Policy and Planning* 9 (4): 371–84.

Fort, Meredith, with Mary Ann Mercer, Oscar Gish and Steve Gloyd, eds. 2004. *Sickness and Wealth: The Corporate Assault on Global Health.* Cambridge: South End Press.

Foster, George M. 1982. "Applied Anthropology and International Health: Retrospect and Prospect." *Human Organization* 41 (3): 189–97.

———. 1984. "Anthropological Research Perspectives on Health Problems in Developing Countries." *Social Science and Medicine* 18 (10): 847–54.

Foster, S. 1989. "A Note on Financing of Health Services: Some Issues and Examples, Briefing Note prepared for DANIDA, WHO Action Programme on Essential Drugs." Geneva: World Health Organization.

Foster, S., and N. Drager. 1988. "How Community Drug Sales Schemes May Succeed." *World Health Forum* 9: 209–28.

Foucault, Michel. 1973. *The Order of Things: An Archeology of the Human Sciences*. New York: Vintage Book.

———. 1979. *Discipline and Punish: The Birth of the Prison*. New York: Vintage Books.

———. 2007. *Security, Territory Population: Lectures at the College de France, 1977–1978*. New York: Picador.

Fowler, Alan. 1991. "The Role of NGOs in Changing State-Society Relations: Perspectives from Eastern and Southern Africa." *Development Policy Review* 9: 43–48.

———. 1997. *Striking a Balance: A Guide to Enhancing the Effectiveness of NGOs in International Development*. London: Earthscan.

Fox, Renee. 1981. "The Medicalization and Demedicalization of American Society." In *The Sociology of Health and Illness: Critical Perspectives*, ed. Peter Conrad and Rochelle Kern, 527–34. New York: St. Martin's Press.

Frankenberg, Ronald. 1988. "Gramsci, Culture, and Medical Anthropology." *Medical Anthropology Quarterly* 2 (4): 324–37.

Frenk, Julio, with José Bobadilla, Claudio Stern, Tomas Frejka, and Rafael Lozano. 1991. "Elements for a Theory of Health Transition." *Health Transition Review* 1 (1): 21–38.

Frenzen, D., and Dennis P. Hogan. 1982. "The Impact of Class, Education and Health Care on Infant Mortality in a Developing Society: The Case of Rural Thailand." *Demography* 19 (3): 391–408.

Frieden, Nancy Mandelker. 1977. "The Russian Cholera Epidemic 1892–1893, and Medical Professionalization." *Journal of Social History* 10: 538–59.

———. 1981. *Russian Physicians in an Era of Reform and Revolution, 1856–1905*. Princeton, NJ: Princeton University Press.

Friedman, Milton. 2002. *Capitalism and Freedom*. Chicago: University of Chicago Press.

Frye, R. N., ed. 1975. *The Cambridge History of Iran*. Vol. 4. Cambridge: Cambridge University Press.

Fuglesang, Andreas. 1982. *About Understanding: Ideas and Observations on Cross-Cultural Communication*. Uppsala: Dag Hammarskjold Foundation.

———. 1984. "The Myth of People's Ignorance." *Development Dialogue* 1 (2): 42–62.

Fukuyama, Francis. 1989. "The End of History?" *National Interest* 18: 21–28.

———. 1992. *The End of History and the Last Man*. New York: Free Press.

Gabe, Jonathan, and Michael Bury. 1996. "Anxious Times: The Benzodiazepine Controversy and the Fracturing of Expert Authority." In *Contested Ground: Public Purpose and Private Interest in the Regulation of Prescription Drugs*, ed. Peter Davis. New York: Oxford University Press.

Gaines, Atwood, and Robert Hahn. 1985. "Among the Physicians: Encounter, Exchange and Transformation." In *Physicians of Western Medicine*. Dordrecht: Kluwer Academic Press.

Galtung, Johan. 1969. "Violence, Peace and Peace Research." *Journal of Peace Research* 6 (3): 167–91.

———. 1993. "Kulturelle Gewalt." *Der Bürger im Staat* 43 (2): 106.

Gantt, W. H. 1937. *Russian Medicine*. New York: Paul B. Hoeber.

Garrett, Laurie. 2000. *Betrayal of Trust: The Collapse of Global Public Health*. New York: Hyperion.

Geertz, Clifford. 1973. *The Interpretation of Cultures*. New York: Basic Books.

Gefenas, Eugenijus. 1995. "Health Care in Lithuania: From Idealism to Reality?" In *Reforming Health Care: The Philosophy and Practice of International Health Reform*, ed. David Seedhouse. New York: John Wiley & Sons.

Gellner, Ernest. 1981. *Muslim Society*. Cambridge: Cambridge University Press.

———. 1983. *Nations and Nationalism*. Ithaca, NY: Cornell University Press.

George, Susan. 1997. "How to Win the War of Ideas: Lessons from the Gramscian Right." *Dissent* 44 (3): 47–53.

Gertler, Paul, with L. Locay and W. Sanderson. 1987. "Are User Fees Regressive?" *Journal of Econometrics* 36: 67–88.

Gertler, Paul, with Luis Locay, Warren Sanderson, Avi Dor, and Jacques van der Gaag. 1988. "Health Care Financing and the Demand for Medical Care." World Bank Living Standards Study, Working Paper No. 37. Washington, DC: World Bank.

Gertler, Paul, and Jacques van der Gaag. 1988. "Measuring the Willingness to Pay for Social Services in Developing Countries." World Bank LSMS Working Paper No. 45. Washington, DC: World Bank.

Ghai, D. 1991. *The IMF and the South: The Social Impact of Crisis and Adjustment*. London: Zed Books.

Giddens, Anthony. 1971. *Capitalism and Modern Social Theory*. Cambridge: Cambridge University Press.

Gilligan, J. 1997. *Violence: Reflections on a National Epidemic*. New York: Vintage Books.

Gilson, L. 1988. *Government Health Care Charges: Is Equity Being Abandoned?* EPC publication 15. London: School of Hygiene and Tropical Medicine.

———. 1997. "The Lessons of User Fee Experience in Africa." *Health Policy Plan* 12: 273–85.

Gilson, L., with D. Kalyalya, F. Kuchler, S. Lake, H. Oranga, and M. Ouendo. 2001. "Strategies for Promoting Equity: Experience with Community Financing in Three African Countries." *Health Policy* 58 (1): 37–67.

Goffman, Erving. 1961. *Asylums: Essays on the Social Situation of Mental Patients and Other Inmates*. Garden City, NY: Anchor.

Goldman, Marshall I. 1972. *The Spoils of Progress: Environmental Pollution in the Soviet Union*. Cambridge, MA: MIT Press.

Goldman, Michael. 2005. *Imperial Nature: The World Bank and Struggles for Social Justice in the Age of Globalization*. New Haven, CT: Yale University Press.

Golladay, Fredrick, and Bernhard Liese. 1980. "Health Problems and Policies in the Developing Countries." World Bank Staff Working Paper no 412. Washington, DC: World Bank.

Good, Byron J. 1977. "The Heart of What's the Matter: The Semantics of Illness in Iran." *Culture, Medicine and Psychiatry* 1: 25–58.

———. 1994. *Medicine, Rationality, and Experience: An Anthropological Perspective*. Cambridge: Cambridge University Press.

Good, Byron, and Mary-Jo DelVecchio Good. 1982. "Toward a Meaning-Centered Analysis of Popular Illness Categories: 'Fright Illness' and 'Heart Distress' in Iran." In *Cultural Conceptions of Mental Health and Therapy*, ed. A. J. Marsella and G. M. White, 141–66. Dodrecht: D. Reidel.

———. 1992. "The Comparative Study of Greco-Islamic Medicine: The Integration of Medical Knowledge into Local Symbolic Contexts." In *Paths to Asian Medical Knowledge*, ed. Charles Leslie and Allan Young. Berkeley: University of California Press.

———. 1994. "In the Subjunctive Mode: Epilepsy Narratives in Turkey." *Social Science and Medicine* 38 (6): 835–42.

Good, Mary-Jo DelVecchio. 1995. "Competence and Clinical Narratives in Oncology." In *American Medicine: The Quest for Competence*. Berkeley: University of California Press.

Good, Mary-Jo DelVecchio, and Byron Good. 1988. "Ritual, the State, and the Transformation of Emotional Discourse in Iranian Society." *Culture Medicine and Psychiatry* 12: 43–63.

Goorin, Allan M. 1991. "Polycythemia." In *Manual of Neonatal Care*, ed. John P. Cloherty and Ann R. Stark, 3rd ed. Boston: Little, Brown.

Gordon, Colin. 1991. "Governmental Rationality: An Introduction." In *The Foucault Effect: Studies in Governmentality*, ed. Graham Burchell, Colin Gordon, and Peter Miller. Chicago: University of Chicago Press.

Gortmaker, Steven L. 1979. "Poverty and Infant Mortality in the United States." *American Sociological Review* 44: 280–97.

Gramsci, Antonio. 1971. *Selections from the Prison Notebooks*. Translated by Quintin Hoare and Geoffrey Nowell Smith. New York: International Publishers.

———. 1985. *Selections from Cultural Writings*. Edited by David Forgacs and Geoffrey Nowell-Smith, translated by William Boelhower. Cambridge, MA: Harvard University Press.

Green, A., and A. Matthias. 1997. *Non-Governmental Organizations and Health in Developing Countries*. New York: St. Martin's Press.

Greenhalgh, T. 1987. "Drug Prescription and Self-Medication in India: An Exploratory Survey." *Social Science and Medicine* 25 (3): 307–18.

Greider, W. 1992. *Who Will Tell the People: The Betrayal of American Democracy*. New York: Simon & Schuster.

Grevenmeyer, Jan-Heeren. 1982. *Herrschaft, Raub und Gegenseitigkeit: Die politische Geschichte Badakhshans 1500–1883*. Weisbaden.

Griffiths, Adrian. 1986. "Drug Supply and Use in Developing Countries: Problems and Policies." In *Health, Nutrition, and Economic Crisis: Approaches to Policy in the Third World*, ed. David E. Bell and Michael R. Reich. Dover: Auburn House.

Gross, Jo-Ann, ed. 1992. *Muslims in Central Asia: Expressions of Identity and Change*. Durham, NC: Duke University Press.

Gu, Qiuping, Charles F. Dillon, and Vicki L. Burt. 2010. "Prescription Drug Use Continues to Increase: U.S. Prescription Drug Data for 2007–2008." NCHS Data Brief 42. Centers for Disease Control, www.cdc.gov/nchs/data/databriefs/db42.pdf.

Gupta, Manisha. 1993. "Health Delivery at the Village Level." In *People's Health in People's Hands, Indian Experiences in Decentralized Health Care: A Model for Health*, ed. Panchayati Raj, N. H. Antia, and Kavita Bhatia, 15–42. Bombay: Foundation for Research in Community Health.

Haaijer-Ruskamp, F. V., and Petra Denig. 1996. "New Approaches to Influencing Physicians' Drug Choices: The Practice-Based Strategy." In *Contested Ground: Public Purpose and Private Interest in the Regulation of Prescription Drugs*, ed. Peter Davis. New York: Oxford University Press.

Haak, H. 1987. "Pharmaceuticals in Two Brazilian Villages: Lay Practices and Perceptions." *Social Science and Medicine* 27 (12): 1415–27.

Habermas, Jürgen. 1971. *Knowledge and Human Interests*. Boston: Beacon Press,

———. 1984. *Theory of Communicative Action*. Vol. 2. Boston: Beacon Press.

———. 1987. *The Philosophical Discourse of Modernity: Twelve Lectures*. Cambridge: MIT Press.

Habib, A., and P. Vaughan. 1986. "The Determinants of Health Services Utilization in Southern Iraq: A Household Interview Survey." *International Journal of Epidemiology* 15 (3): 395–402.

Hackler, Chris. 1995. "Health Care Reform in the United States." In *Reforming Health Care: The Philosophy and Practice of International Health Reform*, ed. David Seedhouse. New York: John Wiley & Sons.

Haegeman, Marc. 2004. "The General Meeting Files of the Mont Pèlerin Society (1947–1998)." Liberaal Archief, www.liberaalarchief.be/MPS2005.pdf.

Hall, Stuart. 1992. "Cultural Studies and Its Theoretical Legacies." In *Cultural Studies*, ed. Lawrence Grossberg, Cary Nelson, Paula Treichler. New York: Routledge.

Hampton, M. D., with L. R. Ward, B. Rowe, and E. J. Threfall. 1998. "Molecular Fingerprinting of Multidrug-Resistant Salmonella enterica Serotype Typhi." *Emerging Infectious Diseases* 4 (2).

Handelman, S. 1994. "The Russian Mafiya." *Foreign Affairs* 73 (2): 85–86.

Hanlon, J. 1991. *Mozambique: Who Calls the Shots?* London: James Currey.

———. 1996. *Peace without Profit: How the IMF Blocks Rebuilding in Mozambique.* Portsmouth: Heinemann.

Hardon, Anita, and Najmi Kanji. 1992. "New Horizons in the 1990s." In *Drugs Policy in Developing Countries*, ed. Najmi Kanji, Anita Hardon, Jan Willem Harnmeijer, Masuma Mamdani, and Gill Walt. London: Zed Books.

Harvard Medical School and Open Society Institute. 1999. *The Global Impact of Drug-Resistant Tuberculosis.* Boston: Program in Infectious Disease and Social Change, Department of Social Medicine, Harvard Medical School.

Hartwell, R. M. 1995. *History of the Mont Pèlerin Society.* Indianapolis, IN: Liberty Fund.

Harvey, David. 1989. "From Managerialism to Entrepreneurialism: The Transformation in Urban Governance in Late Capitalism." *Geografiska Annaler B* 71 (1): 3–45.

———. 1990. *The Condition of Postmodernity.* Cambridge: Blackwell.

———. 2005. *A Brief History of Neoliberalism.* New York: Oxford University Press.

Hayek, Friedrich August. 1949. "The Intellectuals and Socialism." *University of Chicago Law Review* (Spring).

Healy, Judith, Jane Falkingham, and Martin McKee. 2002. "Health Care Systems in Transition." In *Health Care in Central Asia*, ed. Martin McKee, Judith Healy, and Jane Falkingham. European Observatory on Health Care Systems Series. Buckingham: Open University Press.

Hecht, R., with C. Overhold and H. Homberg. 1993. "Improving the Implementation of Cost Recovery for Health: Lessons from Zimbabwe." *Health Policy* 25 (3): 213–42.

Helmstadter, Sarah. 1990. "Splitting Headache: The Soviet Union's Aspirin Famine." *New Republic* 203 (18): 12.

Herxheimer, Andrew. 1984. "Immortality for Old Drugs?" *Lancet* 323 (8392): 1460–61.

———. 1991. "Soviet Union: Supplying Essential Medicines." *Lancet* 338 (8775): 1135–36.

Herzfeld, Michael. 1985. *The Poetics of Manhood: Contest and Identity in a Cretan Village.* Princeton, NJ: Princeton University Press.

———. 1991. *The Social Production of Indifference: Exploring the Symbolic Roots of Western Bureaucracy*. Oxford: Berg.

Hetmanek, Allen. 1990. "The Political Face of Islam in Tajikistan: A Review of Muriel Atkin's *The Subtlest Battle*." *Central Asian Survey* 9 (3): 99–111.

Hibou, Beatrice. 1998. "The Political Economy of the World Bank's Discourse: From Economic Catechism to Missionary Deeds (and Misdeeds)." Translated by Janet Roitman. *Etudes du CERI* 39.

Hirschman, A. O. 1987. *Getting Ahead Collectively: Grassroots Experiences in Latin America*. New York: Pergamon.

Hobsbawm, Eric J. 1964. *Labouring Men: Studies in the History of Labour*. London: Weidenfeld and Nicholson.

———. 1983. "Introduction: Inventing Tradition." In *The Invention of Tradition*, ed. Eric Hobsbawm and Terence Ranger. Cambridge: Cambridge University Press.

———. 1990. *Nations and Nationalism since 1780*. Cambridge: Cambridge University Press.

———. 1994. *The Age of Extremes: A History of the World (1914–1991)*. New York: Pantheon Books.

Hobsbawm, Eric, and Terence Ranger, eds. 1983. *The Invention of Tradition*. Cambridge: Cambridge University Press.

Hollis, Martin, and Steven Lukes, eds. 1982. *Rationality and Relativism*. Cambridge, MA: MIT Press.

Hulme, David, and Michael Edwards. 1997. "NGOs, States and Donors: An Overview." In *NGOs, States and Donors: Too Close for Comfort?*, 3–22. London: McMillan Press.

Huntington, Samuel. 1993. "The Clash of Civilization?" *Foreign Affairs* 72 (3): 22–49.

Hutchinson, John F. 1990. *Politics and Public Health in Revolutionary Russia, 1890–1918*. Baltimore, MD: Johns Hopkins University Press.

Hyde, Gordon. 1974. *The Soviet Health Service: A Historical and Comparative Study*. London: Lawrence and Wishart.

Ibn Khaldun. 2005. *The Muqaddimah: An Introduction to History*. Princeton, NJ: Princeton University Press.

Igun, U. 1979. "States in Health Seeking: A Descriptive Model." *Social Science and Medicine* 13 (4): 445–56.

———. 1992. "The Underdevelopment of Traditional Medicine in Africa." In *The Political Economy of Health in Africa*, ed. Toyin Falola and Dennis Ityavyar, Africa Series no. 60, 143–62. Athens: Ohio University Center for International Studies Monographs in International Studies.

Ilcan, Susan, and Anita Lacey. 2011. *Governing the Poor: Exercises of Poverty Reduction, Practices of Global Aid*. Montreal: McGill-Queen's University Press.

Illich, Ivan. 1976. *Medical Nemesis: The Expropriation of Health.* New York: Bantam.

International Monetary Fund. 1998. "Republic of Tajikistan: Recent Economic Developments." IMF Staff Country Report No. 98/16. Washington, DC: International Monetary Fund.

Iqbal, Muhammad. 1989. "The Spirit of Muslim Culture." In *The Reconstruction of Religious Thought in Islam,* ed. M. Saeed Sheikh, Iqbal. Lahore: Academy Pakistan, Institute of Islamic Culture.

Isenalumhe, A., and O. Oviawe. 1988. "Polypharmacy: Its Cost Burden and Barrier to Medical Care in a Drug-Oriented Health Care System." *International Journal of Health Services* 18 (2): 335–42.

Isin, E. F. 2000. "Governing Cities without Government." In *Democracy, Citizenship and the Global City,* ed. E. Isin, 148–68. London: Routledge.

Ivanov, W. 1932. "Notes sur 'l'Ummu'l-Kitab' des Ismaeliens de l'Asie Centrale." *Revue des Études Islamiques* 418.

Jaffré, Y., and de J. P. O. Sardan, eds. 2003. *Une médicine inhospitalière: Les mauvaises relations entre soignants et soignés dans cinq capitales d'Afrique de l'Ouest.* Paris: Karthala.

Jain, A. K. 1985. "Determinants of Regional Variations in Infant Mortality in Rural India." *Population Studies* 39 (3): 407–24.

Jallade, Lucila, with Eddy Lee and Joel Samoff. 1994. "International Cooperation." In *Coping with Crisis: Austerity, Adjustment and Human Resources.* London: Cassell/UNESCO.

James, C. D., with K. Hanson, B. McPake, D. Balabanova, D. Gawtkin, I. Hopwood, C. Kirunga, R. Knippenberg, B. Meessen, S. S. Morris, A. Preker, Y. Souteyrand, A. Tibouti, P. Villeneuve, and K. Xu. 2006. "To Retain or Remove User Fees? Reflections on the Current Debate in Low- and Middle-Income Countries." *Applied Health Economics and Health Policy* 5 (3): 137–53.

James, Chris, with Saul S. Morris, Regina Keith, and Anne Taylor. 2005. "Impact on Child Mortality of Removing User Fees: Simulation Model." *British Medical Journal* 331: 747–49.

Jameson, Frederic. 1991. *Postmodernism, or the Cultural Logic of Late Capitalism.* Durham, NC: Duke University Press.

Jessop, B. 2002. "Liberalism, Neoliberalism, and Urban Governance: A State-Theoretical Perspective." *Antipode* 34 (3): 452–72.

Jhally, Sut. 1987. *The Codes of Advertising: Fetishism and the Political Economy of Meaning in the Consumer Society.* New York: Routledge.

Johnston, Hank. 1994. *New Social Movements.* Philadelphia: Temple University Press.

Jolly, R., with F. Stewart and G. A. Cornia. 1992. *Adjustment with a Human Face: Protecting the Vulnerable and Promoting Growth.* New York: Clarendon Print.

Jones, Daniel Stedman. 2012. *Masters of the Universe: Hayek, Friedman, and the Birth of Neoliberal Politics*. Princeton, NJ: Princeton University Press.

Kaiser, Paul. 1994. "Culture and Civil Society in International Context: The Case of Aga Khan Health Care and Education Initiatives in Tanzania." PhD diss., Indiana University.

———. 1996. *Culture, Transnationalism, and Civil Society*. Westport, CT: Praeger.

Kanji, Najmi. 1989. "Charging for Drugs in Africa: UNICEF's Bamako Initiative." *Health Policy and Planning* 4 (2): 110–20.

———. 1992. "Action at Country Level: The International and National Influences." In *Drugs Policy in Developing Countries*, ed. Najmi Kanji, Anita Hardon, Jan Willem Harnmeijer, Masuma Mamdani, and Gill Walt. London: Zed Books.

Kanji, Najmi, and Anita Hardon. 1992. "What Has Been Achieved and Where Are We Now?" In *Drugs Policy in Developing Countries*, ed. Najmi Kanji, Anita Hardon, Jan Willem Harnmeijer, Masuma Mamdani, and Gill Walt. London: Zed Books.

Kanji, Najmi, with Anita Hardon, Jan Willem Harnmeijer, Masuma Mamdani, and Gill Walt. 1992. *Drugs Policy in Developing Countries*. London: Zed Books.

Kaplan, Martha. 1995. *Neither Cargo nor Cult: Ritual Politics and the Colonial Imagination in Fiji*. Durham, NC: Duke University Press.

Kapur, Devesh, with John P. Lewis and Richard Webb, eds. 1997. *The World Bank: Its First Half Century*. Washington, DC: Brookings Institute.

Karpat, Kemal. 1986. "Introduction: Elites and the Transmission of Nationality and Identity." *Central Asian Survey* 5 (3/4): 5–24.

Kassalow, Jordan S. 2001. "Why Health Is Important to US Foreign Policy." New York: Milbank Memorial Fund.

Kay, D. A. 1976. "The International Regulation of Pharmaceutical Drugs." Report to the National Science Foundation on the Application of International Regulatory Techniques to Scientific/Technical Problems. Washington, DC: American Society of International Law.

Kelman, S. 1979. "The Social Nature of the Definition in Health." *International Journal of Health Services* 5 (4): 625–42.

Kennedy, B. P., with I. Kawachi and E. Brainerd. 1998. "The Role of Social Capital in the Russian Mortality Crisis." *World Development* 26: 2029–43.

Kennedy, John F. 1961. "Special Message to the Congress on Foreign Aid." Speech delivered on March 22. American Presidency Project, www.presidency.ucsb.edu/ws/index.php?pid = 8545.

Keshavjee, Salmaan. 1996. "Medical Anthropology: Providing an Insight into the Social, Political and Economic Determinants of Health." *Journal of the American Medical Association* 276 (13): 1096–97.

———. 1998. "Medicines and Transitions: The Political Economy of Health and Social Change in Post-Soviet Badakhshan, Tajikistan." PhD diss., Harvard University.

———. 2006. "Bleeding Babies in Badakhshan: Symbolism, Materialism, and the Political Economy of Traditional Medicine in Post-Soviet Tajikistan." *Medical Anthropology Quarterly* 20 (1): 72–93.

Keshavjee, Salmaan, and Mercedes Becerra. 2000. "Disintegrating Health Services and Resurgent Tuberculosis in Post-Soviet Tajikistan: An Example of Structural Violence." *Journal of the American Medical Association* 283 (9): 1201.

Keynes, John Maynard. 1936. *The General Theory of Employment, Interest and Money*. London: Palgrave Macmillan.

Khodjamurodov, Ghafur, and Bernd Rechel. 2010. "Tajikistan: Health System Review." *Health Systems in Transition* 12 (2): 1–154.

Kim, Jim Yong. 1993. "Pills, Production and the Symbolic Code: Pharmaceuticals and the Political Economy of Meaning in South Korea." PhD diss., Harvard University.

Kivumbi, G. W., and F. Kintu. 2002. "Exemptions and Waivers from Cost Sharing: Ineffective Safety Nets in Decentralized Districts in Uganda." *Health Policy and Planning* 17: 64–71.

Kleinman, Arthur. 1978. "Concepts and a Model for the Comparison of Medical Systems and Cultural Systems." *Social Science and Medicine* 12: 85–93.

———. 1980. *Patients and Healers in the Context of Culture: An Exploration of the Borderland between Anthropology, Medicine, and Psychiatry*. Berkeley: University of California Press.

———. 1988. *The Illness Narratives: Suffering, Healing, and the Human Condition*. New York: Basic Books.

———. 1993. "What Is Specific to Western Medicine." In *Encyclopedia of the History of Medicine*, ed. W. F. Bynum and Roy Porter. New York: Routledge.

———. 1994. "An Anthropological Perspective on Objectivity: Observation, Categorization, and the Assessment of Suffering." In *Health and Social Change in International Perspective*.

———. 1995. *Writing at the Margin: Discourse between Anthropology and Medicine*. Berkeley: University of California Press.

Kleinman, Arthur, and Joan Kleinman. 1991. "Suffering and Its Professional Transformation: Toward an Ethnography of Interpersonal Experience." *Culture, Medicine and Psychiatry* 5 (3): 275–301.

———. 1994. "How Bodies Remember: Social Memory and Bodily Experience of Criticism, Resistance and Delegitimation following China's Cultural Revolution." *New Literary History* 25: 707–23.

Kleinman, Arthur, and Lilias H. Sung. 1979. "Why Do Indigenous Practitioners Successfully Heal?" *Social Science and Medicine* 13B: 7–26.

Kloos, H., with A. Etea, A. Defega, H. Aga, et al. 1987. "Illness and Health Behavior in Addis Ababa and Rural Central Ethiopia." *Social Science and Medicine* 25 (9): 1003–19.

Kloos, H., et al. 1988. "Buying Drugs in Addis Ababa." In *The Context of Medicines in Developing Countries: Studies in Pharmaceutical Anthropology*, ed. Sjaak Van der Geest and Susan Reynolds Whyte. Boston: Kluwer Academic.

Knaus, William. 1981. *Inside Russian Medicine: An American Doctor's First-Hand Report*. New York: Everest House.

Knippenberg, R., with E. Alihonou, A. Soucat, K. Oyegbite, M. Calivis, I. Hopwood, R. Niimi, M. P. Diallo, M. Conde, and S. Ofosu-Amaah. 1997. "Implementation of the Bamako Initiative: Strategies in Benin and Guinea." *International Journal of Health Planning and Management* 12 (suppl. 1): S29–47.

Komarov, Boris (pseud.). 1978. *The Destruction of Nature: The Intensification of the Ecological Crisis in the USSR*. Frankfurt/Main: Posev Verlag.

Korn, J. 1984. "Eastern Africa: Perspectives of Drug Usage." *Danish Medical Bulletin* 31 (suppl. 1): 34–37.

Kornai, Janos. 1992. *The Socialist System: The Political Economy of Communism*. Princeton, NJ: Princeton University Press.

Kreutzmann, Hermann. 1996. *Ethnizität im Entwicklungsprozess: Die Wakhi in Hochasien*. Berlin: D. Reimer.

Krishnaswamy, K., with D. Jumar and G. Radhaiah. 1985. "A Drug Survey: Precepts and Practices." *European Journal of Clinical Pharmacology* 29 (3): 363–70.

LaFond, Anne. 1995. *Sustaining Primary Health Care*. London: Earthscan.

Lancaster, Roger Nelson. 1988. *Thanks to God and the Revolution: Popular Religion and Class Consciousness in the New Nicaragua*. New York: Columbia University Press.

Lane, David. 1970. *Politics and Society in the USSR*. New York: Random House.

Lapeyre, F. 2004. "Globalization and Structural Adjustment as a Development Tool." Working Paper no. 31, Policy Integration Department, World Commission on the Social Dimension of Globalization. Geneva: International Labour Office.

Lapidus, Gail, ed. 1982. *Women in Soviet Society: Equality, Development, and Social Change*. Berkeley: University of California Press.

Lash, Scott. 1993. "Pierre Bourdieu: Cultural Economy and Social Change." In *Bourdieu: Critical Perspectives*, ed. Craig Calhoun, Edward LiPuma, and Moishe Postone. Chicago: University of Chicago Press.

Leach, Edmond. 1977. *Political Systems of Highland Burma*. London: Athlone Press.

Leat, D. 1995. *Challenging Management: An Exploratory Study of Perceptions of Managers Who Have Moved from For-Profit to Voluntary Organizations*. London: City University Business School.

Lee, K. 2001. "Globalisation—a New Agenda for Health?" In *International Co-operation and Health*, ed. M. McKee, P. Garner, and R. Stott. Oxford: Oxford University Press.

Lee, Kelley, with Kent Buse and Suzanne Fustukian. 2002. "An Introduction to Global Health Policy." In *Health Policy in a Globalizing World*, 3–17. Cambridge: Cambridge University Press.

Lee, Kelley, and Hilary Goodman. 2002. "Global Policy Networks: The Propagation of Health Care Financing Reform since the 1980s." In *Health Policy in a Globalizing World*, ed. Kelley Lee, Kent Buse, and Suzanne Fustukian, 97–119. Cambridge: Cambridge University Press.

Le Grande, A., and L. Sri Ngernyuang. 1989. *Herbal Drugs in Primary Health Care, Thailand: The Impact of Promotional Activities on Drugs Consumption, Provision and Self-Reliance.* Amsterdam: Royal Tropical Institute.

Leigh, Edward. 1988. *Right Thinking.* London: Ebury Press.

Leitzel, J., with C. Gaddy and M. Alexeev. 1995. *Mafiosi and Matrioshki: Organized Crime and Russian Reform.* Washington, DC: Brookings Review.

Lemke, Thomas. 2001. "The Birth of Bio-Politics: Michel Foucault's Lecture at the College de France on Neo-Liberal Governmentality." *Economy and Society* 30 (2): 190–207.

Lenin, Vladimir Il'ich. 1926. *State and Revolution.* New York: Vanguard Press.

Lerman, S., with D. Shepard and R. Cash. 1985. "Treatment of Diarrhea in Indonesian Children: What It Costs and Who Pays for It." *Lancet* 2 (8456): 651–54.

Leslie, Charles, ed. 1976. *Asian Medical Systems.* Berkeley: University of California Press.

Levi, Primo. 1996. *Survival in Auschwitz: The Nazi Assault on Humanity.* New York: Touchstone.

Levinas, Emmanuel. 1986. "Useless Suffering." In *Face to Face with Levinas*, ed. Richard Cohn, 156–67. Albany: State University of New York Press.

———. 1987. "Meaning and Sense." In *Collected Philosophical Papers*, 75–107. Dordrecht: Martinus Nijhoff.

Lévi-Strauss, Claude. 1963. *Structural Anthropology.* New York: Basic Books.

Levy, Stuart B. 1982. "Microbial Resistance to Antibiotics: An Evolving and Persistent Problem." *Lancet* 2 (8289): 83–88.

Lewis, Bernard. 1980. *The Assassins: A Radical Sect in Islam.* New York: Octagon Books.

Lewis, David. 2007. *The Management of Non-Governmental Development Organizations.* London: Routledge.

Lindenbaum, Shirley, and Margaret Lock, eds. 1993. *Knowledge, Power, and Practice: The Anthropology of Medicine and Everyday Life.* Berkeley: University of California Press.

Litvack, Jennie I. 1992. "The Effects of User Fees and Improved Quality on Health Facility Utilization and Household Expenditure: A Field Experiment in the Adamaoua Province of Cameroon." PhD diss., Fletcher School Of Law and Diplomacy, Tufts University.

Litvack, J., and C. Bodart. 1993. "User Fees Plus Quality Equals Improved Access to Health Care: Results of a Field Experiment in Cameroon." *Social Science and Medicine* 37 (3): 369–83.

Lock, M. 1993. *Encounters with Aging: Mythologies of Menopause in Japan and North America*. Berkeley: University of California Press.

Loewy, Erich H. 1995. "Of Markets, Technology, Patients and Profits." In *Reforming Health Care: The Philosophy and Practice of International Health Reform*, ed. David Seedhouse. New York: John Wiley & Sons.

Lowe, David. 2012. "Idea to Reality: NED at 25." National Endowment for Democracy, www.ned.org/about/history.

Lubin, Nancy. 1982. "Women in Soviet Central Asia: Progress and Contradictions." *Soviet Studies*, 182–203.

Lundberg, Olle. 1993. "The Impact of Childhood Living Conditions on Illness and Mortality in Adulthood." *Social Science and Medicine* 36 (8): 1047–52.

Lurie, P., et al. 1995. "Socioeconomic Obstacles to HIV Prevention and Treatment in Developing Countries: The Roles of the International Monetary Fund and the World Bank." *AIDS* 9 (6): 539–46.

Lyotard, Jean-François. 1984. *The Postmodern Condition: A Report on Knowledge*. Minneapolis: University of Minnesota Press.

———. 1987. "Rewriting Modernity." *Substance* 16 (54): 3–9.

Madison, Bernice Q. 1968. *Social Welfare in the Soviet Union*. Stanford, CA: Stanford University Press.

Makarem, Sami. 1967. "The Philosophical Significance of the Imam in Isma'ilism." *Studia Islamica* 27.

———. 1977. *The Political Doctrine of the Isma'ilis*. New York: Caravan Books.

Mamdani, Masuma. 1992. "Early Initiatives in Essential Drugs Policy." In *Drugs Policy in Developing Countries*, ed. Najmi Kanji, Anita Hardon, Jan Willem Harnmeijer, Masuma Mamdani, and Gill Walt. London: Zed Books.

Mangtani, Punam, with Damien J. Jolley, John M. Watson, and Laura C. Rodrigues. 1995. "Socioeconomic Deprivation and Notification Rates for Tuberculosis in London during 1982–91." *British Medical Journal* 310 (6985): 963–66.

Mann, G. V. 1980. "Food Intake and Resistance to Disease." *Lancet* 1: 1238–39.

Marcus, George E., and Michael M. J. Fischer. 1986. *Anthropology as Cultural Critique*. Chicago: University of Chicago Press.

Marglin, Stephen. 1990. "Toward the Decolonization of the Mind." In *Dominating Knowledge: Development, Culture, and Resistance*, ed. Frédérique Marglin and Stephen Marglin, 1–28. Oxford: Clarendon Press.

———. 1992. *Economics as a System of Knowledge*. Cambridge, MA: Harvard University Press.

Markwell, Donald. 2006. *John Maynard Keynes and International Relations: Economic Paths to War and Peace*. New York: Oxford University Press.

Marmot, M. G., and G. D. Smith. 1989. "Why Are the Japanese Living Longer?" *British Medical Journal* 299: 1547–51.

Marshall, George C. 1947. "The Marshall Plan Speech." George C. Marshall Foundation, www.marshallfoundation.org/library/MarshallPlanSpeech-fromRecordedAddress_000.html.

Martin, Emily. 1992. *The Woman in the Body: A Cultural Analysis of Reproduction*. Boston: Beacon Press.

Martorell, Reynaldo, and Theresa Ho. 1984. "Malnutrition and Mortality." In *Child Survival: Strategies for Research, Population and Development Review*, 10 (suppl.): 49–68.

Marx, Karl. 1962. "The German Ideology." In *Selected Works*, vol. 1. London: Lawrence and Wishart.

———. 1975. "On the Jewish Question." In *Early Writings*. New York: Vintage Books.

———. 1990. *Capital: A Critique of Political Economy*. Translated by Ben Fowkes. New York: Penguin Books.

———. 1997. *The Marx Reader*. Cambridge: Polity Press.

Marx, Karl, and Friedrich Engels. 1964. *On Religion*. New York: Schocken.

Masiye F., with V. Seshamani, C. Cheelo, et al. 2005. *Health Care Financing in Zambia: A Study of the Possible Policy Options for Implementation*. Lusaka: University of Zambia.

Matveeva, Anna. 2009. "The Perils of Emerging Statehood: Civil War and State Reconstruction in Tajikistan: An Analytical Narrative on State-Making." Working Paper No. 46. London: Crisis States Research Centre.

Mauss, Marcel. 1990. *The Gift*. New York: W. W. Norton.

McGovern, William Montgomery. 1939. *The Early Empires of Central Asia: A Study of the Scythians and the Huns and the Part They Played in World History*. Chapel Hill: University of North Carolina Press.

McKeown, Thomas. 1976. *The Role of Medicine: Dream, Mirage, or Nemesis?* Princeton, NJ: Princeton University Press.

———. 1979. "Food, Infection, and Population." *Journal of Interdisciplinary History* 14 (2): 227–48.

———. 1988. *The Origins of Human Disease*. Cambridge: Blackwell.

McKeown, Thomas, and R. G. Brown. 1955. "Medical Evidence Related to English Population Changes in the Eighteenth Century." *Population Studies* 9: 119–41.

McPake, Barbara. 1993a. "Can Health Care User Fees Improve Health Service Provision for the Poor?" *Health Exchange, International Health Exchange* (June/July).

———. 1993b. "User Charges for Health Services in Developing Countries: A Review of the Literature." *Social Science and Medicine* 36 (11): 1397–1405.

———. 2002. "The Globalisation of Health Sector Reform Policies: Is 'Lesson Drawing' Part of the Process?" In *Health Policy in a Globalizing World,* ed. Kelley Lee, Kent Buse, and Suzanne Fustukian, 120–39. Cambridge: Cambridge University Press.

McPake, B., with K. Hanson and A. Mills. 1993. "Community Financing of Health Care in Africa: An Evaluation of the Bamako Initiative." *Social Science and Medicine* 36 (11): 1383–95.

Médecins Sans Frontières. 1993. *Clinical Guidelines: Diagnostic and Treatment Manual.* 3rd ed. Paris: Médecins Sans Frontières.

———. 1995. *Osnovniye Lekarstvyenniye Sredstva: Prakticheskey Spravochnik, Translated from English.* Moscow: MSF.

———. 2008. "Help Wanted: Confronting the Health Care Worker Crisis to Expand Access to HIV Treatment, MSF Experience in South Africa." Johannesburg: Médecins Sans Frontières.

Meegama, S. A. 1980. "Socioeconomic Determinants of Infant and Child Mortality in Sri Lanka: An Analysis of Post-War Experience." World Fertility Scientific Report No. 8. Voorburg, Netherlands: International Statistical Institute.

Melrose, D. 1982. *Bitter Pills: Medicines and the Third World Poor.* Oxford: OXFAM.

Memi, Albert. 1984. *Dependency.* Boston: Beacon.

Meng, Q., with Q. Sun and N. Hearst. 2002. "Hospital Charge Exemptions for the Poor in Shandong, China." *Health Policy and Planning* 17: 56–63.

Mercer, Alex. 1990. *Disease, Mortality and Population in Transition: Epidemiological-Demographic Change in England since the Eighteenth Century as Part of a Global Phenomena.* New York: Leicester University Press.

Meuwissen, L. 2002. "Problems of Cost Recovery Implementation in District Health Care: A Case Study from Niger." *Health Policy and Planning* 17 (3): 304–13.

Meyer C. 1992. "A Step Back as Donors Shift Institution Building from the Public to the 'Private' Sector." *World Development* 20 (8): 1115–26.

Mezentseva, Elena, and Natalia Rimachevskaya. 1990. "The Soviet Country Profile: Health of the USSR Population in the 70s and 80s—An Approach to a Comprehensive Analysis." *Social Science and Medicine* 31 (8): 867–77.

Mills, A. 1997. "Contractual Relationships between Government and the Commercial Private Sector in Developing Countries." In *Private Health Providers in Developing Countries: Serving the Public Interest?*, ed. S. Bennett, B. McPake, A. and Milla. London: Zed Books.

Minder, Raphael. 2013. "After Austerity, Portugal Asks, What's Left?" *International Herald Tribune,* April 24, 1, 3.

Minorsky, V. 1960. "Shughnan." In *The Encyclopedia of Islam.* Leiden: Brill.

Mirowski P., and D. Plehwe, eds. 2009. *The Road from Mont Pelerin: The Making of the Neoliberal Thought Collective.* Cambridge, CA: Harvard University Press.

Mises, Ludwig von. 1949. *Human Action.* New Haven, CT: Yale University Press.

———. 1951. *Socialism: An Economic and Sociological Analysis.* New Haven, CT: Yale University Press.

Mishler, Elliot G., et al. 1981. *Social Contexts of Health, Illness, and Patient Care.* Cambridge: Cambridge University Press.

Mohan, G., and K. Stokke. 2000. "Participatory Development and Empowerment: The Dangers of Localism." *Third World Quarterly* 21 (2): 247–68.

Montagne, Michael. 1996. "The Pharmakon Phenomenon: Cultural Conceptions of Drugs and Drug Use." In *Contested Ground: Public Purpose and Private Interest in the Regulation of Prescription Drugs,* ed. Peter Davis. New York: Oxford University Press.

Mont Pelerin Society. 1947. "Statement of Aims." *The Mont Pelerin Society,* www.montpelerin.org/montpelerin/mpsGoals.html.

Mooney, G. 1983. "Equity in Health Care: Confronting the Confusion." *Effective Health Care* 1: 179–84.

———. 1986. *Economics, Medicine and Health Care.* Brighton: Wheatsheaf.

———. 1987. "What Does Equity in Health Mean?" *World Health Statistics Quarterly* 40: 296–303.

Moore, M. 1993. "Good Government? Introduction." *IDS Bulletin* 24 (1): 1–6.

Moore, Sally Falk. 1987. "Explaining the Present: Theoretical Dilemmas in Processual Anthropology." *American Ethnologist* 14 (4): 727–36.

———. 1989. "The Production of Cultural Pluralism as a Process." *Public Culture* 1 (2): 26–48.

———. 1994. "The Ethnography of the Present and the Analysis of Process." In *Assessing Cultural Anthropology,* ed. Robert Borofsky. New York: McGraw Hill.

Morris, David B. 1991. *The Culture of Pain.* Berkeley: University of California Press.

———. 1996. "About Suffering: Voice, Genre, and Moral Community." *Daedalus* 125 (1): 25–45.

Moses, S., with F. Manji, J. E. Bradley, et al. 1992. "Impact of User Fees on Attendance at a Referral Centre for Sexually Transmitted Diseases in Kenya." *Lancet* 340: 463–66.

Mosley, W. Henry. 1985. "Will Primary Health Care Reduce Infant and Child Mortality?" In *Health Policy, Social Policy and Mortality Prospects: Proceedings of a Seminar in Paris, France,* ed. J. Vallin and A. D. Lopez, 103–37. Liege: Oridana Editions.

Mossialos, E., and J. Le Grand. 1999. "Cost Containment in the EU: An Overview." In *Health Care and Cost Containment in the European Union*. Aldershot: Ashgate.

Murav'ev, Nikolai Nikolaevich. 1977. *Journey to Khiva: Through the Turkoman Country*. London: Oguz Press.

Murray, Christopher J. L., and Lincoln C. Chen. 1993. "In Search of a Contemporary Theory for Understanding Mortality Change." *Social Science and Medicine* 36 (2): 143–55.

———. 1994. "Dynamics and Patterns of Mortality Change." In *Health and Social Change in International Perspective*, ed. Lincoln Chen, Arthur Kleinman, and Norma Ware, 3–24.

Murray, M. J., and A. B. Murray. 1977. "Starvation Suppression and Refeeding Activation of Infection: An Ecological Necessity?" *Lancet* 1 (8003): 123–25.

Nagar, R., and S. Raju. 2003. "Women, NGOs and the Contradictions of Empowerment and Disempowerment: A Conversation." *Antipode* 35 (1): 1–13.

Nanji, Azim. 1980. "Shi'a Isma'ili Interpretations of the Qur'an." In *Selected Proceedings of the International Congress for the Study of the Qur'an*, 39–49. Canberra: Australian National University.

———. 1987. "Isma'ilism. Islamic." In *Spirituality*, ed. S. H. Nasr. New York: Crossroads.

Nasr, Seyyed Hossein. 1966. *Ideals and Realities of Islam*. London: George Allen and Unwin.

———. 1968. *Science and Civilization in Islam*. Cambridge, MA: Harvard University Press.

National Endowment for Democracy. 2012. "Statement of Principles and Objectives." National Endowment for Democracy, www.ned.org/publications/statement-of-principles-and-objectives.

Navarro, Vicente. 1976. *Medicine under Capitalism*. New York: PRODIST.

———. 1977. *Social Security and Medicine in the USSR: A Marxist Critique*. Lexington: Lexington Books.

———. 1984. "A Critique of the Ideological and Political Positions of the Willy Brandt Report and the WHO Alma Ata Declaration." *Social Science and Medicine* 18 (6): 467–74.

———. 1993. *Dangerous to Your Health: Capitalism in Health Care*. New York: Cornerstone Books.

———. 2007. *Neoliberalism, Globalization and Inequalities: Consequences for Health and Quality of Life*. Amityville: Baywood Publishing.

Newhouse, Joseph P., and the Insurance Experiment Group. 1993. *Free for All? Lessons from the RAND Health Insurance Experiment*. Cambridge, MA: Harvard University Press.

Newland, K. 1981. "Infant Mortality and the Health of Societies." Worldwatch Paper 47. Washington DC: Worldwatch Institute.

New Scientist. 1990. "'Medical Famine' Blights USSR, Says Official Journal." *New Scientist* 127 (1726): 20.

Nichols, Mark. 1991. "Deadly Shortages: Decay Sabotages Care in the Soviet Union." *Maclean's* 104 (32): 38.

Nichter, Mark. 1989. "Pharmaceuticals, Health Commodification, and Social Relations: Ramifications for Primary Health Care." In *Anthropology and International Health: South Asian Case Studies*, 233–76. Dordrecht: Kluwer Academic Publishers.

Nobel Prize. 1974. Press release, October. Nobel Prize, www.nobelprize.org /nobel_prizes/economics/laureates/1974/press.html.

Nove, Alec. 1982. "Is There a Ruling Class in the USSR?" In *Classes, Power, and Conflict: Classical and Contemporary Debates*, ed. Anthony Giddens and David Held. Berkeley: University of California Press.

Nuraliev, Iusuf N. 1981. *Meditsina Epokhi Avitsenny*. Dushanbe: Irfon.

Obermeyer, Carla Makhlouf. 1992. "Islam, Women, and Politics: The Demography of Arab Countries." *Population and Development Review* 18 (1): 33–60.

OCHA (United Nations Office for the Coordination of Humanitarian Affairs). 1998. "Tajikistan Humanitarian Situation Report, May 1998." Relief Web, www.reliefweb.int/files.

O'Connell, B. 1999. *Civil Society: The Underpinnings of American Democracy*. Hanover, NH: University Press of New England.

O'Connor, Ronald W., ed. 1980. *Managing Health Systems in Developing Areas: Experiences from Afghanistan*. Lexington: Lexington Books.

Olcott, Martha B. 1991. "Women and Society in Central Asia." In *Soviet Central Asia: The Failed Transformation*, ed. William Fierman. Boulder, CO: Westview Press.

———. 1995. "Islam and Fundamentalism in Independent Central Asia." In *Muslim Eurasia: Conflicting Legacies*, ed. Ro'i Yaacov. London: Frank Cass.

Olufsen, Ole. 1904. *Through the Unknown Pamirs: The Second Danish Pamir Expedition, 1898–99*. London: William Heinemann.

Omran, Abdel R. 1971. "The Epidemiologic Transition: A Theory of the Epidemiology of Population Change." *Milbank Memorial Fund Quarterly* 49 (4): 509–38.

———. 1977. "Epidemiologic Transition in the U.S.: The Health Factor in Population Change." *Population Bulletin* 32 (2): 3–42.

Ong, Aihwa. 2006. *Neoliberalism as Exception*. Durham, NC: Duke University Press.

Orosz, Eva. 1990. "The Hungarian Country Profile: Inequalities in Health and Health Care in Hungary." *Social Science and Medicine* 31 (8): 847–57.

Paganini, Agostino. 2004. "The Bamako Initiative Was Not about Money." *Health Policy and Development* 2 (1): 11–13.

PAHO. 1991. "Surveillance of Living Conditions and the Health Situation." *Epidemiological Bulletin* 12 (3), www.paho.org/english/dd/ais/EB_v12n3.pdf.

Palley, Thomas I. 2005. "From Keynesianism to Neoliberalism: Shifting Paradigms in Economics." In *Neoliberalism: A Critical Reader,* ed. Alfredo Saad-Filho and Deborah Johnston, 20–29. London: Pluto Press.

Paphassarang, C., with K. Philavong, B. Boupha, and E. Blas. 2002. "Equity, Privatization and Cost Recovery in Urban Health Care: The Care of Lao PDR." *Health Policy and Planning* 17: 72–84.

Pappu, K. 1993. "Strategies for Community-Based Health Action." In *People's Health in People's Hands, Indian Experiences in Decentralized Health Care: A Model for Health,* ed. Panchayati Raj, N. H. Antia, and Kavita Bhatia, 113–23. Bombay: Foundation for Research in Community Health.

Paredes, Patricia, with Manuela De La Peña, Enrique Flores-Guerra, Judith Diaz, and James Trostle. 1996. "Factors Influencing Physicians' Prescribing Behavior in the Treatment of Childhood Diarrhoea: Knowledge May Not Be the Clue." *Social Science and Medicine* 42 (8): 1141–53.

Parsons, Talcott. 1972. "Definition of Health and Illness in the Light of American Values and Social Structure." In *Patients, Physicians, and Illness,* ed. E. Gartly Jaco, 107–27. Glencoe: Free Press.

Pashaev, K. P., with A. V. Alimskii, G. G. Ashurov and A. I. Aliev. 1997. "The Incidence Dynamics of Dental Caries and Periodontal Diseases in the Population of Different Territorial and Administrative Areas of Tajikistan [in Russian]." *Stomatologiia* 76 (5): 62–64.

Paul, Benjamin. 1955. "Health and Human Behavior: Areas of Interest Common to the Social and Medical Sciences." *Current Anthropology* 3: 159–205.

Pauly, Mark V. 1968. "The Economics of Moral Hazard." *American Economic Review* 58: 231–37.

Payer, Lynn. 1988. *Medicine and Culture: Varieties of Treatment in the United States, England, West Germany, and France.* New York: H. Holt.

Pearson, Mark. 2004. "Issues Paper: The Case for Abolition of User Fees for Primary Health Services." London: DFID Health Systems Resource Center.

Penkala-Gawecka, Maria Danuta. 1980. "Two Types of Traditional Medicine in Afghanistan." *Ethnomedizin* 6 (1/4): 201–28.

———. 1988. "Medical Pluralism in Afghanistan: Conflict between, Coexistence or Integration of Various Medical Systems?" In *Poland at the 12th Congress of Anthropological and Ethnological Sciences,* ed. S. Szynkiewicz, 235–47. Wroclaw, Poland: Zakład Narodowy im. Ossolińskich.

Perry, Seymore, and Flora Chu. 1986. "Selecting Medical Technologies in Developing Countries." In *Health, Nutrition, and Economic Crisis: Approaches to Policy in the Third World,* ed. David E. Bell and Michael R. Reich. Dover: Auburn House.

Pfeiffer, James. 2004. "International NGOs in the Mozambique Health Sector: The 'Velvet Glove' of Privatization." In *Unhealthy Health Policy: A Critical Anthropological Examination*, ed. Arachu Castro and Merrill Singer, 43–62. New York: Altamira Press.

Pigg, Stacy Leigh. 1992. "Constructing Social Categories through Place: Social Representations and Development in Nepal." *Comparative Studies in Society and History* 34 (3): 491–513.

Pipes, Daniel. 1993. "The Politics of the 'Rip Van Winkle' States: The Southern Tier States of the Ex-Soviet Union Have Moved the Borders of the Middle East North." *Middle East Insight* (November–December): 30–40.

Pipes, Richard. 1990. *The Russian Revolution*. New York: Knopf.

Pliskin, Karen L. 1987. *Silent Boundaries: Cultural Constraints on Sickness and Diagnosis of Iranians in Israel*. New Haven, CT: Yale University Press.

Poladi, Hassan. 1989. *The Hazaras*. Stockton: Mughal Publishing.

Poliakov, Sergei P. 1992. *Everyday Islam—Religion and Tradition in Rural Central Asia*. Armonk: M. E. Sharpe.

Pollitt, C. 1993. *Managerialism and Public Services*. Oxford: Blackwell.

Polyani, Karl. 1954. *The Great Transformation*. Boston: Beacon Press.

———. 1977. *The Livelihood of Man*. New York: Academic Press.

Powell, G. B., Jr. 1982. *Contemporary Democracy: Participation, Stability, and Violence*. Cambridge, MA: Harvard University Press.

Powell, Lewis F., Jr. 1971. "Attack of American Free Enterprise System." Memorandum to Eugene B. Sydnor, Jr., chairman of the Education Committee, U.S. Chamber of Commerce, August 23, www.webcitation.org/64jAmJkKB.

Powell, M., and Seddon, D. 1997. "NGOs and the Development Industry." *Review of African Political Economy* 71: 3–10.

Prescott, Nicholas, and David de Ferranti. 1985. "The Analysis and Assessment of Health Programs." *Social Science and Medicine* 20 (12): 1235–40.

Price, L. 1989. "In the Shadow of Biomedicine: Self-Medication in Two Ecuadorian Pharmacies." *Social Science and Medicine* 28 (9): 905–15.

Price-Smith, A. T. 1999. "The Health of Nations: Infectious Disease and Its Effects on State Capacity, Prosperity, and Stability." PhD diss., University of Toronto.

Przeworski, Adam. 1991. *Democracy and the Market: Political and Economic Reforms in Eastern Europe and Latin America*. New York: Cambridge University Press.

Putnam, Robert D. 1976. *The Comparative Study of Political Elites*. Englewood Cliffs, NJ: Prentice-Hall.

———. 1995. "Bowling Alone." *Journal of Democracy* 6 (1): 65–78.

Rabinow, Paul, ed. 1984. *The Foucault Reader*. New York: Pantheon Books.

———. 1986. "Representations Are Social Facts: Modernity and Post-Modernity in Anthropology." In *Writing Culture: The Poetics and Politics of Ethnogra-*

phy, ed. James Clifford and George E. Marcus, 234–61. Berkeley: University of California Press.

Rahman, Fazlur. 1987. *Health and Medicine in the Islamic Tradition—Change and Identity.* New York: Crossroad.

Ranelagh, John. 1991. *Thatcher's People: An Insider's Account of the Politics, the Power, and the Personalities.* London: HarperCollins.

Rapp, Rayna. 1993. "Accounting for Amniocentesis." In *Knowledge, Power and Practice,* ed. Shirley Lindenbaum and Margaret Locke. Berkeley: University of California Press.

Rapp, Rayna, and Marilyn Young, eds. 1989. *Promissory Notes: Women in the Transition to Socialism.* New York: Monthly Review Press.

Ravitch, Michael L. 1937. *The Romance of Russian Medicine.* New York: Liveright Publishing.

Readings, B. 1991. *Introducing Lyotard.* New York: Routledge.

Reagan, Ronald. 1982. "Address to Members of the British Parliament." Speech at the Palace of Westminster, London, June 8, http://teachingamericanhistory.org/library/index.asp?document=926.

Reddy, S., and J. Vandermoortele. 1996. "User Financing of Basic Social Services: A Review of Theoretical Arguments and Empirical Evidence." New York: Office of Evaluation, Policy and Planning, United Nations Children's Fund.

Remnick, David. 1993. *Lenin's Tomb: The Last Days of the Soviet Empire.* New York: Random House.

Ridde, Valery. 2003. "Entre efficacité et équit: Qu'en est-il de l'Initiative de Bamako? Une revue des experiences oust-africaines." Paper presented at the 26th Journées des Economistes Français de la Santé: Santé et Développment, Clermont-Ferrand, www.cerdi.org/Colloque/PDFSante2003/ridde.pdf.

———. 2011. "Is the Bamako Initiative Still Relevant for West African Health Systems?" *International Journal of Health Services* 41 (1): 175–84.

Riddell, R. 1999. "Evaluation and Effectiveness in NGOs." In *International Perspectives on Voluntary Action: Reshaping the Third Sector,* ed. D. Lewis. London: Earthscan.

Rist, Gilbert. 2008. *The History of Development: From Western Origins to Global Faith.* 3rd ed. London: Zed Books.

Robinson, Mark. 1993. "Governance, Democracy and Conditionality: NGOs and the New Policy Agenda." In *Governance, Democracy and Conditionality: What Role for NGOs?,* ed. A. Clayton. Oxford: INTRAC.

Robinson, William I. 1995. "Pushing Polyarchy: The US-Cuba case and the Third World." *Third World Quarterly* 16 (4).

Rodin, J., and D. de Ferranti. 2012. "Universal Health Coverage: The Third Global Health Transition?" *Lancet* 380 (9845): 861–62.

Ro'i, Yaacov. 1991. "Central Asian Riots and Disturbances, 1989–1990: Causes and Context." *Central Asian Survey* 10 (3): 21–54.

Rose, R. 1994. "Post-Communism and the Problem of Trust." *Journal of Democracy* 5 (3).

Rosenau, Pauline Vaillancourt, and Christine Thoer. 1996. "The Liberalization of Access to Medication in the United States and Europe." In *Contested Ground: Public Purpose and Private Interest in the Regulation of Prescription Drugs*, ed. Peter Davis. New York: Oxford University Press.

Rosenthal, F., and W. Newbrander. 1996. "Public Policy and Private Sector Provision of Health Services." *International Journal of Health Planning and Management* 11: 203–16.

Rostow, W. W. 1960. *Stages of Economic Growth: A Non-Communist Manifesto.* Cambridge: Cambridge University Press.

Rouse, Joseph. 1987. *Knowledge and Power: Toward a Political Philosophy of Science.* Ithaca, NY: Cornell University Press.

Rowden, Rick. 2009. *The Deadly Ideas of Neoliberalism.* London: Zed Books.

Roy, Olivier. 1993. "The Civil War in Tajikistan: Causes and Implications." Washington, DC: United States Institute of Peace.

Rubin, Barnett. 1993. "The Fragmentation of Tajikistan." *Survival* 35 (4): 71–91.

Ruderman, A. 1990. "Economic Adjustment and the Future of Health Services in the Third World." *Journal of Public Health Policy* 11 (4): 481–90.

Rumer, Boris Z. 1989. *Soviet Central Asia: A Tragic Experiment.* Boston: Unwin Hyman.

———. 1993. "The Gathering Storm in Central Asia." *Orbis: A Journal of World Affairs* 37 (1): 89–105.

Ryan, Michael. 1978. *The Organization of Soviet Medical Care.* Oxford: Basil Blackwell.

———. 1989. *Doctors and the State in the Soviet Union.* London: Macmillan.

Ryan, T. M. 1972. "Primary Medical Care in the Soviet Union." *International Journal of Health Services* 2 (2): 243–53.

Ryan, William. 1971. *Blaming the Victim.* New York: Pantheon Books.

Rylko-Bauer, Barbara, and Paul E. Farmer. 2002. "Managed Care or Managed Inequality? A Call for Critiques of Market-Based Medicine." *Medical Anthropology Quarterly* 16 (4): 476–502.

Saad-Filho, A., and D. Johnson. 2005. *Neoliberalism.* London: Pluto Press.

Sabine, George Holland. 1963. *A History of Political Theory.* London: G. Harrap.

Sachs, Jeffrey. 1990. "What Is To Be Done?" *Economist,* January 13.

Sachs, Wolfgang. 1992. *The Development Dictionary: A Guide to Knowledge as Power.* London: Zed Books.

Sacks, Jonathan. 1991. *The Persistence of Faith: Religion, Morality and Society in a Secular Age.* London: Weidenfeld and Nicolson.

Sahlins, Marshall. 1976. *Culture and Practical Reason*. Chicago: University of Chicago Press.

———. 1985. *Islands of History*. Chicago: University of Chicago Press.

Sahn, David E. 1992. "Public Expenditures in Sub-Saharan Africa during a Period of Economic Reforms." *World Development* 20 (5): 673–93.

Salamon, L. 1993. "The Global Associational Revolution: The Rise of the Third Sector on the World Scene." Occasional Paper 15. Baltimore, MD: Institute for Policy Studies, Johns Hopkins University.

Saltman, Richard B., and Casten Von Otter. 1995. *Implementing Planned Markets in Health Care: Balancing Social and Economic Responsibility*. Philadelphia: Open University Press.

Samoff, Joel. 1994. "Responses to Crisis: (Re)Setting the Education and Training Policy Agenda." In *Coping with Crisis: Austerity, Adjustment and Human Resources*. London: Cassell/UNESCO.

Sandel, Michael J. 2012. *What Money Can't Buy: The Moral Limits of Markets*. New York: Farrar, Straus and Giroux.

SAPRIN (Structural Adjustment Participatory Review International Network). 2002. *The Policy Roots of Economic Crisis, Poverty and Inequality*. Washington, DC: SAPRIN.

Sartre, Jean-Paul. 1956. *Being and Nothingness*. London: Methuen.

Sauerborn, R., with A. Nougtara and J. Diesfeld. 1989. "Low Utilization of Community Health Workers: Results from a Household Interview Survey in Burkina Faso." *Social Science and Medicine* 29 (10): 1163–74.

Schecter, Kate. 1992. "Soviet Socialized Medicine and the Right to Health Care in a Changing Soviet Union." *Human Rights Quarterly* 14 (2): 206–15.

Scheper-Hughes, Nancy. 1984. "Infant Mortality and Infant Care: Cultural and Economic Constraints on Nurturing in Northeast Brazil." *Social Science and Medicine* 19 (5): 533–46.

———. 1990. "Three Propositions for a Critically Applied Medical Anthropology." *Social Science and Medicine* 30 (2): 189–97.

———. 1992. *Death without Weeping: The Violence of Everyday Life in Brazil*. Berkeley: University of California Press.

Schmemann, Serge. 1993. "War Bleeds Ex-Soviet Land at Central Asia's Heart—Soviet Outpost in Asia, Freed, Is Engulfed by War." *New York Times*, February 21, 1, 12.

Schoeberlein-Engel, John S. 1994. "Conflict in Tâjikistân and Central Asia: The Myth of Ethnic Animosity." *Harvard Middle Eastern and Islamic Review* 1 (2).

Scholte, J. A. 2000. *Globalization: A Critical Introduction*. London: MacMillan Press.

Schubert-Lehnhardt, Viola. 1995. "Who Should Be Responsible for a Nation's Health." In *Reforming Health Care: The Philosophy and Practice of International Health Reform*, ed. David Seedhouse. New York: John Wiley & Sons.

Schwartz, Rebecca K., with Stephen B. Soumerai and Jerry Avorn. 1989. "Physician Motivations for Nonscientific Drug Prescribing." *Social Science and Medicine* 28 (6): 577–82.

Scott, James C. 1976. *The Moral Economy of the Peasant: Rebellion and Subsistence in Southeast Asia.* New Haven, CT: Yale University Press.

———. 1977. "Protest and Profanation: Agrarian Revolt and the Little Tradition." *Theory and Society* 4: 1–38, 211–46.

———. 1985. *Weapons of the Weak: Everyday Forms of Peasant Resistance.* New Haven, CT: Yale University Press.

———. 1990. *Domination and the Arts of Resistance: Hidden Transcripts.* New Haven, CT: Yale University Press.

Scrimshaw, Susan C. 1978. "Infant Mortality and Behavior in the Regulation of Family Size." *Population and Development Review* 4 (3): 383–404.

Seedhouse, David. 1995. "The Logic of Health Reform." In *Reforming Health Care: The Philosophy and Practice of International Health Reform.* New York: John Wiley & Sons.

Segal, R., and C. D. Helper. 1982. "Prescribers' Beliefs and Values as Predictors of Drug Choices." *American Journal of Hospital Pharmacy* 39: 1391–97.

Sekhar, C., with R. Raina and G. Pillai. 1981. "Some Aspects of Drug Use in Ethiopia." *Tropical Doctor* 11: 116–18.

Sen, Amartya. 1992. *Inequality Reexamined.* Cambridge, MA: Harvard University Press.

———. 1994. "Objectivity and Position: Assessment of Health and Well-Being." In *Health and Social Change in International Perspective,* ed. Lincoln C. Chen, Arthur Kleinman, and Norma C. Ware. Boston: Department of Population and International Health, Harvard School of Public Health.

———. 2009. "Capitalism beyond the Crisis." *New York Review of Books,* March 26, www.nybooks.com/articles/archives/2009/mar/26/capitalism-beyond-the-crisis/.

Sergeyev, L. 1965. "Impiriyi Oghkhoni Chorum (Empire of Aga Khan IV)." *Badakhshoni Sovyeta* (in Tajik).

Shah, Parmesh, and Meera Kaul Shah. 1996. "Participatory Methods for Increasing NGO Accountability: A Case Study from India." In *Beyond the Magic Bullet: NGO Performance and Accountability in the Post–Cold War World,* ed. Michael Edwards and David Hulme, 1–22. West Harford: Kumarian.

Shahrani, M. N. 1995. "Islam and the Political Culture of 'Scientific Atheism' in Post-Soviet Central Asia: Future Predicaments." In *The Politics of Religion in Russia and the New States of Eurasia,* ed. Michael Bourdeaux, 273–92. London: M. E. Sharpe.

Shepard, Donald S., with Guy Carrin and Prosper Nyandagazi. 1987. "Self Financing of Health Care at Government Health Centers in Rwanda." Antwerp: Centre for Development Studies, University of Antwerp, UFSIA.

———. 1992. "The Role of User Fees in Financing Health Care at Government Health Centers in Rwanda." In *Strategies for Health Care Finance in Developing Countries: With a Focus on Community Financing in Sub-Saharan Africa*, ed. Guy Carrin and Marc Vereecke, 96–116. London: Macmillan.

Shimkim, Michael B. 1958. "Book reviews: *Sorok let Sovetskovozdravookhraneniya (Forty years of Soviet health protection), 1917–1957.*" *Science* 127 (3311): 1384–85.

Shore, C. N. 1989. "Patronage and Bureaucracy in Complex Societies." *Journal of the Anthropological Society of Oxford* 20 (1): 56–73.

Shore, Chris, and Susan Wright. 1997. "Policy: A New Field of Anthropology." In *Anthropology of Policy: Critical Perspectives on Governance and Power*, ed. Cris Shore and Susan Wright, 3–39. London: Routledge.

Sigerist, Henry E. 1947. *Medicine and Health in the Soviet Union*. New York: Citadel Press.

Silverman, Milton. 1982. *Prescriptions for Death: The Drugging of the Third World*. Berkeley: University of California Press.

Skaar, C. M. 1998. "Extending Coverage of Priority Health Care Services through Collaboration with the Private Sector: Selected Experiences of USAID Cooperating Agencies." Bethesda, MD: Partnerships for Health Reform, Abt Associates.

Slim, Randa, and Faredun Hodizoda. 2001. "Tajikistan: From Civil War to Peacebuilding." In *Searching for Peace in Europe and Eurasia*, ed. Paul van Tongeren, Hans van der Veen, and Juliette Verhoeven, 516–35. Boulder, CO: Lynne Rienner.

Slonimskaia, I. A. 1965. "V. I. Lenin ob okhrane zdrov'ia naroda." In *Cherki istoriografii sovetskogo zdravookhraneniia*, ed. M. I. Barsukov. Moscow: Meditsina.

Smirnov, Iu. 1988. "Strannyi' Islam." *Pamir* 2: 104–55.

Smith, Adam. 1982a. *The Theory of Moral Sentiments*. Edited by A. L. Macfie and D. D. Raphael. Indianapolis, IN: Liberty Classics.

———. 1982b. *The Wealth of Nations*. New York: Penguin Books.

Smith, M. G. 1989. "The Nature and Variety of Plural Unity." In *The Prospects for Plural Societies*, ed. David Maybury-Lewis, 146–85. Washington, DC: American Ethnological Society.

Snoy, Peter. 1975. *Bagrot: Eine dardische Talschaft im Karakorum*. Graz, Austria: Akademische Druck- u. Verlagsanst.

Sollis, P. 1992. "Multilateral Agencies, NGOs and Policy Reform.' *Development in Practice* 2 (3): 163–78.

Soloviev, Z. P. 1940. "Tezisi doklada 'Profilakticheskie zadachi lechebnoi pomoshchi.'" In *Voprosy Zdravookhraneniia*, 137–38. Moscow.

Spicker, Stuart F. 1995. "Going off the Dole: A Prudential and Ethical Critique of the 'Healthfare' State." In *Reforming Health Care: The Philosophy and*

Practice of International Health Reform, ed. David Seedhouse. New York: John Wiley & Sons.

Stark, Evan. 1977. "The Epidemic as a Social Event." *International Journal of Health Sciences* 7: 681–705.

Starr, Paul. 1982. *The Social Transformation of American Medicine.* New York: Basic Books.

Steil, Benn. 2013. *The Battle of Bretton Woods: John Maynard Keynes, Harry Dexter White, and the Making of a New World Order.* Princeton, NJ: Princeton University Press.

Stein, Howard. 2004. "The World Bank and the IMF in Africa: Strategy and Routine in the Generation of a Failed Agenda." In *Global Politics and Africa.* London: Routledge.

———. 2008. *Beyond the World Bank Agenda: An Institutional Approach to Development.* Chicago: University of Chicago Press.

Stein, Howard, and E. W. Nafziger. 1991. "Structural Adjustment, Human Needs and the World Bank Agenda." *Journal of Modern African Studies* 29 (1): 173–89.

Stein, Howard, and Machiko Nissanke. 1999. "Structural Adjustment and the African Crisis: A Theoretical Appraisal." *Eastern Economic Journal* 25 (4): 399–420.

Stein, Sir Aurel. 1933. *On Ancient Central-Asian Tracks.* London: Routledge.

Steinberg, Jonah. 2011. *Isma'ili Modern: Globalization and Identity in a Muslim Community.* Chapel Hill: University of North Carolina Press.

Stephens, B., with J. P. Mason and R. B. Isely. 1985. "Health and Low-Cost Housing." *World Health Forum* 6: 59–62.

Stewart, S. 1997. "Happy Ever After in the Market Place: Non-Government Organizations and Uncivil Society." *Review of African Political Economy* 71: 11–34.

Stites, Richard. 1992. *Russian Popular Culture: Entertainment and Society since 1900.* Cambridge: Cambridge University Press.

Stock, Robert. 1983. "Distance and the Utilization of Health Facilities in Rural Nigeria." *Social Science and Medicine* 17 (9): 563–70.

Stuckler, D., with L. P. King and S. Basu. 2008. "International Monetary Fund Programs and Tuberculosis Outcomes in Post-Communist Countries." *PLoS Med* 5 (7): e143, doi:10.1371/journal.pmed.0050143.

Stuckler, David, and Sanjay Basu. 2013. *The Body Economic: Why Austerity Kills.* New York: Basic Books.

Sugar, J., with A. Kleinman, and K. Heggenhougen. 1991. "Development's 'Downside': Social and Psychological Pathology in Countries Undergoing Social Change." *Health Transition Review* 1 (2): 211–20.

Suny, Ronald. 1992. "Nationalist and Ethnic Unrest in the Soviet Union." In *The "Nationality" Question in the Soviet Union,* ed. Gail Lapidus, 307–32. New York: Garland Publishers.

Szreter, Simon. 1988. "The Importance of Social Intervention in Britain's Mortality Decline, c. 1850–1914: A Re-Interpretation of the Role of Public Health." In *Social History of Medicine* 1: 1–37.

Tadjbakhsh, Shahrbanou. 1993a. "Causes and Consequences of the Civil War." *Central Asia Monitor* 1: 10–14.

———. 1993b. "The Bloody Path of Change: The Case of Post-Soviet Tajikistan." *Harriman Institute Forum* 6 (11): 1–10.

———. 1993c. "The Tajik Spring of 1992." *Central Asia Monitor* 2: 21–29.

Tandon, Y. 1996. "An African Perspective." In *Compassion and Calculation: The Business of Private Foreign Aid*, ed. D. Sogge, K. Biekart, and J. Saxby. London: Pluto Press.

Taussig, Michael T. 1980. *The Devil and Commodity Fetishism in South America*. Chapel Hill: University of North Carolina Press.

Taylor, Carl E. 1976. "The Place of Indigenous Medical Practitioners in the Modernization of Health Services." In *Asian Medical Systems*, ed. Charles Leslie, 285–99. Berkeley: University of California Press.

Tendler, J. 1982. "Turning Private Voluntary Organizations into Development Agencies: Questions for Evaluation." Program Evaluation Discussion Paper 12. Washington, DC: USAID.

Ten Have, Henk A. M. J. 1995. "Choosing Core Health Services in the Netherlands." In *Reforming Health Care: The Philosophy and Practice of International Health Reform*, ed. David Seedhouse. New York: John Wiley & Sons.

Tett, Gillian. 1994. "Guardians of Faith: Women in Soviet Tajikistan." In *Muslim Women's Choices*, ed. Camillia El-Solh and Judy Mabro, 128–51. Providence: Berg Publishers.

Thatcher, Margaret. 1978. "I Believe—A Speech on Christianity and Politics." Speech at St. Lawrence Jewry, London, March 30, www.margaretthatcher.org/document/103522.

———. 1993. *The Downing Street Years*. New York: HarperCollins.

———. 1995. *The Path to Power*. New York: HarperCollins.

"The Bamako Initiative" (editorial). 1988. *Lancet* 332 (8621): 1177–78.

Think Tank Watch. 2007. "The Mont Pèlerin Society." Think Tank Watch, http://thinktank-watch.blogspot.com/2007/12/mont-pelerin-society.html.

Thobani, Akbarali. 1993. *Islam's Quiet Revolutionary: The Story of Aga Khan IV*. New York: Vantage.

Thompson, E. P. 1968. *The Making of the English Working Class*. Harmondsworth: Penguin.

Tipton, Steven M. 1982. *Getting Saved from the Sixties: Moral Meaning in Conversion and Cultural Change*. Berkeley: University of California Press.

Tocqueville, Alexis de. 1969. *Democracy in America*. Edited by J. P. Mayer. Translated by George Lawrence. Garden City, NY: Doubleday.

Tohidi, Nayereh. 1991. "Gender, Islamism and Feminist Politics in Iran." In *Third World Women and the Politics of Feminism*, ed. Chandra Mohanty, Ann Russo, and Lourdes Torres, 251–71. Bloomington: Indiana University Press.

———. 1995. "Soviet in Public, Azeri in Private: Gender, Islam, and Nationalism in Soviet and Post-Soviet Azerbaijan." Paper presented at the annual meeting of the Middle East Studies Association, Washington, DC.

Tomaro, John B. 2005. "Programme Visit to Tajikistan, May 14th–21st." Aga Khan Foundation, internal memo, May 20.

Tomson, G., and G. Sterky. 1986. "Self-Prescribing with the Aid of Pharmacies in Three Asian Developing Countries." *Lancet* 13: 620–22.

Townsend, J. G., with G. Porter and E. Mawdsley. 2004. "Creating Spaces of Resistance: Development NGOs and their Clients in Ghana, India and Mexico." *Antipode* 36 (5): 871–89.

Turshen, M. 1999. *Privatizing Health Services in Africa*. New Brunswick, NJ: Rutgers University Press.

Tvedt, T. 1998. *Angels of Mercy or Development Diplomats NGOs and Foreign Aid*. Oxford: James Currey.

Ugalde, A., and J. Jackson. 1995. "The World Bank and International Health Policy: A Critical Review." *Journal of International Development* 7 (3): 525–42.

UNICEF. 1988a. *The Bamako Initiative: Panel 188 in UNICEF's The State of the World's Children*. London: Oxford University Press.

———. 1988b. *Recommendations to the Executive Board for Programme Cooperation, 1989–1993, the Bamako Initiative*. E/ICEF/1988/P/L.40.

———. 1990a. *Revitalizing Primary Health Care/Maternal and Child Health: The Bamako Initiative*. Progress report, Executive Board Doc. E/ICEF/1990/L.3, 20 February, New York.

———. 1990b. *The Bamako Initiative Planning Guide*. New York: Bamako Initiative Management Unit, UNICEF.

UNICEF/WHO Mission. 1992. "The Invisible Emergency: A Crisis of Children and Women in Tajikistan." Report of UNICEF/WHO mission with participation of UNDP, UNFPA, WFP.

UNDP (United Nations Development Programme). 1990. *Human Development Report 1990*. New York: Oxford University Press.

———. 1995. *Republic of Tajikistan: Human Development Report 1995*. Istanbul: Detay/Kamex Printing.

———. 1998. *Tajikistan: Human Development Report 1998*. UNDP.

———. 2003. *Human Development Report 2003*. UNDP.

USAID (U.S. Agency for International Development). 1995. *Policy Guidance: USAID–U.S. PVO Partnership*. Washington, DC: USAID.

———. 1997. *Strategic Plan for Tajikistan*. USAID Regional Mission for Central Asia, Almaty, Kazahkstan, April 1997.

———. 2013. "Who We Are." *US Agency for International Development,* www. usaid.gov/who-we-are.

U.S. Department of State, Office of the Historian. 2012. "Milestones: 1937–1945. The Bretton Woods Conference, 1944." U.S. Department of State, Office of the Historian, http://history.state.gov/milestones/1937–1945/BrettonWoods.

Vakhabov, Abdulla. 1980. *Muslims in the USSR.* Moscow: Novosti Press Agency Publishing House.

Vaksberg, Arkadii. 1991. *The Soviet Mafia.* Translated by John and Elizabeth Roberts. London: Weidenfeld and Nicolson.

Van der Geest, Sjaak, and Susan Reynolds Whyte. 1988. *The Context of Medicines in Developing Countries: Studies in Pharmaceutical Anthropology.* Boston: Kluwer Academic Publishers.

———. 1989. "The Charm of Medicine: Metaphors and Metonyms." *Medical Anthropology Quarterly* 3 (4): 345–67.

Velkoff, Victoria Averil. 1992. "Trends and Differentials in Infant Mortality in the Soviet Union for the Years 1970–1988." PhD diss., Princeton University.

Verba, Sidney, with Kay Lehman Schlozman and Henry E. Brady. 1995. *Voice and Equality: Civic Voluntarism in American Politics.* Cambridge, MA: Harvard University Press.

Veressayev, Vikenty V. 1916. *The Memoirs of a Physician.* Translated by Simeon Linden. New York: Alfred A. Knopf.

Vitek, C. R. M. Wharton. 1998. "Diphtheria in the Former Soviet Union: Reemergence of a Pandemic Disease." *Emerging Infectious Diseases* 4 (4).

Vivian, J. 1994. "NGOs and Sustainable Development in Zimbabwe: No Magic Bullets." *Development and Change* 25: 181–209.

Waddington, C. J., and K. A. Enyimayew. 1989. "A Price to Pay: The Impact of User Charges in Ashanti-Akim District of Ghana." *International Journal of Health Planning and Management* 4: 17–47.

Wade, Robert. 2002. "US Hegemony and the World Bank: The Fight over People and Ideas." *Review of International Political Economy* 9 (2): 214–43.

Waning, Brenda, with Jason Maddix and Lyne Soucy. 2010. "Balancing Medicine Prices and Business Sustainability: Analyses of Pharmacy Costs, Revenues and Profit Shed Light on Retail Medicine Mark-Ups in Rural Kyrgyzstan." *BMC Health Services Research* 10: 205.

Ware, Norma C., with Nicholas A. Christakis and Arthur Kleinman. 1992. "An Anthropological Approach to Social Science Research on the Health Transition." In *Advancing Health in Developing Countries: The Role of Social Research,* edited by Lincoln C. Chen, Arthur Kleinman, and Norma C. Ware. New York: Auburn House.

Weber, Max. 1930. *The Protestant Ethic and the Spirit of Capitalism.* Translated by Talcott Parsons. London: HarperCollins.

———. 1946. *From Max Weber: Essays in Sociology*. Edited and translated by H. H. Gerth and C. Wright Mills. New York: Oxford University Press.

———. 1968. *Economy and Society*. Edited by Guenther Roth and Claus Wittich. Berkeley: University of California Press.

White, Hayden. 1979. "Michel Foucault." In *Structuralism and Since*, ed. John Sturrock, 81–115. New York: Oxford University Press.

White, Stephen, with Graeme Gill and Darrell Slider. 1993. *The Politics of Transition: Shaping a Post-Soviet Future*. Cambridge: Cambridge University Press.

WHO (World Health Organization). 1988. "Guidelines for Implementing the Bamako Initiative." Regional Committee for Africa, 38th Session, Brazzaville, September 7–14, AFR/RC38/18 Rev. 1.

———. 1991. *The Public/Private Mix in National Health Systems and the Roles of Ministries of Health: Report of an Interregional Meeting*. Geneva: World Health Organization.

———. 1996. *National Essential Drugs Programme Tajikistan*. Copenhagen: World Health Organization.

———. 1997a. *The World Health Report 1997: Conquering Suffering Enriching Humanity*. Geneva: World Health Organization.

———. 1997b. WHO *Global Database on Child Growth and Malnutrition*. Compiled by Mercedes de Onis and Monika Blössner, Programme of Nutrition. Geneva: World Health Organization.

———. 1999. *Country Health Report: Republic of Tajikistan*. Copenhagen: WHO Regional Office for Europe.

———. 2008. *World Health Report 2008: Primary Health Care Now More Than Ever*. Geneva: World Health Organization.

Wiktorowicz, Q. 2001. "The Political Limits to Nongovernmental Organizations in Jordan." *World Development* 30 (1): 77–93.

Wilkinson, R. G. 1992. "National Mortality Rates: The Impact of Inequality?" *American Journal of Public Health* 82 (8): 1082–84.

Williams, Raymond Bradley. 1977. *Marxism and Literature*. Oxford: Oxford University Press.

———. 1980. "Advertising: The Magic System." In *Problems in Materialism and Culture*, 170–95. London: Verso.

———. 1988. *Religions of Immigrants from India and Pakistan: New Threads in the American Tapestry*. New York: Cambridge University Press.

Winiecki, Jan. 1991. *Resistance to Change in the Soviet Economic System: A Property Rights Approach*. London: Routledge.

Wise, P. H., with M. Kotelchuck, M. L. Wilson, and M. Mills. 1985. "Racial and Socioeconomic Disparities in Childhood Mortality in Boston." *New England Journal of Medicine* 313: 360–66.

Wnuk-Lipinski, Edmund. 1990. "The Polish Country Profile: Economic Crisis and Inequality in Health." *Social Science and Medicine* 31 (8): 859–66.

Wolf, Eric. 1969. *Peasant Wars of the Twentieth Century.* New York: Harper & Row.

Wood, Allen W. 1990. *Hegel's Ethical Thought.* Cambridge: Cambridge University Press.

Wood, Ellen Meiksins. 1995. *Democracy against Capitalism: Renewing Historical Materialism.* Cambridge: Cambridge University Press.

———. 2012. *The Ellen Meiksins Wood Reader.* Edited by Larry Patriquin. Boston: Brill Academic.

Woodhall, Maureen. 1994. "The Context of Economic Austerity and Structural Adjustment." In *Coping with Crisis: Austerity, Adjustment and Human Resources.* London: Cassell/UNESCO.

World Bank. 1973. "Address to the Board of Governors by Robert S. McNamara, President, World Bank Group, Nairobi Kenya, September 24, 1973." World Bank, http://siteresources.worldbank.org/EXTARCHIVES/Resources/Robert_McNamara_Address_Nairobi_1973.pdf.

———. 1975. *Health Sector Policy Report.* Washington, DC: World Bank.

———. 1980. *World Development Report 1980.* Washington, DC: World Bank.

———. 1987. *Financing Health Services in Developing Countries: An Agenda for Reform.* Washington, DC: World Bank.

———. 1992. *Measuring the Incomes of Economies in the Former Soviet Union.* Washington, DC: World Bank.

———. 1993. *World Development Report 1993: Investing in Health.* Washington, DC: World Bank.

———. 1997. *Health, Nutrition, and Population Sector Strategy Paper.* Washington, DC: World Bank.

———. 1998. "Tajikistan." World Bank Group, www.worldbank.org/gtml/extdr/offrep/eca/tajcb.htm.

———. 2004. *African Development Indicators, 2004.* Washington, DC: World Bank.

———. 2009. *Republic of Tajikistan: Poverty Assessment.* Washington, DC: World Bank.

World Health Organization and Health Action International. 2008. *Measuring Medicine Prices, Availability, Affordability and Price Components.* 2nd ed. Geneva: World Health Organization.

Wuthnow, Robert. 1987. *Meaning and Moral Order: Explorations in Cultural Analysis.* Berkeley: University of California Press.

Yalman, Nur. 1967. *Under the Bo Tree.* Berkeley: University of California Press.

Yates, Rob. 2006. *International Experiences in Removing User Fees for Health Services.* London: DFID Health Systems Resource Center.

———. 2009. "Universal Health Care and the Removal of User Fees." *Lancet* 373: 2078–81.

Yoder, R. A. 1989. "Are People Willing and Able to Pay for Health Services?" *Social Science and Medicine* 29: 35–42.

Yonowitch, Murray. 1977. *Social and Economic Inequality in the Soviet Union: Six Studies*. New York: M. E. Sharpe.

Young, Allen. 1983. "The Relevance of Traditional Medical Cultures to Modern Primary Health Care." *Social Science and Medicine* 17 (16): 1205–11.

Yuval-Davis, Nira, and Floya Anthias, eds. 1989. *Women-Nation-State*. London: Macmillan Press.

Zaidi, S. A. 1999. "NGO Failure and the Need to Bring Back the State." *Journal of International Development* 11: 259–71.

ZdravReform. 1994. *Semi-Annual Performance Report, July 1, 1994–December 31, 1994*, pdf.usaid.gov/pdf_docs/Pdabt563.pdf.

———. 1996. *Zdravreform Regional Technical Conference Report*, pdf.usaid.gov/pdf_docs/Pnacl738.pdf.

———. 1999. *ZdravReform Program Strategies*, pdf.usaid.gov/pdf_docs/Pnacg430.pdf.

Zeckhauser, Richard J. 1970. "Medical Insurance: A Case Study of the Tradeoff between Risk Spreading and Appropriate Incentives." *Journal of Economic Theory* 2 (1): 10–26.

Zwi, A., and A. Mills. 1995. "Health Policy in Less Developed Countries: Past Trends and Future Directions." *Journal of International Development* 7 (3): 299–328.

Index

Abt Associates, 69–70
Aeroflot, 35
affordability of health programs, 95
Afghanistan, 35, 40
Africa, 96–97, 127, 173nn66,68
Aga Khan, Hasan Ali Shah, 158–59n11
Aga Khan Development Network. *See* AKDN
Aga Khan Foundation. *See* AKF
Aga Khan Fund for Economic Development (AKFED), 43
Aga Khan Health Services, 124
Aga Khan III, 40–41, 159n11, 160nn18,19,20,21
Aga Khan IV, 8–9, 39, 41–44, 157n8, 161–62nn27,31,36, 176–77n49
Aga Khan's family, 41, 160n21
agency/responsibility, 12, 148n34
ahl al-sunna wa'l-jama'ah (Sunni), 157n6
Ahmad Shah, 40
AIDS patients, treatment for, xxvii
AKDN (Aga Khan Development Network), 16, 43–44, 162n31
AKF (Aga Khan Foundation), 2–3; creation of, 43; food assistance by, 6; health and nutrition study by, 58, 59 (table), 61–64, 126–27, 163n10; health programs of, 6; humanitarian assistance phase shifts to development

phase at, 68; ideological language of donor adopted by, 109, 133–34, 177n49; Khorog headquarters of, 115; as a large international NGO, 8; as nondenominational, 161n23; Pharmaceutical Use Survey, 59–60, 163n13, 164n17; on providing medicines in Badakhshan, 76, 166n40; reputation/success of, 8, 16, 44, 77; on the revolving drug fund, 10–11, 109, 124, 177n49 (*see also* Bamako Initiative); on sustainability, 70; USAID funding for, 6, 9, 70–71, 109; water and sanitation study by, 163n6. *See also under* Badakhshan
AKFED (Aga Khan Fund for Economic Development), 43, 116
Akin, John: "Financing Health Services in Developing Countries," 96
Aksartova, Sada (Saadat), 165n6
Alamut (eagle's nest; Iran), 158n11
Alexander II, Tsar, 23
Alexander the Great, 38–39, 156n2
Ali Ibn Abu Talib, 39, 157n6
Alma Ata Declaration (1978), xx, 72, 97
American Association of Retired Persons (AARP), 178n2
American Enterprise Institute, 103, 183n28
American Political Foundation, 105